Preface

Seventy years ago, the Russian Revolution of 1917 "shook the world" and ushered in an era. In the summer of 1991, the failed coup of Soviet hardliners confirmed that a second Russian revolution had occurred, one that seems likely to sweep away the decaying institutions of Soviet communism planted in 1917. The coup itself and the response to it marked also the end of a dramatic effort by Mikhail Gorbachev to reform communism.

The coup's failure created an opening through which the republics that had made up the Soviet Union rushed toward nationhood. Many of the newly independent states were lands conquered in Stalin's reign or in earlier times during the expansionist period of Russia's Tsars. Most had suffered enormously. They face great obstacles.

While Americans are familiar with Russia, the largest of the newly independent states, Kazakhstan, Moldova, Belarus, and even Ukraine are largely unknown entities. This guide is intended to provide a point of entry to help understand the new nations, their current leaders, and the policy issues which face them and the United States. Any such guide is a snapshot in time. We have, therefore, endeavored to provide the tools to help understand not only what has happened, but what may happen.

The present volume is one of a series of ACCESS "guides" to resources and issues. Like all ACCESS publications it relies on the cooperation and expertise of specialists from many viewpoints who help us make sure that the material we provide is accurate, timely, and high quality. We are grateful to Nick Babiah of the US-Ukraine Foundation, David Clingman at the World Bank, Paul Goble of the Carnegie Endowment for International Peace, Rose Gottemoeller at RAND, Jonathan Halperin of FYI, Aram Hamparian of the Armenian National Committee, Kent Lee of Eastview Publications, Dunbar Lockwood at the Arms Control Association, James Molloy of the American University, Stan Norris at the Natural Resources Defense Council, Brian St. David Reed of Radio Free Europe/Radio Liberty, David Shorr of British American Security Information Council (BASIC), and Greg Webb at the Arms Control Association for their time, expert review, and advice. Special thanks are also due ACCESS Board members Stephen Atkins of Texas A&M, Gloria Duffy of Global Outlook, Susan Graseck of the Center for Foreign Policy Development at Brown University, William Kincade of American University, and John Redick at the University of Virginia for their expertise and help on this project. The assistance of all these experts has greatly improved *One Nation Becomes Many*. ACCESS is responsible for any errors or omissions that occurred in the final text. The quality of the guide most reflects, however, the commitment of the editors (Stephen Young, Ronald Bee, and Bruce Seymore) and other ACCESS staff for whose dedication I am most grateful.

One Nation Becomes Many: The ACCESS Guide to the Former Soviet Union involved the entire staff of ACCESS. They are: Editor Stephen Young, Ronald Bee (Publications and Research), and Bruce Seymore (Information Services). Mr. Young was responsible for the overall publication. The guide to organizations was assembled by Mr. Seymore, Intern John Coffin, and ACCESS Information Specialists Lisa Alfred and Vineta Beinikis. The narrative and bibliography on Change and Challenge were written by Mr. Bee with assistance from Intern Renee Zimmerman and expert reviewers acknowledged above. Chee Huan ensured that computer systems operated smoothly. Editing, proofing, production, and marketing were aided by Gillian Ament (Office Management), Wendy Hyatt (Outreach Director), Barbara Kelley (Publication Sales Fulfillment), and Intern Amy Nguyen. Ms. Alfred has overseen preparations for the second printing.

This guide was made possible through the generosity of major donors who choose to remain anonymous. ACCESS general support is provided by ACCESS Associates and by the Carnegie Corporation of New York, the Ford Foundation, and the John D. and Catherine T. MacArthur Foundation.

Founded in 1985, ACCESS is a nonprofit, nonpartisan information clearinghouse on international relations, peace, and security. It is our mission to identify and track more than 2500 institutes, think tanks, advocacy groups and university programs in more than 100 countries, that work on these issues. Through our database, inquiry service, and publications, ACCESS serves as a link between the specialists and the journalists, teachers, librarians and concerned citizens seeking authoritative information. ACCESS is founded in the belief that an informed and involved citizenry is the surest road to a secure and lasting peace.

Mary E. Lord
Executive Director

ISBN 1-878597-07-8

ACCESS: A Security Information Service
1730 M Street NW., Suite 605
Washington, DC 20036

Printed in the United States of America
Entirely on Recycled Paper

NOTE: In the second printing, errata have been corrected and transliteration of proper names made consistent with that favored by the new nations. The leaders of each of the former republics has been updated as of September 1992. All other text remains identical to the first printing.

Contents

CHRONOLOGY

The Russian Empire

7th Century Eastern Slavs, ancestors of Russians, Belorussians, and Ukrainians, begin expanding European Russia.

978-1054 The zenith of the Kiev Rus', a Slavic state that controls parts of what is today Ukraine, Byelarus, the Baltics and Russia.

13th Century Mongols defeat the Russian princes and the Golden Horde settles in southern Russia

1325-1341 Ivan I founds the Musccvite state.

1462-1505 Reign of Ivan the Great, the first Tsar of Russia, who expands Muscovy to Novgorod and Tver.

1533-84 Reign of Ivan the Terrible, who expands Muscovy east into Siberia and south to the Caspian Sea.

1682-1725 Reign of Peter the Great, who defeats Sweden, capturing much of the Baltics and founding St. Petersburg, the first "window to the West," on the Gulf of Finland. Russians reached the Pacific in the 1640s.

1762-96 Reign of Catherine the Great, who annexed the Crimean pennisula and a large portion of Poland. In the early 1800s, Russia acquires Finland from Sweden, and Bessarabia from the Ottoman Turks.

19th Century Russia loses the Crimean War to France and Britain but takes control of Georgia, northern Azerbaijan, eastern Armenia, Turkistan, and in the east as far south as Vladivostok. In 1867, Russia sells Alaska to the US.

1904-05 The Russo-Japanese War, won by Japan, costs Russia parts of the Manchurian coast and the sourthern half of the Sakhalin islands.

1905 The first Russian revolution, a failed attempt to overthrow the Tsarist system.

The Building of the Soviet Union

1917 The February and October Russian Revolutions overthrow Tsarist rule and bring Lenin's Bolsheviks to power.

1918-1921 Red Army troops win the civil war and retain most of the former Russian empire.

Dec. 30, 1922 The Union of Soviet Socialist Republics (USSR) or Soviet Union is formed by the Treaty of Union.

August 23, 1939 Nazi Germany and the Soviet Union sign a non-aggression pact, also known as the Hitler-Stalin pact. A secret protocol divides Eastern Europe into Soviet and German spheres.

June 27, 1940 The Soviet Union annexes Bessarabia (now part of Moldova) and Northern Bukovina (now part of Ukraine).

August 1940 The Soviet Union annexes Estonia, Latvia, and Lithuania, as arranged for in the Hitler-Stalin pact.

June 22, 1941 Nazi Germany invades the Soviet Union. Over 20 million Soviets die during the war. Millions more are killed by Soviet leader Joseph Stalin in purges and repressive policies before, during and after the war.

August 14, 1945 Japan surrenders, ending World War II. Soviet occupation of Japan's Kuril Islands, north of Japan, is the key issue preventing improvement in Japanese-Soviet relations to this day.

The Cold War

February 26, 1946 Stalin makes his "Cold War" speech, stating the Soviet Union will continue pre-war policies.

March 5, 1946 Winston Churchill declares an "Iron Curtain" has fallen over the countries of Eastern Europe.

February 24, 1948 Soviet-backed Communist coup succeeds in Czechoslovakia.

June 24, 1948 Stalin blocks all land routes to West Berlin. In response, U.S. President Harry S Truman institutes the "Berlin Airlift" with Great Britain and France. Stalin lifts the blockade on May 15, 1949.

April 4, 1949 The North Atlantic Treaty Organization (NATO) is formed.

September 23, 1949 President Truman announces that the Soviet Union has exploded its own atomic bomb, four years after the first U.S. explosion.

1950 Following the victory of Communist forces in China, the Soviet Union and China form an alliance calling for world-wide revolution. Communist North Korea, with Soviet backing, launches an attack on South Korea.

March 5, 1953 Stalin dies. After a lengthy power struggle, Nikita Khrushchev attains full power in 1957.

May 14, 1955 The Warsaw Treaty Organization, or Warsaw Pact, is formed.

November 1956 Soviet troops roll into Hungary, crushing a move by Budapest to declare itself neutral.

August 13, 1961 The Berlin Wall goes up.

October 1962 During the Cuban Missile Crisis, U.S. President John F. Kennedy blockades Cuba, forcing Soviet Premier Khrushchev to remove Soviet nuclear missiles being deployed there.

August 5, 1963 The Limited Test-Ban Treaty, prohibiting atmospheric nuclear tests by the United States and the Soviet Union, goes into effect.

October 14, 1964 Khrushchev is deposed as Soviet leader and replaced by Leonid Brezhnev.

July 1, 1968 The Nuclear Non-Proliferation Treaty is signed.

August 21, 1968 Soviet troops invade Czechoslovakia, crushing the "Prague Spring" reform movement.

May 5, 1972 The SALT I agreement, creating a 5 year freeze on testing and deployment of intercontinental ballistic missiles (ICBM) and submarine-launched ballistic missiles (SLBM), is signed by the US and the USSR.

May 26, 1972 The Anti-Ballistic Missile (ABM) Treaty is signed, severely restricting the testing or deployment of anti-ballistic missile systems.

June 18, 1979 The SALT II Treaty, placing ceilings on strategic nuclear forces, is signed in Vienna. In the aftermath of the Soviet invasion of Afghanistan, the US never ratifies the treaty but abides by its limits informally until 1986.

December 1979 The Soviet Union invades Afghanistan.

November 10, 1982 Leonid Brezhnev dies; Yuri Andropov replaces him as General Secretary.

March 23, 1983 US President Ronald Reagan introduces the Strategic Defense Initiative (SDI or Star Wars).

February 10, 1984 Andropov dies and, three days later, is replaced by Konstantin Chernenko.

The Gorbachev Era of Reforms

March 11, 1985 Konstantin Chernenko dies and is replaced by Mikhail Gorbachev as General Secretary of the Central Committee of the Communist Party.

February 1986 Gorbachev annouces the USSR must pursue *"glasnost"* or openness to move into the 21st Century.

April 25, 1986 The Chernobyl nuclear reactor accident in Ukraine kills more than 20; over 100,000 are evacuated from the region. Radiation released from the accident is detected worldwide.

October 11-12, 1986 At the Reykjavik summit, Gorbachev and Reagan discuss abolishing all nuclear weapons; talks break down over the issue of the U.S. Strategic Defense Initiative.

November 1986 The Supreme Soviet approves legislation allowing limited private-sector activities. Individuals and families can for the first time since 1922 start their own small businesses and offer their skills for a fee.

December 19, 1986 Andrei Sakarov, Nobel Peace Prize winner and father of the dissident movement in the Soviet Union, is released from exile in Gorky.

June 12, 1987 Elections for local soviets or assemblies are held. Some races have more than one candidate, although all candidates are approved by the Communist Party.

December 8, 1987 Gorbachev & Reagan sign the INF Treaty abolishing intermediate-range nuclear missiles.

December 7, 1988 Speaking at the United Nations, Gorbachev promises large unilateral cuts in conventional forces by 1991 and a shift to a defensive military posture.

February 15, 1989 The last Soviet troops withdraw from Afghanistan.

March 26, 1989 In the first multi-candidate elections for the Congress of People's Deputies since 1917, many official Communist candidates are defeated. (The Congress is the Soviet equivalent of a parliament)

April 9, 1989 Soviet troops put down a demonstration in Tbilisi, Georgia. Up to thirty people die and 200 are injured.

June 3-15, 1989 Over 90 people die in Uzbekistan during riots between Uzbeks and ethnic Meskhetians.

Eastern Europe Breaks Off

June 4, 1989 Poland holds partially open parliamentary elections. Candidates from Solidarity, the labor union, win 92 of the 100 seats in the Senate and 160 of the 161 open in the 460-seat Sejm.

September 10, 1989 Hungary announces it will no longer prevent East Germans from passing through to Austria. Within the next month, nearly 50,000 East Germans leave for the West, the vast majority going to West Germany.

October 1989 Gorbachev announces that the USSR "has no right, moral or political right, to interfere in the events happening in Eastern Europe."

November 9, 1989 The Berlin Wall falls. Free travel is allowed.

November 10, 1989 Bulgarian President Todor Zhivkov resigns after 35 years in power.

December 4, 1989 The Warsaw Pact (excluding Romania) condemns the 1968 invasion of Czechoslovakia.

December 25, 1989 Following a week of protests and armed clashes, Romanian leader Nicolae Ceausescu and his wife are captured, summarily tried and executed. Former and current Communists dominate the new government.

December 29 Dissident playwright Vaclav Havel is elected president of Czechoslovakia by the parliament.

January 2, 1990 Soviet troops are sent to Azerbaijan to quell mounting violence against ethnic Armenians.

January 5-16, 1990 The Communist Party chief in Azerbaijan resigns in the face of increasing violence. Over 10,000 Azerbaijanis demonstrate in Baku. In the following days, over 30 people, primarily ethnic Armenians, are killed. The Soviet Union declares a state of emergency in parts of Azerbaijan.

January 20, 1990 One day after airlifting thousands of Soviet troops into Azerbaijan, Gorbachev orders Soviet troops into Baku. Soviet officials report 83 people are killed. Azerbaijani sources claim over 300 are killed. Soviet troops control the capital, but an estimated one million Azerbaijanis gather in a funeral procession for those killed.

February 13, 1990 The Communist Party's new platform plays down the role of doctrine, opens the door to a multiparty system, commits the party to a market economy, calls for separation of powers, and supports the right of "self-determination including secession."

March 18, 1990 Free elections in East Germany give victory to a Christian Democratic-led coalition that seeks unification with West Germany.

March 25, 1990 In free elections in Hungary, anti-communist and pro-free market parties are the big winners.

The Beginning of the End of the Soviet Union

March 11, 1990 Lithuania declares independence from the Soviet Union. Soviet authorities respond with an economic blockade, which ends 72 days later when Lithuania announces a moratorium on its declaration.

March 13, 1990 The Congress of People's Deputies repeals the Communist Party's constitutionally guaranteed monopoly on power and creates a new presidential office which Gorbachev is elected to fill.

March 30, 1990 The Estonian Supreme Soviet passes a resolution announcing that Estonia is in a transitional period leading to the republic's full independence. The resolution states that Estonia does not recognize the USSR's authority on Estonian territory and that Estonia considers itself occupied territory.

May 1, 1990 Thousands jeer the Politburo, or ruling cabinet, at the annual May Day Parade, the traditional high point of Soviet pomp and ceremony.

May 4, 1990 The Latvian Supreme Soviet declares Latvia's independence from the Soviet Union and calls for independence to be established after a transition period.

May 29, 1990 Boris Yeltsin is elected president of Russia by the Russian parliament.

June 8-12, 1990 The Russian parliament asserts that in Russia its laws take precedence over Soviet laws. Three days later, it proclaims Russia a sovereign country.

July 2-12, 1990 At the 28th Congress of the Communist Party, Gorbachev faces down a challenge from conservatives. Yeltsin resigns from the Party citing the slow pace of reform; the mayors of Moscow and Leningrad follow his example.

July 15, 1990 Gorbachev decrees an end to the Communist monopoly on radio and television broadcasts.

July 21, 1990 The Belorussian Supreme Soviet declares Belorussia's sovereignty. The declaration asserts the supremacy of Belorussian laws and Belorussia's right to form its own army and issue currency.

July 25, 1990 Gorbachev orders illegal militias throughout the USSR to surrender arms. Few comply.

August 6, 1990 The UN Security Council, including the Soviet Union, votes to establish mandatory economic sanctions against Iraq for its invasion of Kuwait.

September 13, 1990 Gorbachev presents the republic parliaments and the Supreme Soviet with a radical 500-day economic reform plan drawn up by Stanislav Shatalin.

September 14, 1990 The "Two-Plus-Four" Treaty is signed between the two Germanies and four victors of World War II, granting a united Germany full sovereignty.

October 15, 1990 Mikhail Gorbachev is awarded the Nobel Peace Prize.

October 16, 1990 Gorbachev presents a new compromise plan for economic reform that is a weakened version of the Shatalin 500-day economic reform plan. The USSR Supreme Soviet approves the new plan. Yeltsin rejects the compromise and vows to go ahead with the radical plan in Russia.

October 27, 1990 In the first direct elections for president of a Soviet republic, Turkmen Communist Party First Secretary Saparmurad Niyazov, running unopposed, is elected president of Turkmenistan.

November 19, 1990 U.S. President George Bush, with Gorbachev and European leaders, signs the Conventional Forces in Europe (CFE) Treaty, calling for large reductions, particularly on the Soviet side, of armed forces in Europe.

November 24, 1990 Gorbachev introduces the first draft of a Union Treaty, designed to replace the 1922 version, that will grant substantial power to the republics. Four republics refuse to sign.

December 25, 1990 The Congress of People's Deputies approves a constitutional amendment expanding the authority of Gorbachev's presidential office.

January 13, 1991 Soviet paratroopers and tanks attack the radio and television center in Vilnius, the capital of Lithuania. Fourteen people are killed and more than 160 wounded.

March 4, 1991 The USSR Supreme Soviet ratifies the Two-Plus-Four Treaty allowing German unification.

March 17, 1991 In a first-ever nationwide referendum, more than 70% of Soviets vote to keep the union as a "federation of equal sovereign states." Armenia, Georgia, Moldavia, and the Baltic republics boycott the referendum.

March 31, 1991 The military structure of the Warsaw Pact is officially dissolved.

April 4, 1991 The Russian Congress of People's Deputies votes to give Boris Yeltsin expanded powers, including the right to rule by decree.

April 10-14, 1991 The Georgian Supreme Soviet unanimously approves a declaration of the republic's independence. Four days later it unanimously elects its chairman, Zviad Gamsakhurdia, to the newly created post of president.

April 24, 1991 Gorbachev reaches agreement with nine of the 15 republican leaders to work on an economic treaty that would give the republics a greater voice in how they will reform their economies. The agreement is known as the "9-plus-1" Accord.

May 26, 1991 Georgia elects Zviad Gamsakhurdia president of the republic in the first contested election of a republic leader. Gamsakhurdia, a former Communist who appealed to nationalist voters, receives 86% of the vote.

June 11, 1991 The White House announces that President Bush has approved $1.5 billion in farm credit guarantees for the Soviet Union.

June 12, 1991 Boris Yeltsin, with 60% of the vote, wins free multicandidate elections for president of Russia.

July 24, 1991 Gorbachev announces accord with nine republics on the union treaty, to be signed August 20.

July 31, 1991 In Moscow, Bush and Gorbachev sign the START Treaty. After nine years of negotiation, the treaty is the first that reduces strategic nuclear weapons.

August 19, 1991 The newly created State Committee for the State of Emergency announces that Gorbachev, for health reasons, has been temporarily replaced by Vice-President Gennadi Yanayev. A six month state of emergency is announced. Gorbachev, vacationing in the Crimea, is cut off from public view. Yeltsin declares the coup illegal, calls for Gorbachev's reinstatement, and appeals to Moscow's citizenry to stage protests. This occurs one day before the new union treaty is scheduled to be signed.

August 20, 1991 President Bush issues a written statement condemning the unconstitutional removal of President Gorbachev. Moscow citizens surround the Russian parliament building where Yeltsin and his government are operating. Three demonstrators are killed in minor clashes with the Army and KGB.

August 21, 1991 The Supreme Soviet Presidium declares the removal of Gorbachev illegal. Soviet television announces that the attempted coup has failed.

August 22, 1991 Gorbachev returns to Moscow. Coup leaders are arrested.

August 24, 1991 Gorbachev resigns as head of the Communist Party.

August 26, 1991 Yeltsin claims Russia reserves the right to "re-examine borders" with neighboring republics that are declaring themselves independent.

August 30-31, 1991 Azerbaijan, Uzbekistan and Kyrgystan (formerly Kirghizia) vote to declare themselves independent of the Soviet Union.

September 2, 1991 Bush announces that the United States officially recognizes the independence of Estonia, Latvia, and Lithuania. In Tbilisi, demonstrators demand the resignation of Georgian President Zviad Gamsakhurdia. Six people are wounded when police fire on the crowd.

September 6, 1991 The Soviet Union officially recognizes the independence of the Baltic states.

September 12, 1991 The twelve republics and the Baltic nations agree to maintain a collective defense framework and single control over the Soviet nuclear arsenal.

September 17, 1991 Estonia, Latvia, and Lithuania are admitted as member countries to the United Nations.

September 23-24, 1991 In Tbilisi, protestors backed by rebel national guard units take control of the capital's television center. President Gamsakhurdia places the city under a state of emergency.

September 27, 1991 President Bush announces unilateral nuclear arms cuts, including the removal and destruction of US tactical nuclear weapons and nuclear-armed cruise missiles, stopping planned rail-basing of MX ballistic missiles, and the end of the round-the-clock alert status for nuclear weapons.

October 5, 1991 Following Bush's initiative, President Gorbachev announces the removal of short-range nuclear weapons from Soviet ships, submarines, and land-based naval aircraft, a year-long moratorium on nuclear tests and says the USSR will reduce its strategic nuclear forces to 5,000 warheads. The International Monetary Fund (IMF) grants associate member status to the Soviet Union, which had requested full membership. Associate members can receive technical assistance but not IMF credit.

October 6, 1991 The European Community approves a $1.5 billion food and aid package for the USSR.

October 8, 1991 Japan announces $2.5 billion in aid for the Soviet Union, largely in export credit insurance.

October 9, 1991 The Soviet Union reestablishes relations with Estonia and Lithuania, broken since 1940.

October 12, 1991 President Askar Akayev runs unopposed in the first direct presidential elections in Kyrgyzstan and wins 95% of the vote.

October 17, 1991 Levon Ter-Petrossyan wins Armenia's presidency in the republic's first direct elections.

October 18, 1991 Eight Soviet republics sign the Treaty on an Economic Community, aimed to form a common economic space and foster inter-republic cooperation. Ukraine, Moldova, Azerbaijan and Georgia reject it.

October 22, 1991 The Ukraine Supreme Soviet approves plans to create a 400,000 to 450,000-strong Ukrainian national armed forces.

October 26, 1991 Gorbachev agrees to withdraw all 45,000 Soviet troops from Poland by the end of 1992.

November 4, 1991 Ukraine agrees to sign the Treaty on Economic Union.

November 24, 1991 Rakhmon Nabiyev, chairman of the Tajik Supreme Soviet, is elected president of Tajikistan. Nabiyev was former first secretary of the Tajik Communist Party.

November 25, 1991 A planned ceremony for the signing of the new Union treaty for the twelve remaining republics is called off. The draft, which called for a "union of sovereign states," was rejected by Yeltsin and leaders of other republics. In Tbilisi, Georgia, demonstrators call for the resignation of President Zviad Gamsakhurdia and the release of arrested opposition leaders.

December 1, 1991 Ukraine holds its first direct presidential elections and a referendum on independence. Ukrainian Supreme Soviet Chairman Leonid Kravchuk wins 60% of the vote for president; 90% approve of the August 24 declaration of Ukrainian independence. Kazakhstan holds its first direct presidential elections; appointed President Nursultan Nazarbayev, running unopposed, wins approximately 90 % of the vote.

The Soviet Union Breaks Up

December 8, 1991 Russian President Boris Yeltsin, Belorussian Supreme Chairman Stanislau Shushkenvich, and Ukrainian President Leonid Kravchuk form a "Commonwealth of Independent States" (CIS), open to all republics of the former Soviet Union. They agree to create economic ties, develop market mechanisms, preserve a unified economic space, and retain the ruble while introducing national currencies. Mensk (formerly Minsk) will be the center of the Commonwealth.

December 17, 1991 Yeltsin and Gorbachev agree that the Soviet Union will cease to exist on January 1, 1992.

December 21, 1991 Eight republics (all but Georgia) vote to join the Commonwealth of Independent States established by Belarus (formerly Byelorussia), Russia and Ukraine. Russia will take the Soviet Union's seat on the UN Security Council. Belarus and Ukraine agree to remove strategic weapons from their territory and sign the Nuclear Non-

Proliferation Treaty (NPT); the nuclear weapons in Kazakhstan are not covered in the agreement.

December 22, 1991 Fighting breaks out in Tbilisi, Georgia between rebel National Guard troops and forces loyal to President Gamsakhurdia, who takes refuge in the basement of the parliament.

December 25, 1991 Gorbachev announces his resignation as President of the Soviet Union. He hands over codes for the use of Soviet nuclear weapons to Yeltsin. Yeltsin states he will keep the codes but will not use the weapons without the authorization of the three other nuclear republics (Ukraine, Belarus, and Kazakhstan). President Bush recognizes the independence of the eleven members of the Commonwealth of Independent States as well as Georgia.

December 30, 1991 The leaders of the Commonwealth of Independent States (CIS) opened a meeting in Mensk on the future form and direction of the CIS. Agreements are signed on military and strategic forces, on establishing a CIS council, and on the distribution of foreign aid, among other topics. Ukraine, Moldova, and Azerbaijan restate their intent to create their own national armed forces.

January 2, 1992 Opposition leaders in Tbilisi, Georgia form a provisional government headed by a Military Council. Prime Minister Tengiz Sigua heads the Council.

January 6, 1992 Georgian President Gamsakhurdia, under siege in the parliament building for two weeks, flees Tbilisi, seeking asylum in Armenia. He returns to northwest Georgia January 16, calling for a civil war, but opposition forces hold most of the republic's territory.

February 10, 1992 US cargo planes begin an airlift of Western humanitarian aid to Moscow and other cities in the former Soviet Union. The airlift is criticized both in the East and West as too little. European nations and private groups have been providing food and pharmaceuticals for months.

February 17, 1992 Meeting in Moscow, Russian President Yeltsin and US Secretary of State James Baker agree to plans for US assistance for dismantling Russian nuclear weapons. They also agree to a science and technology institute to employ nuclear scientists from the former USSR to keep them from providing secrets to other nations.

March 1, 1992 Azerbaijani sources claim Armenian forces killed hundreds in the town of Khojaly in the Nagorno-Karabakh region of Azerbaijan.

March 6, 1992 Azerbaijan President Ayaz Mutalibov resigns after growing protests following the alleged massacre in Khojaly. Protestors were seeking better efforts to defend Azerbaijanis in the Nagorno-Karabakh region, officially under Azerbaijani control but populated largely by Armenians.

March 10, 1992 Former Soviet Foreign Minister Eduard Shevardnardze, a Georgian, is appointed head of a newly created State Council that will be given executive and legislative powers to adminster Georgia until new elections can be held. The State Council replaces the provisional Military Council that had ruled following the ouster of President Zviad Gamsakhurdia.

March 12, 1992 Ukraine's leader Leonid Kravchuk announces that he is halting the transfer of nuclear weapons from Ukraine to Russia until he is reassured that they will be destroyed. The policy is reportedly reversed three weeks later; all weapons are scheduled to be transferred to Russia by July 1992.

March 16, 1992 Russia's leader Boris Yeltsin announces the creation of a Russian Ministry of Defense, which he will head. This is widely perceived as a blow to hopes for continued control over the armed forces of the former Soviet Union by the Commonwealth of Independent States.

March 21, 1992 Over 60% of the voters in Tatarstan vote to become a "sovereign state." Tatarstan, the largest of 17 autonomous enclaves within Russia, has been a part of Russia for 300 years.

March 31, 1992 The International Monetary Fund (IMF) endorses Russia's economic reform plan, paving the way for the republic to receive up to $4 billion in IMF aid over the next year. In Moscow, 18 of 20 of Russia's autonomous areas sign an agreement granting them more political and economic freedom but binding them to the Russian state. Tatarstan and Chechen-Inguish, two regions that have made moves toward independence, refuse to sign.

April 1, 1992 President Bush in Washington and German Chancellor Helmut Kohl in Bonn announce a $24 billion aid program for Russia. Seven countries will contribute to the program that will include $11 billion in bilateral aid, $4.5 billion in IMF and World Bank loans, $2.5 billion in debt rescheduling, and a $6 billion ruble stabilization fund.

April 13, 1992 Yeltsin's entire Cabinet offers to resign after the Russian Congress of People's Deputies efforts to scale back the ambitious economic reform program Russia has undertaken. In addition to changing the economic program, the Congress asks Yeltsin to resign his post as prime minister (he would remain president) and name a replacement.

Sources: *The Washington Post, The New York Times,* **The Columbia History of the World,** *Toward Freedom* (American Enterprise Institute), *U.S. Department of State Dispatch, CRS Report for Congress, Soviet Union* (National Geographic), **Looking the Tiger in the Eye,** *Change in Eastern Europe* (ACCESS).

ARMENIA

Land area: 11,620 square miles, the smallest of the former Soviet republics, slightly larger than Maryland.

Population: 3,283,000 (1989), the 13th largest republic population of the former Soviet Union.
93% Armenian
3% Azeri
2% Kurds
2% Russians and other nationalities

Many if not most Azeris have left Armenia since 1989. The Armenian Church, the first established Christian church, is the dominant religion.

Leaders: President: Levon Ter-Petrossyan, Armenian National Movement candidate; Prime Minister: Khosrof Harutunyan; Foreign Minister: Raffi Hofanesyan (an American citizen).

Location: Borders Turkey, Georgia, Iran, and Azerbaijan. The capital is Yerevan. The Nakhichevan Autonomous Republic of Azerbaijan is separated from Azerbaijan by Armenian territory.

History: The region of Armenia has been controlled by the Byzantine, Persian, Arab, Ottoman, Mongol and Russian empires. During World War I, perhaps a million Armenians were deported from Turkish Armenia, with hundreds of thousands massacred or starved to death. With Turkey's defeat in World War I, Armenia enjoyed a brief period of independence, but fell to the Red Army shortly thereafter. In 1988, a massive earthquake struck Armenia, killing 25,000 people. Hundreds of thousands of people were left homeless, a problem exacerbated by an equally large number of ethnic Armenian refugees fleeing the strife in Azerbaijan.

Politics: Political parties are allowed. Multicandidate elections for the Supreme Soviet were held in May 1990. The country is administered by a Council of Ministers. In a September 21, 1991 referendum, 92 percent of the population favored independence from the Soviet Union. The leading political party is the Armenian National Movement. Armenia has joined the Commonwealth of Independent States.

Economics: Per capita GNP (1989): $4,710. The economic situation in Armenia is desperate. Azerbaijan has instituted a rail, road, and fuel blockade of Armenia through its territory. Armenia must import 65% of foodstuffs and 80% of its fuel from other republics. The crisis recently forced the shut-down of all industry in Armenia. The government has followed Russia's economic model, freeing prices while raising some wages. The majority of the collective farms have been redistributed to peasants and some state enterprises have been privatized.

Current issues: The largest issue is the Nagorno-Karabakh region of Azerbaijan, where over 75 percent of the population of 200,000 is Armenian. Over 1,000 deaths have resulted from fighting between Armenian and Azerbaijani nationalists. The region had been an Autonomous Oblast within Azerbaijan until November 1991, when Azerbaijan proclaimed direct rule. On December 10, 1991, the Armenian population in the region voted for independence in a referendum. In January 1992 Armenia proposed the region become an independent republic in the Commonwealth of Independent States. Negotiations between President Ter-Petrossyan and leaders in Azerbaijan, mediated by Russian President Yeltsin and Kazakh President Nazerbayev, have failed to resolve the issue. Both sides have alleged bloody massacres of civilians. The departure of most Azeris from Armenia has made it the most homogenous of any of the republics of the former Soviet Union.

AZERBAIJAN

Land area: 33,774 square miles, slightly larger than Maine.

Population: 7,000,000 (1989), the sixth most populous of the former Soviet republics.
    83% Azeri
    6% Russian
    6% Armenian
    5% other nationalities

Turkic Azeris are predominantly Shiite Muslim, the only non-Sunni Muslim republic.

Leaders: President: Ebulfez Elcibey; Parliamentary Chairman: Isa Gamberov; Prime Minister: Rakhim Guseynov; Foreign Minster: Tofig Kasimov.

Location: Borders Russia, Georgia, Armenia, Iran, and the Caspian Sea. The capital is Baku. The Nakhichevan Autonomous Republic is separated from Azerbaijan by Armenia. Armenia has claimed sovereignty over the region of Nagorno-Karabakh within Azerbaijan, a territory largely populated by Armenians.

History: The region of Azerbaijan has been dominated by Turks, Iranians, and Russians. The Republic is largely Muslim. The Azerbaijani language is in the Turkic family. There are 7 million Azerbaijanis in northern Iran. An independent republic was formed in 1918 but overthrown by the Red Army in 1920. Azerbaijan, along with Georgia and Armenia, were made into the Transcaucasian Soviet Federal Socialist Republic from 1922 until 1936, when the Soviet government re-established three separate republics. The Nagorno-Karabakh region, which had been part of the Armenian homeland, was transferred to Azerbaijan control by Soviet leader Joseph Stalin.

Politics: Former President Mutalibov was placed in power by Soviet leadership following the intervention of Soviet troops in Baku in January 1990. He resigned following widespread protests after allegations of a massacre of Azerbaijanis in the Nagorno-Karabakh region. He had won presidential elections in September 1991 after an opponent dropped out citing an unfair electoral process. Open elections in the fall of 1990 gave an opposition coalition 40 seats in the 350 Azerbaijan Supreme Soviet. Azerbaijan joined the Commonwealth of Independent States but has opposed assuming a share of the foreign debt of the Soviet Union.

Economics: Per capita GNP (1989): $3,750. The Azerbaijani economy is based on the production of oil and natural gas. Although oil output has declined in recent years, some experts believe Azerbaijan has significant unexploited oil and gas resources. Over half of Soviet oil extraction machinery is produced in Azerbaijan. Agriculture has been hurt by drought. Overall, the population subsists at a level substantially lower than other republics of the former Soviet Union.

Current issues: The major issue in Azerbaijan is the future of Nagorno-Karabakh. Continuing violence has plagued the region; an estimated 1,000 have been killed and hundreds of thousands made refugees since 1989. Soviet troops sent into the region in January 1990 began to withdraw in December 1991. Violence flared again in March 1992 with both sides shelling opposing villages. Azerbaijan revoked the autonomous status of Nagorno-Karabakh, which had declared itself an independent republic. Former President Mutalibov had rejected outside intercession in the region despite calls by some for a United Nations role.

BELARUS

(FORMERLY BELORUSSIA)

Land area: 80,154 square miles, slightly smaller than Kansas.

Population: 10,200,000 (1989), the fifth most populous former Soviet republic.
78% Belorussian
13% Russian
4% Polish
5% other nationalities

Leaders: Chairman of the Supreme Soviet: Stanislau Shushkevich; Prime Minister: Vyacheslau Kebich; Foreign Minister: Petr Kravchanka.

Location: Borders Russia, Ukraine, Lithuania, Latvia, and Poland. Mensk (formerly Minsk), the capital, is also the coordinating center of the Commonwealth of Independent States.

History: Belorussians, or White Russians, along with Russians and Ukrainians, are the only Slavic peoples of the former Soviet Union. The region has been ruled, at various times, by Poles, Lithuanians, and Russians. An independent Belorussian Democratic Republic was founded in 1918 but became part of the Soviet Union shortly thereafter.

Politics: Belarus was one of the strongest supporters for maintaining the Soviet Union, both in government and populace. Over 80 percent of the population favored preserving the union in the March 1991 referendum. The activities of the Belorussian Communist Party (BCP) were suspended following its support of the failed August coup, but the Party of Communists of Belarus, which declared itself the successor to the BCP, is largely made up of the same leadership. Belarus, Ukraine, and the Russian Federation were the founding members of the Commonwealth of Independent States. Political parties are allowed; the largest opposition party is the Belorussian Popular Front, an anti-communist, nationalist movement. Elections for the Supreme Soviet in March 1990 were dominated by traditional Communists, although opposition candidates won some victories.

Economics: Per capita GNP (1989): $5,960. The economy is fairly industrialized, including production of automobiles and agricultural machinery, with substantial consumer durables and chemical industries. Agricultural products include potatoes, grain, and flax. Belarus is a net exporter of foodstuffs but must import raw materials for industry. Inter-republic fights over raw materials have hurt the economy, which declined by over 12% in 1991.

Current issues: Belarus has pledged to remove or destroy all nuclear weapons, both long and short-range, deployed on its territory by the former Soviet Union. An estimated 1,250 nuclear weapons of all types were in Belarus in 1990. Plans are moving forward for the creation of a 90,000-strong Belarus national army.

The leadership has been moving slowly toward a more open political and economic system, although Chairman Shushkevich has gone on record opposing "uncontrolled capitalism." Potential border disputes with Poland and Lithuania have apparently been avoided through negotiation.

ESTONIA

Land area: 17,590 square miles, slightly larger than Massachusetts and Vermont combined.

Population: 1,566,000 (1989), the smallest population of the former Soviet republics.
　62% Estonians
　30% Russians
　3% Ukrainians
　5% others nationalities

The majority of Estonians are Lutherans.

Leaders: President and Chairman of the Supreme Council: Arnold Ruutel; Prime Minister: Tiit Vahi; Foreign Minister: Jaan Manitski.

Location: Borders Russia, Latvia, and the Baltic Sea. The capital is Tallinn.

History: From the 13th to 16th centuries, Estonia was under Germanic rule. Sweden ruled from then until 1721, when Estonia and Latvia were ceded to the Russian Empire. It stayed in the Empire until its fall in 1917. By 1918, Estonia was an independent state. In 1940, under the terms of the secret Hitler-Stalin non-aggression pact, the Soviet Union invaded and annexed Estonia and the other Baltic states. During World War II, Germany controlled Estonia until the Soviet Union recaptured the territory in 1944. In the years following, tens of thousands of Estonians were executed, imprisoned, or deported as a policy of forced sovietization took place. Additionally, hundreds of thousands of Russians migrated into Estonia and Latvia.

Politics: On March 30, 1990, Estonia declared a transitional period toward independence. In March 1991, 78% of Estonians voted for independence in a referendum. On August 20, 1991, Estonia declared full independence. The Communist Party was banned shortly thereafter. By September 6, 1991, Russia, the United States, and the Soviet Union, along with most of the world, had recognized Estonia. The Estonian People's Front, the umbrella organization calling for independence, was organized in 1988. It is the foremost political organization in Estonia.

Economics: Estonia has few natural resources except for some oil shale and peat deposits used as fuel. The economy is industrialized but depends on raw materials imported from the former Soviet Union. The electronics and electrical industries are substantial, and Estonia produces computers, electric motors, and computer-controlled equipment. Estonia is a net exporter of foodstuffs. Under the leadership of Prime Minister Savisaar, Estonia has moved toward privatization of farms and industry, has freed most retail and wholesale prices, is encouraging private entrepeneurs and foreign investors, and is planning its own currency.

Current issues: As in Latvia and Lithuania, the future of the troops from the former Soviet Union stationed in Estonia is a major issue. Current plans are to withdraw all troops by 1994.

As in Latvia, the ethnic Russian minority is sizable but has, at least in part, supported independence for Estonia. Estonia has close ties with its neighbor to the north, Finland, where a similar language is spoken.

GEORGIA

Land area: 26,872 square miles, slightly larger than West Virginia.

Population: 5,400,000 (1989), the seventh most populous former Soviet republic.
69% Georgian
9% Armenian
5% Azerbaijani
3% South Ossetian
14% other nationalities

Leaders: Chairmen of the State Council: Eduard Shevardnadze; Acting Prime Minister of the Provisional Government: Tenghiz Sigua; Foreign Minister: Alexandr Chikvaidze.

Location: Borders Russia, Azerbaijan, Armenia, Turkey, and the Black Sea. The capital is Tbilisi.

History: The Georgian people trace their ancestors back to settlers as far back as the 12th century BC They have been conquered by Romans, Turks, Arabs, Iranians, and Mongols. Georgia established an independent republic in 1918, but the Red Army invaded and conquered the country in February 1921. Georgia, Azerbaijan and Armenia were united into the Transcaucasian Soviet Federal Socialist Republic from 1922 until 1936, when the Soviet government re-established them as three separate republics.

Politics: Over 90% of the Georgian population voted for independence on March 21, 1991; the parliament unanimously approved the referendum ten days later. Former President Zviad Gamsakhurdia was ousted in early January 1992 following a revolt led by rebellious national guard units. Although Gamsakhurdia won 87% of the vote for President in May 1991, his dictatorial actions, including censorship of the press, jailing and harassment of opponents, quickly turned many against him. Gamsakhurdia was replaced by a provisional government under a Military Council which included the Prime Minister and several officials from the national guard, which lead the fight against Gamsakhurdia. After seeking asylum in Armenia, Gamsakhurdia returned to his home territory in northwest Georgia and called for a civil war to oust the Military Council. Although fighting ensued, the Military Council forces quickly assumed control of most of the country.

Economics: Per capita GNP (1989): $4,410. The Georgian economy revolves around fruits and teas, some mining, and tourism. Georgia is the largest producer of grapes, citrus fruits, and tea in the former Soviet Union. The republic has significant manganese deposits and coal. The tourism industry focuses on spas on the Black Sea coast. Georgia has banned the export of almost all foodstuffs and has made little movement toward privatization and marketization.

Current issues: On March 10, 1992, Eduard Shevardnadze, former Soviet foreign minister and architect with Mikhail Gorbachev of perestroika, was named chairman of a newly formed State Council. Shevardnadze was also former head of the Communist Party in Georgia, and for that reason is not universally approved of in Georgia. The State Council includes most members of the provisional Military Council and will hold executive and legislative powers until elections can be held. Elections for a new parliament are scheduled for spring 1992.

The region of South Ossetia has claimed independence and, in a referendum on January 19, 1992, voted for unification with the North Ossetian region of the Russian Federation. Reports indicate that over 200 Ossetians have been killed since 1990, with tens of thousands fleeing to North Ossetia. Fighting between Georgian nationalist guerillas and Ossetian fighters continues while Georgian National Guard units have been massively deployed in the region. An economic blockade of South Ossetia has been in effect for months.

KAZAKHSTAN

Land area: 1,059,750 square miles, the second largest former Soviet republic, almost twice the size of Alaska.

Population: 16,500,000 (1989), the fourth most populous of the former Soviet republic.
40% Kazakh
38% Russian
6% German
5% Ukrainian
11% other nationalities

Kazakhs are predominantly Sunni Muslim by nationality. Kazakhstan is the most heterogeneous of the former Soviet republics.

Leaders: President: Nursultan Nazarbayev; Vice President: Yerik Asanbayev; Chairman of the Supreme Council: Serikbolsyn Abdildan; Prime Minister (Chairman of the Cabinet of Ministers): Sergey Tereshchenko; Foreign Minister: Tolevtay Suleymenov.

Location: Borders Russia, China, Kyrgyzstan, Uzbekistan, Turkmenistan, the Aral and Caspian Seas. The capital is Alma-Ata.

History: Kazakhs are descended from Turkic Muslim and Mongols who inhabited the area from the fifteenth century. Russians took control in the nineteenth century, ruling a vast region of primarily nomadic Kazakhs. Kazakhstan was briefly independent after the 1917 Russian revolution, but became a part of the Russian Federation shortly thereafter. It became a separate republic in 1936. In December 1986, Soviet leader Gorbachev appointed an ethnic Russian as Kazakh Communist Party leader, citing accusations of corruption in Kazakh leadership. Major riots in Alma-Ata and other cities followed. In 1989, Gorbachev appointed Nazarbayev, the current president, to head the Kazakh Communist Party. Kazakh was made the official language of the republic in 1989; many Russians have left since then.

Politics: The Supreme Soviet (now called the Supreme Council) was elected in partly open elections in March 1990. President Nazarbayev obtained his office after an election in the Supreme Soviet in April 1990. The Communist Party changed its name to the Socialist Party of Kazakhstan and still holds the large majority of leadership positions. There are a number of other political parties, most of which are nationalist in nature, but all are fairly small. Kazakhstan joined the Commonwealth of Independent States in December 1991. Popular elections for president and the Supreme Council are reportedly to be held in early 1992.

Economics: Per capita GNP (1989): $3,720. Kazakhstan is rich in natural resources. It is a major source of copper, zinc, titanium, magnesium, and chromium, has significant oil reserves, and was the third largest producer of grain among the former Soviet republics. Some moves have been made toward privatization. The environment, especially around the Aral and Caspian Seas, has been severely degraded by pesticides, nuclear wastes, and other toxins.

Current issues: Kazakhstan is one of four former Soviet republics containing strategic nuclear weapons. Originally, Kazakhstan threatened to retain its tactical and strategic weapons as long as Russia did. In December 1991, however, Nazarbayev agreed to place strategic forces under control of the Commonwealth of Independent States and agreed to move all tactical weapons to Russia by mid-1992. The Supreme Council has endorsed making Kazakhstan a nuclear-free state. The Semipalatinsk nuclear test area, heavily contaminated with radioactive wastes, has been closed down, largely because of protests by environmentalists.

Tensions with Russia flared when, following the August 1991 coup, Russian leader Boris Yeltsin declared that borders with secessionist republics may be reviewed. Officials from the two republics met later to reaffirm the current borders and call for protection of the rights of ethnic minorities.

KYRGYZSTAN

(FORMERLY KIRGHIZIA OR THE KIRGHIZ REPUBLIC)

Land area: 77,415 square miles, about the size of South Dakota.

Population: 4,291,000 (1989), the 10th largest population of the former Soviet republics.
52% Kyrgyz
21% Russian
13% Uzbek
3% Ukrainian
2% German
9% other nationalities

The Kyrgyz are predominantly Sunni Muslim.

Leaders: President: Askar Akayev; Chairman of the Presidium of the Supreme Soviet: Medetbek Sherimkulov; Prime Minister: Tursunbek Chyngyshev.

Location: Borders China, Kazakhstan, Uzbekistan, and Tajikistan. The capital is Bishkek (formerly Frunze).

History: The region of Kyrgyzstan has been controlled by Mongols, Kaluyks, Manchus, the Kokland Khanate, and Russians. The Kyrgyz, a nomadic tribe who speak a Turkic language, never formed an independent state. This area was part of the Russian Empire from 1876, became part of the Turkestan Autonomous Republic after the Revolution in 1917, part of the Kara-Kyrgyz Autonomous Oblast, and finally a full republic in the Soviet Union in 1936. Kyrgyz fiercely opposed the forced collectivization of farms in the 1920s. From that time, ethnic Russians have held most government positions and leadership of the Communist Party in the republic. In 1990, major ethnic conflict broke out between ethnic Kyrgyz and Uzbeks, resulting in 250 deaths.

Politics: The Supreme Soviet was elected in March 1990 in partially free elections. Ninety-five percent of the elected deputies were Communists. In October 1990, the Supreme Soviet elected the reformist Askar Akayev president over Communist Party leader Absamat Masaliyev. Akayev won uncontested direct presidential elections on October 12, 1991 with 95% of the vote. Activities of the Communist Party were suspended following its support for the August 1991 coup, but Akayev has not abandoned the Party. Akayev strongly supported Yeltsin during the coup. Kyrgyzstan joined the Commonwealth of Independent States in December 1991 and has supported continuation of some form of union of the former republics.

Economics: Per capita GNP (1989): $3,030. Kyrgyzstan is the third poorest former Soviet republic, ahead of only Uzbekistan and Tajikistan. The republic is the third largest producer of wool among the former Soviet republics, after Russia and Kazakhstan. The republic is self-sufficient agriculturally despite the fact that only seven percent of the land is arable. Akayev has called for the creation of a market economy and a national currency. On January 4, 1992, Akayev announced the liberalization of most prices, excluding fuels and basic foodstuffs. Many salaries were raised to lessen the hardship.

Current issues: Continuing tensions exist between the Kyrgyz majority and the Uzbek minority. Many Russians and Ukrainians reportedly left during 1990 because of ethnic tension. Opposition to the Communist-dominated Supreme Soviet continues. Akayev has promoted reformist policies for the most part, and would like to keep strong ties to other republics of the former Soviet Union.

LATVIA

Land area: 25,200 square miles, slightly larger than West Virginia.

Population: 2,680,000, the second smallest population of the former Soviet republics.
   52% Latvian
   34% Russian
   5% Byelorussian
   4% Ukrainian
   2% Poles
   3% other nationalities

Over two-thirds of Latvians are Lutheran, most of the remaining population is Catholic.

Leaders: President and Chairman of the Parliament: Anatolijs Gorbunovs; Chairman of the Council of Ministers: Ivars Godmanis; Foreign Minister: Janis Jurkans.

Location: Borders Estonia, Russia, Belarus, Lithuania, and the Baltic Sea. The capital is Riga.

History: Latvians are descendents of the ancient Balts and speak one of two surviving Baltic languages, the other being Lithuanian. The region of Latvia was first organized above the tribal level by German conquerors in the late 13th and early 14th century. Later, Latvia fell under Polish-Lithuanian control and then Swedish domination, until the territory was ceded to Peter the Great, the Russian Tsar, in 1721. In 1918, Latvia established a widely recognized independent state, which existed until 1940. That year, under the terms of the secret Hitler-Stalin non-aggression pact, the Soviet Union invaded and annexed Latvia and the other Baltic states. Nazi Germany invaded in World War II and killed or deported 90% of Latvia's Jewish population. When it became clear that the Soviet Union would retake the country, hundreds of thousands of Latvians left for the West. Additionally, hundreds of thousands of Russians migrated into Latvia and Estonia.

Politics: On May 4, 1990, the Latvian Parliament declared the republic was in a transitional stage moving toward independence. On January 20, 1991, Soviet troops stormed the Latvian Interior Ministry, killing five. On March 3, 1991, the vast majority of Latvians voted for independence in a referendum. Latvia declared full independence on August 21, 1991. By September 6, Russia, the United States, and the Soviet Union had recognized the independence of Latvia. The Communist Party was banned after the failed August 1991 coup. Chairman Gorbunovs was a member of the Party but is a political moderate reformist who is extremely popular.

Economics: Latvia has few natural resources, but has an excellent port and transportation systems. The economy is heavily industrialized but depends critically on imported raw materials, and over 90% of Latvia's fuel must be imported. The electrical industry is substantial, and Latvia produces large numbers of buses, railway cars, and motorcycles. Agricultural production is low; Latvia must import most of its foodstuffs. Latvia has moved toward privatization of farms and industry, and is planning its own currency.

Current issues: A major issue is the future of troops from the former Soviet Union still stationed in Latvia. All Baltic states have demanded the troops leave; the Soviet Defense Ministry has stated it is not possible until all troops are withdrawn from Poland and Germany, which may not be until 1994.

The treatment of the sizable Russian minority has also been an issue. Many Russians supported Latvian independence but are now worried about their future.

Latvian economic dependence upon the Soviet Union was substantial; finding products and markets to replace those lost will be difficult.

LITHUANIA

Land area: 25,400 square miles, slightly larger than West Virginia.

Population: 3,675,000 (1989).
    80% Lithuanian
    9% Russian
    7% Poles,
    2% Byelorussians
    2% other nationalities

The majority of Lithuanians are Roman Catholic.

Leaders: Chairman of the Supreme Council (Parliament): Vytautas Landsbergis; Prime Minister: Gediminas Vagnorius; Foreign Minister: Algirdas Saudargas.

Location: Borders Latvia, Belarus, Poland, and the Baltic Sea. Kaliningrad, still a part of Russia, lies south of Lithuania. The capital of Lithuania is Vilnius.

History: Lithuanians are descendents of the ancient Balts and speak one of two surviving Baltic languages, the other being Latvian. They have inhabited the region for over 2000 years. In the fourteenth century, Lithuanians ruled what is today Belarus and parts of Ukraine and Russia. In 1385, Lithuania formed an empire with Poland which was the main state in central Europe. In the 18th century, Poland was partitioned and Lithuania became part of the Russian empire. Following World War I and the overthrow of the Russian Tsar, Lithuania became an independent country in 1918. In 1940, under the secret Hitler-Stalin non-aggression pact that divided up Eastern Europe, the Soviet Union invaded and annexed Lithuania and the other Baltic states.

Politics: On March 11, 1990, Lithuania declared independence from the Soviet Union. Soviet authorities responded with an economic blockade that lasted 72 days, when Lithuania announced a moratorium on its declaration. On January 13, 1991, Soviet paratroopers and tanks attacked the radio and television center in Vilnius. Fourteen people were killed and over 160 wounded. On February 9, 1991, over 90% of the population of Lithuania voted for independence from the Soviet Union. At the end of July 1991, seven Lithuanian border guards were killed in a raid, presumably by Soviet forces. During the August 1991 coup, Soviet forces deployed throughout the Baltics, but withdrew to military bases once the coup failed. By September 6, 1991, Lithuanian independence had been recognized by Russia, the United States, the Soviet Union, and most of the world.

Economics: Lithuania has few natural resources and depends on imports from the former Soviet Union for its industry. The transportation system, including several Baltic ports, is excellent. Two nuclear power reactors similar in design to the Chernobyl plant provide electricity. Agriculture is fairly well developed, providing most of Lithuanians basic foodstuffs.

Current issues: As in the other Baltic states, the continued presence of troops from the former Soviet Union is an issue. Current plans hold that the troops will not be withdrawn until 1994, after withdrawal from Germany and Poland is complete.

Lithuania has the smallest Russian population of the Baltic states. In November 1989, it passed a citizenship law granting citizenship to all who were Lithuanians in 1940 and their descendents. Permanent residents would also be granted citizenship if they were born in Lithuania or one of their parents or grandparents had been. Others wanting citizenship must pass several tests. These criteria have worried the Russian minority.

The troubled economy is also a major issue. Privatization is underway but the previous extreme dependence on the Soviet Union makes getting materials and markets difficult.

MOLDOVA

(FORMERLY THE MOLDAVIAN SOVIET SOCIALIST REPUBLIC)

Land area: 13,012 square miles, the second smallest former Soviet republic, about twice the size of Hawaii.

Population: 4,341,000, the most densely populated former Soviet republic.
- 65% Moldovan
- 14% Ukrainian
- 13% Russian
- 4% Gagauzi
- 4% eight other nationalities

Leaders: President: Mircea Snegur; Speaker of the Parliament: Alexandru Mosanu; Prime Minister: Andrei Sangheli; Minister of Foreign Relations: Nicolae Tau. On December 8, 1991, President Snegur, the only candidate, won 98% of the vote in direct popular presidential elections.

Location: Borders Romania and Ukraine. The capital is Chisinau (formerly Kishinev).

History: Moldova, part of a region known as Bessarabia, has been transferred between Romanian and Russian control. Following World War I, Bessarabia declared independence from Russia and united with Romania. In June 1940, under the Hitler-Stalin Non-Agression Pact, Soviet troops occupied and annexed the area, creating the Moldavian Soviet Socialist Republic from a section of Bessarabia and giving another section to Ukraine.

Politics: Moldova declared its independence from the Soviet Union on August 27, 1991. It has joined the Commonwealth of Independent States. The Communist Party was banned in 1990. Laws developing the basics of a multiparty system were adopted in September 1991.

Economics: Per capita GNP (1989): $3,830. Moldova's economy is based on agriculture and food processing, with a small industrial base. The economy has declined in recent years. The government has sought to promote privatization of land and enterprises.

Current issues: A major issue for Moldova concerns a second unification with Romania. The government's official line recently has been "one people, two lands," and President Snegur has called for a long independence phase before consideration of unification. Romania has not taken a strong position on the issue, stating that unification could take place in five years or in fifty.

Two ethnic conflicts confront Moldova. The Turkic-speaking Gagauzi population announced the creation of a Republic of Gagauzia in August 1990. In September 1990, the majority Russian population in the east Dnestr valley proclaimed a Dnestr Soviet Republic, with the intention of seceding from Moldova. The Moldovan government has announced that the declarations of secession were invalid. The secessionist regions again declared independence following Moldova's withdrawal from the Soviet Union.

RUSSIAN FEDERATION

(ALSO RUSSIA OR THE RUSSIAN SOVIET FEDERATION OF SOCIALIST REPUBLICS)

Land area: 6,600,000 square miles, over three-quarters of the territory of the former Soviet Union, almost twice the size of the United States.

Population: 147,386,000 (1989), just over half the population of the former Soviet Union.
82% Russians
4% Tatar
3% Ukrainian
11% over 100 additional ethnic groups and nationalities

The major religion of the population is Russian Orthodox.

Leaders: President: Boris Yeltsin; Vice President: Lt. General Aleksandr Rutskoi; Foreign Minister: Andrey Kozyrev; Prime Minister: Yegor Gaidar; Chairman of the Supreme Soviet: Ruslan Khasbulatov; Mayor of Moscow: Gavriil Popov.

Location: Borders the Arctic Ocean, the Bering Sea, the Pacific Ocean, the Sea of Japan, North Korea, China, Mongolia, Kazakhstan, the Caspian Sea, Azerbaijan, Georgia, the Black Sea, Ukraine, Belarus, Latvia, Estonia, the Baltic Sea, Finland, and Norway. Two-fifths of the land is permafrost. One small region, the military port of Kaliningrad, is separated from the rest of Russia. It rests between Lithuania, Poland, and the Baltic Sea. The capital of Russia is Moscow.

History: Slavs settled in what is now Ukraine in the early Christian era. The Kievan Rus' state of the eleventh century is the origin of "Russian." The Mongols, first led by Genghis Khan, captured the region and created vassal states, including one centered around Moscow. During the reigns of Ivan the Great (1462-1505), Ivan the Terrible (1533-84), Peter the Great, (1682-1724), and Catherine the Great (1762-96), Russians freed themselves from Mongol domination and vastly expanded the territory they controlled. The Russian Empire reached from Warsaw in the west to Vladivostock in the east. The 19th century saw additional expansion southward, as Russians took control of what is today Azerbaijan, and westward, as Bessarabia and parts of Poland came under Russian control.

Following World War I and the overthrow of Tsar Nicolas, the Bolsheviks took control of Russia. They initially allowed Armenia, Azerbaijan, Georgia, Ukraine, Belorussia, and the Baltic States to declare themselves independent, but in 1922 all except the Baltics were forcibly incorporated in the Union of Soviet Socialist Republics by the Treaty of Union. Soviet leader Joseph Stalin (1924-1952) killed millions of Soviet citizens through purges, forced collectivization of farms, and government-engineered famine. The Baltic states were annexed in 1940 under the secret Hitler-Stalin non-aggression pact which divided up eastern Europe. Millions more died during World War II. Mikhail Gorbachev took power in 1985 and, attempting reform of the stagnating Soviet system, undertook policies that eventually led to the disintegration of the Soviet Union and the re-emergence of Russia and the other republics as independent states.

Politics: In March 1990, mostly free elections were held for the Russian Congress of People's Deputies. In May 1990, Boris Yeltsin was narrowly elected president by the Russian Congress. In June 1991, Yeltsin won direct elections with 58 percent of the vote, defeating five opponents. Yeltsin has undertaken a dizzying number of reforms, placing Soviet ministries under Russian control and reorganizing or abolishing government institutions, often ruling by decree. The Communist Party was suspended following the failed August 1991 coup, then dissolved and its properties seized in November 1991. Some hard-line opponents of Yeltsin have been attempting to reorganize the remnants of the party. Russia has assumed the Soviet Union's seat at the United Nations and on the UN Security Council. Russia was one of the original three members of the Commonwealth of Independent States.

Economics: Per capita GNP (1989): $5,810. Russia is blessed with an incredible wealth of natural resources. Russia has over 30% of the world's proven natural gas reserves, 20% of the coal, 20% of the gold, and 6% of the oil. Uranium, diamonds, copper, lead, silver, and many other materials are also abundant. Heavy industry is the dominant sector in the Russian economy, although its agricultural production of grain, potatoes, and vegetables is approximately half of the production of the former Soviet Union. The economy has declined substantially in the last year, a fall caused by consumer shortages and inflation. In January 1992, President Yeltsin began a radical economic reform program, liberalizing most prices, encouraging foreign trade, and moving toward privatization of industry and farms. Many observers expected riots over high prices and shortages during the 1991-92 winter, but little violence developed.

Current issues: Many issues confront Russia. Some worry that Yeltsin is moving toward authoritarian rule as he assumes more power. He has sought strong ties among the former Soviet republics. However, his announcement on March 16, 1992 that Russia was forming its own ministry of defense, which he would head, led many to doubt the viability of the Commonwealth of Independent States.

Russia has agreed to take control of all the tactical nuclear weapons of the former Soviet Union, most of which it has promised to destroy. Along with the other republics that possess nuclear weapons, Russia has pledged to abide by all treaties, including the START Treaty reducing nuclear arsenals. Yeltsin has proposed reducing strategic warheads to 2,000-2,500, well below the 7,000 to 9,500 limits proposed in the START Treaty.

Russia also faces a wealth of ethnic and nationality issues, with at least two regions seeking to declare themselves independent states. Threats of a second coup are occasionally heard. For a more thorough discussion of these and other issues, see the **Change and Challenge in the Former USSR** section of this guide.

TAJIKISTAN

(FORMERLY TADZHIKISTAN OR THE TADZHIK SOVIET SOCIALIST REPUBLIC)

Land area: 55,809 square miles, slightly smaller than Iowa.

Population: 5,112,000 (1989), the 8th largest populace of the former Soviet republics.
    62% Tajik
    23% Uzbek
    7% Russian
    8% other nationalities

The Tajik's are predominatly Sunni Muslim by nationality.

Leaders: President: (At the time we went to press, this position was vacant. Former president Nabiyev, former first secretary of the republic's Communist Party Central Committee resigned on September 7, 1992) ; Parliamentary Speaker: Akbarsho Iskandarov; Minister of Foreign Affairs: Khudoberdi Kholiqnazarov.

Location: Borders Uzbekistan, Kyrgyzstan, China, and Afghanistan. The western half is rugged mountain territory, with the highest peak in the former Soviet Union, Mt. Communism at 24,500 feet. The capital of Tajikistan is Dushanbe.

History: Tajiks trace their history to Persia, and they speak a dialect similar to Farsi. The region has been controlled by Arabs (seventh century), Mongols (13th century), Uzbeks (15th century), Afghans and Bukhanas (18th century), and Russians (late 19th century). The Red Army invaded in 1921 and the Tajik Autonomous Republic was created with the Uzbek Soviet Socialist Republic in 1924. Tajikistan became a separate republic in 1929.

Politics: Tajikistan is the most conservative of the Central Asian republics. In February 1990, government troops killed 21 demonstrators who were protesting reported favored treatment of Armenian refugees. Opposition candidates were then banned from the March elections for the Supreme Soviet; as a result Communist candidates won 94% of the seats. The Communist Party was banned and the president was forced to resign following protests over his support of the August 1991 coup. A Communist coup followed and the Party was reinstated on September 23, 1991 by acting President Rakhmon Nabiyev. Following more protests, Nabiyev stepped down and the Party was again suspended. In presidential elections in November, Nabiyev won with 58 percent of the vote. He then again reinstated the Communist Party. Tajikistan joined the Commonwealth of Independent States in December 1991.

Economics: Per capita GNP (1989): $2,340. Tajikistan is the least developed and poorest of the former Soviet republics. The economy is almost entirely based on cotton production, although only 6 percent of the land is arable. Cattle and sheep raising predominate in the rest of the land. Tajikistan must import the vast majority of its foodstuffs. Prices and salaries were freed in January 1992 and subsidies increased by cutting defense funds.

Current issues: The ban on religious parties was lifted in October 1991, leading to the formation of several Islamic parties that are gaining support. Relations with neighboring republics, which are dominated by Turkic rather than Persian populations, have been strained recently. Tajiks have a long tradition of antagonism with Uzbeks; many claim parts of Uzbekistan are historically Tajik territory.

In 1989, the Supreme Soviet made Tajik the official language, causing a minor exodus of Russian and other minorities.

Reports have surfaced that the republic may be trying to sell enriched uranium and uranium processing technology abroad, but the government has denied these reports. Tajikistan does have substantial deposits of uranium but does not have any processing or enrichment facilities.

TURKMENISTAN

Land area: 190,359 square miles, slightly smaller than twice the size of Wyoming.

Population: 3,534,000 (1989), the 12th largest population of the former Soviet republics.
72% Turkmen
9% Russian
9% Uzbek
10% other nationalities

Turkmen are largely Sunni Muslims and speak a Turkic language.

Leaders: President: Saparmurad Niyazov; Vice President: Atta Charyyev; Chairman of the Presidium of the Supreme Soviet: Sakhat Muradov; Foreign Minister: Avdy Kuliyev.

Location: Borders Uzbekistan, Afghanistan, Iran, Kazakhstan, and the Caspian Sea. Ninety percent of Turkmenistan's territory is covered by desert. The capital of Turkmenistan is Ashkhabad.

History: From the sixth century until the 13th, the region of Turkmenistan had been controlled by Turkic tribes or Muslim Arabs. In the 13th century, the Mongols took control. The region fell under Russian control in the late 19th century. A provisional Turkmen government was established following the 1917 revolution, but the Red Army took over in 1920. Turkmenistan was made a republic of the Soviet Union in 1924. The Soviet policy of forced collectivization of farms, carried out in the 1920s and 1930s, was strongly opposed by the nomadic Turkmen. Open rebellion broke out in 1928, and years of fighting and repression followed.

Politics: Elections for the Supreme Soviet were held in January 1990. As the elections were only partially open, over 90 percent of the elected deputies were members of the Communist Party. Party Chief Saparmurad Niyazov was elected president by the Supreme Soviet in November 1990. Following the August 1991 coup, Niyazov resigned from the USSR Communist Party Politburo and later declared that the Turkmenistan Communist Party no longer had property rights. On December 16, 1991, the Party changed its name to the Democratic Party of Turkmenistan. No opposition parties have been allowed to participate in elections. Turkmenistan declared independence on October 27, 1991 and joined the Commonwealth of Independent States in December 1991.

Economics: Per capita GNP (1989): $3,370. Turkmenistan is one of the poorest of the republics of the former Soviet Union. The republic's primary exports are gas and cotton, although other natural resources such as salt, sulphur, and nitrogen are also exported. Turkmenistan depends heavily on imported foodstuff and textiles. Prices were somewhat liberalized in January 1992, although food prices were not allowed to rise more than three times above 1991 prices. This has kept prices considerably lower than in other republics.

Current issues: Turkmenistan is establishing trade relations with both Iran and Turkey, as well as the other central Asian republics (Kazakhstan, Tajikistan, Kyrgyzstan, and Uzbekistan), Russia, and Japan.

Ethnic tensions are fairly low. Free press has not been allowed. Some opposition leaders and activists were arrested following protests over Niyazov's temperate reaction to the August 1991 coup.

UKRAINE

(FORMERLY THE UKRAINE OR THE UKRAINIAN SOCIALIST SOVIET REPUBLIC)

Land area: 235,443 square miles, about the size of Texas.

Population: 51,704,000 (1989), the 2$^{\underline{nd}}$ largest population of the former Soviet republics.
73% Ukrainian
22% Russian
5% other nationalities

Leaders: President: Leonid Kravchuk; Chairman of the Presidium of the Ukrainian Supreme Rada: Ivan Plyushch; Prime Minister: Vitol'd Fokin; Foreign Minister: Anatolii Zlenko.

Location: Borders Russia, Belarus, Moldova, Romania, Hungary, Czechoslovakia, Poland, and the Black Sea. The capital is Kiev.

History: Like Russians and Belorussians, Ukrainians trace their roots to the Kievan Rus' of the 9th-13th centuries. From the 17th century, what is today Ukraine was divided by Poland and Russia. When Poland was partitioned in the 18th century, Russia took control of most of Ukraine. Following the collapse of the Russian Empire in 1917, Ukraine was again divided by Poland and Soviet Russia. Ukrainian communists, under Soviet control, ruled for about a decade, but in 1932-33 Soviet leader Joseph Stalin began a Russification program and a government-engineered famine that killed millions. Following World War II, Polish Ukraine and parts of Romania dominated by ethnic Ukrainians were added to the Ukraine republic. In 1954, Khruschev ceded the Crimea to Ukraine.

Politics: In open elections in March 1990, the Ukrainian Communist Party won a clear majority of the 450-seat Supreme Soviet over Rukh candidates, the opposition organization that supported Ukrainian independence. The Ukrainian Communist Party was implicated in the failed August 19-21, 1991 coup. In the aftermath, Party activity was banned and its property nationalized. Ukraine declared independence three days after the coup failed. On December 1, 1991, over 90% of the population voted in a referendum for independence. In presidential elections held on the same day, Supreme Soviet Chairman Leonid Kravchuk was elected President, defeating the Rukh nominee Vyacheslav Chornvil with 61% of the vote. Kravchuk has adopted many of the nationalist positions of the opposition. Ukraine was one of the original three members (with Russia and Belarus) of the Commonwealth of Independent States, but views the CIS as more of a coordinating body than the precursor to a renewed union.

Economics: Per capita GNP (1989): $4,700. Ukraine was often called the breadbasket of the Soviet Union, producing almost half the total agricultural output of all the republics, focusing on wheat, corn, and beets. Ukraine also produces large amounts of coal and has a large steel production industry. Ties with the Russian economy are very close. Russia's price liberalization forced Ukraine to follow suit. Ukraine plans to issue its own currency and has already introduced a coupon system designed to parallel the ruble. Although Kravchuk has pledged to move toward free markets and privatization, little progress has been made in that direction.

Current issues: Leader Kravchuk has explicitly fought what he sees as Russian domination. He temporarily stopped the transfer of tactical nuclear weapons to Russia until he was reassured they were being destroyed. He has claimed the Black Sea fleet as Ukrainian, an issue Russia disputes. He has also opposed the pace of economic reform undertaken by Russia. Ukraine is creating its own armed forces, including from 100,000 to 450,000 men and women under arms. This has caused worry in Russia and around the world, as 450,000 troops would be one of the largest forces in Europe. Ukrainian leaders counter this point by noting it would still be substantially less than the number of troops posted in Ukraine when it was in the Soviet Union.

UZBEKISTAN

Land area: 174,486 square miles, slightly smaller than Nebraska and Wyoming combined.

Population: 19,900,000 (1989), the third largest of the former Soviet republics.
71% Uzbek
8% Russian
5% Tajik
4% Kazakh
12% other nationalities

The Uzbeks are the most numerous of the Sunni Muslim nationalities of the former Soviet Union.

Leaders: President: Islam Karimov; Vice President: Shakurulla Mirsaidov; Chairman of Presidium of Supreme Soviet: Shavkat Yuldashev; Prime Minister: Abdulkhashim Mutalov; Foreign Minister: Ubaidulla Abdurazzakou.

Location: Borders Kyrgyzstan, Tajikistan, Afghanistan, Turkmenistan, Kazakhstan, and the Aral Sea. Nearly four-fifths of Uzbekistan is desert. The capital is Tashkent.

History: Uzbekistan is named after the 14th century ruler of the Golden Horde, Uzbek Kahn, who ruled over Turkic tribes within the Mongol Empire. Uzbeks conquered much of the surrounding region in the 16th century, and were influenced by Iranian, Turkic, and Arab societies. The 19th century saw the entrance of Russians into the region. Muslim and Russian forces struggled to control the region in the early 20th century, with the Red Army taking command in 1923. The Uzbek Republic was created in 1936. In 1982, the Uzbek government was shaken when it was discovered Uzbekistan had sold cotton to the Soviet central government but never actually transferred any product. Much of the Uzbek government was imprisoned and thousands expelled from the Communist Party in the aftermath.

Politics: Following the August 1991 coup, the Communist Party in Uzbekistan broke with Moscow's Communist Party, changing its name to the Popular Democratic Party of Uzbekistan, but retaining its leadership role. Partly free elections for the Supreme Soviet were held in February 1990, with many Communist candidates running unopposed or for reserved seats. Karimov was appointed president in March 1990 by the Supreme Soviet and won relatively open elections for president in December 1991, drawing 86% of the vote. He has been accused of authoritarian leadership. Uzbekistan joined the Commonwealth of Independent States although Karimov has opposed Russian leadership of the military forces.

Economics: Per capita GNP, (1989): $2,750. Uzbekistan is the second poorest republic after Tajikistan. President Karimov has opposed the radical economic reforms taken by Russia and other republics, instead calling for "market socialism." The economy is heavily dependent on cotton production - two-thirds of the cotton grown in the former Soviet Union was produced here even though only nine percent of the land is arable. Environmental degradation and economic decline have seriously lowered the standard of living - almost half the population lives below the poverty line. Uzbekistan is heavily dependent on imported grain and other foodstuffs.

Current issues: Protests against Karimov and continued rule by former communists have occurred in several cities. Pro-democracy rallies in the fall of 1991 were forcibly broken up. Karimov promised on January 17, 1992 to register all political parties. He may, however, exclude the Islamic Rebirth Party, a fundamentalist Muslim party organizing in all the Central Asian republics. Islamic-inspired protests are growing in the republic.

Sources: *Congressional Research Service Report for Congress; Transcaucasus: A Chronology; The New York Times; The Washington Post; The Soviet Union at the Crossroads: Facts and Figures on the Soviet Republics; ACCESS Resource Brief* "Independence for the Baltic States;" *Foreign Affairs, " America and the World 1989/90"; The Economist.*

WHO IS WHO AND WHO WAS WHO

The following short biographies provide information on some of the key individuals in the former Soviet Union. The leaders of each republic are included; where available, other significant figures in the new nations are also included. Key historical figures are listed as well. Individuals whose description ends with an (FYI) notation were identified as up-and-coming leaders in democracy, ecology, peace, and entrepreneurship by FYI Information Resources for a Changing World.

Askar Akayev, President of Kyrgyzstan, won direct uncontested elections to that office on October 12, 1991. The former head of the Kyrgyz Academy of Sciences, Akayev is a reformer who was originally elected president by the Kyrgyz Supreme Soviet in October 1990. He defeated Absamat Masaliyev, a hard-line member of the Communist Party who had opposed a Kyrgyz declaration of sovereignty. While Akayev has endorsed democratization and the creation of a market economy, he also maintains support for the communist-dominated Supreme Soviet.

Victor Alksnis was leader of the hard-line faction in the now defunct Supreme Soviet or parliament. He is known as the "Dark Colonel." During the failed August 1991 coup, he and his supporters remained aloof. Many cite him as one who could lead a coup attempt against Yeltsin and try to bring back the Soviet Union.

Azat Zhalgasbayevich Allamuratov, president of the Karakalpakistan Cooperative Union in western Uzbekistan, is striving to overcome traditional resistance to democratic and market-oriented reforms in this Central Asian region. Although subject to harassment in the past, the Union continues to operate as a force in bringing the market economy to Karakalpakistan; Dr. Allamuratov's role in the Karakalpak economy will certainly increase. (FYI)

Michail Ananjan is the president of the International Conversion Foundation in Moscow. The Foundation is a private intermediary organization using Ananjan's contacts in the defense and military sectors to connect production facilities with foreign organizations interested in working with them. As the Russian economy continues to privatize and as defense enterprises convert to consumer goods production, Mr. Ananjan will be well positioned as a matchmaker for foreign and Russian firms. (FYI)

Aleksei Arbatov, Chief, Arms Control Department, Institute of World Economics and International Relations (IMEMO). One of the first foreign policy scholars to take part in arms control negotiations and a leading expert on disarmament and security policy for former Soviet President Mikhail Gorbachev.

Georgi Arbatov, Director of the Institute of the USA and Canada since its founding in 1967 and known as Russia's leading expert on the United States. He still has access to current Russian leadership and is a strong supporter of reform and a critic of the military.

Igor Yuryevich Artemyev serves as the chair of the St. Petersburg (formerly Leningrad) City Council Standing Committee for Environmental Control. Eighty percent of the legislation suggested by Artemyev's committee is eventually approved by the St. Petersburg City Council, the highest acceptance rate in Russia; it was instrumental in establishing one of the first effective "ecological banks," which uses fines and fees paid by enterprises to support environmental projects. The committee would like to institute a requirement for environmental impact statements for new construction and environmental assessments for existing facilities. Artemyev is also quite involved in preventing abuse of Russian environmental regulations by foreigners. The committee should continue to provide a model of effective environmental legislation for the rest of the former Soviet Union. (FYI)

Oleg D. Baklanov, former First Deputy Chairman of the USSR Defense Council, one of eight members of the coup committee, was elected to the Central Committee in 1986 after years in the Soviet defense industry. He was known for his faith in Communism and his belief it would eventually prevail. He was arrested following the coup and is in jail.

Nina Belyaeva is currently the head of the Interlegal Research Center, an organization of attorneys, researchers, and scholars dedicated to promoting the growth of a civil society in the former Soviet Union. She has previously served as a journalist for the popular independent weekly "Moscow News"; and at the International Foundation for the Survival and Development of Humanity. Belyaeva is frequently quoted as an expert on the emerging Russian democratic movement and on reforms in the legal system. As the reforms continue, she will become more prominent in these movements and in portraying them to the West. (FYI)

Aleksandr Bolyubash is the head of the independent Ecological Center of the Green Movement in Lugansk, Ukraine. To provide independent financing for the center, Bolyubash teaches an environmental course at the local university that offers certification to industry managers who successfully complete the course. His work is being recognized as a potential model for similar programs around the former Soviet Union. (FYI)

Leonid Brezhnev gradually emerged as the dominant figure in the USSR after Khrushchev was ousted in 1964. In power until his death in November 1982,

Brezhnev's 15 year reign was characterized by cautious domestic policies, a steady growth of Soviet military power and the massive central bureaucracy, and economic stagnation. It was Brezhnev who ordered Soviet tanks into Czechoslovakia in 1968, crushing Czech efforts to reform socialism. The "Brezhnev doctrine" justified the action on the basis that the USSR had an obligation to defend socialism in Warsaw Pact nations.

Gennadi Burbulis is State Secretary for the Russian Federation. He is a long-time Yeltsin supporter. He recently resigned a second position, First Deputy Premier, that he had held simultaneously with his current position. He frequently serves as a spokesman for Yeltsin.

Alim Ivanovich Chabanov, general director of the Rotor Scientific Production Association in Cherkassy, Ukraine, also serves as the president of Ekoprom, a consortium of defense and heavy machinery enterprises involved in development of environmental technology as part of the conversion process. Ekoprom's products have included water and wastewater treatment equipment, air pollution control equipment, and environmentally sound equipment for use in agriculture. Chabanov was an enterprise manager who faced resistance to implementation of new technologies; he was subsequently elected to the USSR Supreme Soviet. Although Ekoprom's activities have not been well publicized, the organization is likely to play a long-term, growing role in the Russian economy. (FYI)

Andriy Oleksiyovich Demydenko came out of the grassroots environmental tradition of Green World (Zelenyi Svit) and has since made a name for himself at the Ukrainian Ministry of the Environment as the head of the Department of Environment Information and Public Relations. Demydenko is a key link for both governmental and private environmental leaders in the Ukraine and internationally. (FYI)

Yegor Gaidar is Deputy Premier in charge of economic reform for Russia. He has been under increasing pressure from conservatives to resign in the aftermath of the worsening economic situation in Russia. Only in his mid-thirties, he and his assistants are holding firm in their efforts to force the command-style Soviet economic system to transform into a free-market system. Gaidar still has Yeltsin's full support.

Zviad Gamsakhurdia, former President of Georgia, was ousted in early January 1992. Pushing strong nationalist themes, he was elected with 87% of the vote in March 1991. However, his harsh, authoritarian rule, including arresting opposition leaders, censorship of the press, and moves to increase his own power, led to the rise of a movement to oust him. After rebel national guard groups trapped him in the parliament for two weeks, he sought asylum in Armenia, then returned to Georgia calling for an uprising to reinstate himself. Although he has some support, opposition groups have effectively taken control of the country.

Oleg Ivanovich Gapanovich is the chairman of the St. Petersburg (formerly Leningrad) City Council Commission on Defense Conversion. The Commission is working to inventory military and defense production facilities in St. Petersburg, where much of the industry was based; they are also working to connect those facilities with international investors and companies interested in conversion. As the Russian movement toward conversion continues, Gapanovich and the Commission will continue to attract attention with their forward-looking methods. (FYI)

Fedor Grigoryevich Gasparyan is a poet and writer deeply involved in Chernobyl/radiation issues in Bryansk (SW of Moscow); he was elected to the Russian Supreme Soviet and now serves as the head of the Committee on Ecology and Natural Resources' Subcommittee on Radiation Safety. He is working closely with American organizations on the development of legislation dealing with radiation safety and will continue to have a large part in the grassroots environmental movement dealing with Chernobyl and other nuclear issues. (FYI)

Ivars Godmanis is Prime Minister of Latvia. He is directing the country's gradual transition to a market economy, creating a central bank, starting to free prices, and allowing privatization of small retail shops. He has a leadership role in the Latvian People's Front, the main political organization brought together to press for Latvian independence.

Mikhail Gorbachev was the leader of the Soviet Union from 1985 until 1991. He became General Secretary of the Central Committee of the Communist Party in 1985, following the death of Konstantin Chernenko. Gorbachev introduced a series of reforms designed to open up Soviet society and re-invigorate the economic and political system. He vastly improved relations with the West and signed several major arms control treaties. While his economic reforms proved weak, other changes set up a chain of events that led to the end of Soviet domination of Eastern Europe. On August 19, 1991, Gorbachev was placed under house arrest by a hard-line Communist faction. The coup collapsed two days later and Gorbachev returned to power, but was overshadowed by Russian leader Boris Yeltsin, who led the opposition to the coup. Gorbachev continued attempts to preserve the union, but Yeltsin and other republic leaders rebuffed him. When the formation of the CIS was finalized, Gorbachev agreed to step down, and he resigned on December 25, 1991. He now heads a private research institute in Moscow.

Anatolijis Gorbunovs, Chairman of the Supreme Council of Latvia (or President), started out in the Latvian Communist Party and worked his way up to the Party's ideology secretary. He was one of the first apparatchiks (Communist party functionary) to publicly support the nationalist Latvian People's Front. He has close ties to the current Russian leadership, and is using those connections to help solve Latvia's interethnic problems with its large Russian minority.

Maira Adyrbekovna Junusova is the general director of the Ecological Foundation of Kazakhstan, an environmental organization involved in performing independent environmental assessments and environmental impact statements (EA/EIS) for local industry, including petroleum and natural gas processing. The Foundation is also working on a database of Kazakh environmental problems. The idea of EA/EIS is spreading in the former Soviet Union and the Ecological Foundation of Kazakhstan's work should serve as a model of how to perform and apply these analyses. (FYI)

Yusup Kamalov researches alternative energy sources as the Chief of the Wind Energy Group at the Karakalpakistan branch of the Uzbekistan Academy of Sciences. He is also deeply involved with the issue of the dying Aral Sea. Kamalov is vice president of the Union for the Protection of the Aral Sea and the Amu Darya River; he is also a charter member of the Aral Sea Information Committee, an international grassroots environmental information group. (FYI)

Islam Karimov, President of Uzbekistan, withdrew from the Communist Party of the Soviet Union following the failed August 1991 coup, but remains the head of the renamed Uzbek Communist Party. Now called the Democratic Party of Uzbekistan, it does not enjoy wide popular support but, with Karimov's continued backing, remains in power. Karimov, an ethnic Uzbek, has stated he prefers the Chinese model of economic over political reform. His somewhat authoritarian rule has been called "national communism."

Vladimir A. Kruchkov, former Chairman of the KGB, one of eight members of the coup committee, was arrested and remains in jail. He was a protege of Yuri Andropov.

Nikita Khrushchev was premier of the Soviet Union from 1958 to 1964. Following Stalin's death in 1953, Khrushchev became General Secretary of the Communist Party; he later denounced Stalin and Stalinism and sought to institute reforms in political and economic policy. Following the withdrawal of Soviet missiles from Cuba during the Cuban Missile Crisis and the failure of his agricultural reforms, Khrushchev was ousted and replaced by Leonid Brezhnev.

Andrei Kokoshin, Deputy Director of the Institute of the USA and Canada, focuses on defense conversion. Prominent author in foreign and domestic press, commentator on arms control and military-related issues.

Andrey Vadimovich Kortunov, Department Chief, Institute of USA and Canada; a prominent civilian expert on defense and security policy. Early proponent of the military doctrine of "reasonable sufficiency" - a doctrine that stresses maintaining only a minimal level of forces necessary for defensive purposes. Publishes in both foreign and domestic press.

Leonid Kravchuk, President of Ukraine and Chairman of the Presidium of the Ukrainian Supreme Soviet, a former Communist Party official who now is a strong supporter of Ukrainian nationalism. Kravchuk has fought what he (and others) perceive as Russian efforts to dominate the CIS and the former Soviet republics. He was one of the three original signatories of the agreement founding the CIS but views it as a transitory arrangement designed to ease the formation of new states. He agreed to transfer all strategic and nuclear weapons to Russia but, in March, temporarily stopped shipments until he was reassured they were being destroyed. Has argued with Russia over control of the Black Sea naval fleet and the pace of economic reforms.

Vytautas Landsbergis, Chairman of the Supreme Council (or President) of Lithuania, is the popular leader of the resistance to Soviet rule. He was a rallying point for nationalists in the Baltics. Landsbergis, a former music professor, emerged in the public eye in 1988, when he became chairman of the Sajudis Seimas Council, the nationalist organization leading the fight for Lithuanian independence. He has survived an economic blockade by Moscow and several internal squabbles.

Vladimir Ilyich Lenin was founder of the Bolshevik (later Communist) Party, a leader in the Bolshevik Revolution in 1917 and organized the foundation of the Soviet Union. Following the intellectual path of Karl Marx, Lenin developed Marxian socialism and applied it to the Soviet Union. He led the Soviet Union until his death in 1924.

Yagub Mamedov, Acting President of Azerbaijan, took on that role in early March 1992 when Ayaz Mutalibov, the former president, was forced to step down amid the continuing violence and protests over the disputed Nagorno-Karabakh region.

Viktor Mikhaylov, Deputy Minister, Atomic Energy and Industry of the Russian Federation and a veteran arms control negotiator. Has proposed using the $400 million given by the US Congress to aid in dismantling nuclear weapons to build storage dumps for radioactive waste. Also proposed joint US-Soviet projects in nuclear sciences to employ nuclear scientists.

Nataliya Ivanovna Mironova is the chairperson of the Nuclear Safety Committee of the Chelyabinsk regional council (south central Russia); she previously worked on the Chelyabinsk Ecological Fund, an organization which was instrumental in bringing to light the 1957 accident in Chelyabinsk and the contamination of the Techa River with radioactive wastes from the defense industry. Several nuclear-weapons-producing facilities are located in and around Chelyabinsk; the Nuclear Safety Committee is working on arms control and other peace issues. As the clean up of former military sites gets into full swing, the activities of the Chelyabinsk activists will serve as a model for other affected areas. (FYI)

Ayaz Mutalibov, former President of Azerbaijan, was originally placed in power by Soviet leadership following the 1990 intervention in Baku, the capital, by Soviet troops. He grew in popularity and won direct but uncontested elections for president in September 1991. He was forced to resign after Armenians in the Nagorno-Karabakh region reportedly massacred much of the population of a small, Azerbaijani-dominated town.

Rakhmon Nabiyev, President of Tajikistan, won direct contested election to that post in November 1991, after a long series of leadership changes. Nabiyev is former chairman of the Tajik Supreme Soviet and first secretary of the republic's Communist Party Central Committee. He replaced Kadreddin Aslonov, who had replaced former Party Chief and President Kakhar Makhkamov after the latter's support for the failed August 1991 coup. Aslonov, after suspending Communist Party activities, was forced aside by hard-liners and replaced by Nabiyev, who in turn was forced to step down temporarily following protests by opposition forces. Nabiyev was restored to office as a result of the November elections, in which he won 58% of the vote to 30% for the opposition candidate. Nabiyev has reinstated the Communist Party but has sought to downsize the government by 40 percent.

Nursultan Nazarbayev, President of Kazakhstan and chair of its security council. Nazarbayev is a respected political moderate who rejects Islamic fundamentalism, a growing issue in Muslim-dominated Kazakhstan. In early 1992, he pledged to eventually rid Kazakhstan of nuclear weapons. Previously, Kazakhstan had threatened to keep some nuclear weapons as long as Russia did.

Saparmurad Niyazov, President of Turkmenistan, was elected to that office by the Supreme Soviet in November 1990. Niyazov resigned from the U.S.S.R. Communist Party Politburo after the failed August 1991 coup. One month later, he declared the Turkmen Communist Party no longer had any property rights. In December, the party changed its name to the Demo-cratic Party of Turkmenistan, and stated it was a parliamentary party. Although Communist Party structures and former members still dominate the government, Niyazov has brought about market reforms, introducing free prices in January 1992. He has sought relations with both Turkey, Turkmenistan's cultural ally, and Iran, the republic's powerful southern neighbor.

Dmitry Oreshkin is an engineer and a senior fellow at the Institute of Geography of the Academy of Sciences. Oreshkin also serves as the foreign commercial liaison for the Institute, which is the leading state research center for geography and demography. The Institute publishes a journal, environmental and nuclear radiation maps, and many scholarly studies and has monitored the world environment and man's place in the planet's ecology for 20 years. (FYI)

V.S. Pavlov, former Prime Minister of the USSR, one of eight members of the coup committee, was an economist by training. As the USSR's Minister of Finance in 1989, his tax reforms received widespread disapproval. He was appointed Prime Minister in January 1991. He opposed seeking aid from the West. He was arrested following the coup and is in jail.

Dmytro Pavlychko, is Chairman of the Ukrainian Surpreme Council Committee on Foreign Affairs and a leading figure in Rukh, the opposition umbrella organization that pushes nationalist issues. Pavlychko and Rukh support independence from Moscow. Rukh candidates captured almost one-third of the seats in the Ukrainian Supreme Soviet.

Boris K. Pugo, former Director of the Interior Ministry of the USSR, was perhaps the most feared leader of the failed August 1991 coup. Pugo, a child of ethnic Latvians, used the Interior Ministry's special forces to attempt to crush Latvian and other Baltic states' independence movements. With Pugo's support, many thought the KGB, the armed forces, and the Interior Ministry's troops would support the coup. Pugo committed suicide on August 21, 1991, the last day of the failed coup, after he was told troops were coming to arrest him.

Victor Reshetin is the general director of the IIA Sistema-Reserve, which evolved from the Reserve Cooperative, one of the first Ukrainian cooperatives registered to engage in foreign trade. IIA Sistema-Reserve provides a range of business, engineering, market research, and information services (utilizing a network of dozens of organizations providing business information from across the former Soviet Union). Reserve was one of the first organizations to understand the importance of retrievable business information on the former Soviet Union. (FYI)

Sergey Rogov, Deputy Director of the Institute of the USA and Canada, head of its political-military section. Is a proponent of the military doctrine of "reasonable sufficiency" and has argued with the military in the past.

Maj. Gen. Aleksandr Rutskoy, Vice President of Russia, supported Yeltsin during the coup attempt. Rutskoy, from a military family and a war hero in Afghanistan, has cast himself as both a defender of the military and a promoter of military reform. He received his post for splitting from a hard-line faction and backing Yeltsin's campaign for president of Russia. He has opposed Yeltsin's economic plans and other reforms, and has been stressing Russian nationalist themes.

Arnold Ruutel, President of Estonia, has overseen the restoration of Estonian independence. Widely popular in Estonia, Ruutel is seeking to establish relations with the Commonwealth of Independent States, on which his country heavily depends economically, and with the West as well.

Andrei Sakharov was a nuclear physicist and human rights leader, who was awarded the Nobel Peace Prize in 1975 for his willingness to publicize repression and civil rights abuse in the Soviet system. After playing a pivotal role in the development of Soviet nuclear weapons, Sakharov became concerned about the destructiveness of nuclear weapons and advocated a ban on nuclear testing. Persecuted for his human rights work, Sakharov was exiled by Brezhnev in 1980 for condemning the invasion of Afghanistan, and allowed to return by Gorbachev in 1986. At his death in 1989, Sakharov was the most respected political figure in the Soviet Union and regarded by Soviet colleagues as a "moral compass."

Aleksandr Savelev is affiliated with IMEMO, the Academy of Sciences' Institute of World Economics and International Relations; he is also one of the key people at the Institute for National Defense and Security Studies, an organization that arose from IMEMO. Savelev's specialty is nuclear weapons and START issues; his academic background is in international relations and diplomacy. Having worked on START issues for years, Savelev is likely to serve in an advisory capacity for Russian START negotiations. (FYI)

Edgar Savissar is Prime Minister of Estonia and leader of the Estonian People's Front, the political organization brought together to press for Estonian independence. He has led the way in reforming Estonia's economy, developing a plan in 1988 that has led to free prices, initialized privatization of small businesses and farms, and encouraged private entrepreneurs and foreign investors.

Marshal Yevgeni Shaposhnikov, Commander-in-Chief of the Commonwealth of Independent States military forces, was appointed Defense Minister of the former USSR after the failed coup. He has attempted to maintain a unified control over the armed forces of the former Soviet Union, but has also acknowledged the right of sovereign states to create their own military. He has stated the army will not support a second coup attempt.

Yuri Shchekochikhin is an outspoken investigative journalist and has served as a USSR People's Deputy. He has been a visible and well-connected member of the Russian democratic movement since the rise of political pluralism began in the former Soviet Union. Shchekochikhin is quoted in the Western and Russian press as a leading figure in the struggle for democratic government; as part of his ongoing investigative work on the KGB, he is currently working on a project publishing interviews and "confessions" of KGB agents. As this book and Shchekochikhin's other works become more widely known, his role in moving democracy forward in Russia will continue to expand. (FYI)

Yuri Shcherbak is the current Minister of Environmental Protection of Ukraine. He has long been an environmentalist and a Ukrainian nationalist. His outspoken reaction to the accident at Chernobyl gave him some publicity. Although he is already well-known in certain sectors, with the advent of Ukrainian independence, Shcherbak should gain even greater political power in the future. (FYI)

Eduard Shevardnadze, Chairman of the State Council of Georgia, was Foreign Minister of the Soviet Union under former president Mikhail Gorbachev and, previous to that, Communist Party boss in Georgia. Shevardnadze, widely respected by the West in recent years, was one of Gorbachev's chief allies during the moves to reform the Soviet Union. He resigned following military crack-downs in several republics, saying he feared a return to hard-line rule, but returned following the failed August 1991 coup. Following the ouster of Georgian President Gamsakhurdia in January 1992, Shevardnadze agreed to return to Georgia to help restore order to the republic and serve as chair of the ruling State Council.

Stanislau Shushkevich is Chairman of the Presidium of the Supreme Soviet of Belarus. Trained as a nuclear physicist, he has repeatedly stressed Belarus' intention to become a nuclear-free state. He became politically active in the aftermath of the Chernobyl disaster. He is a political moderate who delegated the organization of the Belorussian army to military professionals.

Tengiz Sigua, acting Prime Minister of Georgia, led the coalition that ousted former President Zviad Gamsakhurdia. Sigua was Prime Minister until Gamsakhurdia fired him in August 1991. Despite this, he argued against vendettas toward the former president and sought to avoid bloodshed. He has sought ties with Russia and will probably support joining the CIS. He is a member of the ruling State Council of Georgia.

Mircea Snegur, President of Moldova, won direct uncontested election to that office on December 8, 1991, with 98% of the vote. He has emphasized developing legislative and executive structures; a new democratic constitution is being prepared. On the issue of unification with Romania (Moldova was part of Romania until the early 19th century and again between the two world wars), Snegur has stated that Moldova must go through a long independence phase before unification can be considered.

Joseph Stalin was the dictatorial leader of the Soviet Union from the mid-1920s until his death in 1953. He was made General Secretary of the Communist Party in 1922 and beat out several rivals to replace Vladimir Lenin, who died in 1924. Stalin instituted forced collectivization of farms, mass industrialization, "russianization" of the population (forcing the language and culture of Russia on other nationalities), and several purges of leadership and the middle classes. These policies killed millions and destroyed Soviet society. Following a costly victory in World War II, Stalin took control of eastern Europe, installing governments submissive to his will. His death led to some reduction in dictatorial rule but no change in most Soviet policies.

V.A. Starodutsev, chairman of the Farmer's Union of the USSR, one of eight members of the coup committee, was a peasant by birth who rose to power as an agricultural reformer in the 1970s. He was not widely known before the coup and is now in jail.

Olzhas Suleymenov, Chairman of the Nevada-Semipalatinsk Movement and of the Kazakhstan People's Congress Party. Suleymenov is a long-time anti-nuclear activist and was key in the movement that closed the Semipalatinsk nuclear test site. He is a strong supporter of Kazakh autonomy and was an outspoken representative in the former USSR Supreme Soviet.

Levon Ter-Petrossyan, President of Armenia, won direct election for that office on October 16, 1991. A former Chairman of the Armenian Supreme Soviet and a former dissident, Ter-Petrossyan is a member of the Armenian National Movement, the majority party in the parliament. Most of his efforts are focused on resolving the issue of the Nagorno-Karabakh region, an Armenian-dominated enclave in Azerbaijan.

A.I. Tizyakov, former President of the Association of State Enterprises and Industrial, Construction, Transport, and Communications Facilities of the USSR, one of eight members of the coup committee, was arrested following the coup and is in jail.

Yevgeniy Velikov, Vice President of the Russian Academy of Sciences. Recently named chairman of a commission to develop a plan for dismantling nuclear weapons. Was director of the emergency scientific measures to contain the Chernobyl disaster. Is well known in scientific forums as a proponent of disarmament and critic of the Strategic Defense Initiative.

Gennadi I. Yanayev, former Vice President of the USSR, acting president during the short-lived coup of August 1991. Widely perceived as a Communist Party functionary, Yanayev was never seen as an actual leader in the coup, but rather a quasi-constitutionally correct replacement and a malleable personality others could control. He had risen through the ranks of the Communist Youth Organization, then became chair of the Soviet Trade Unions in 1990, and was elected to the Politburo in July 1990. Gorbachev, for reasons never quite clear, nominated him for vice president in December 1990; he was elected to the post after a surprisingly pitched battle in the Parliament. After the coup collapsed, he was arrested and is now in jail.

Dmitri T. Yazov, former Defense Minister of the USSR, one of eight members of the coup committee, a career military man who was opposed to Gorbachev's economic and military reforms. Erroneously reported to have committed suicide, Yazov was arrested following the coup and is in jail.

Boris Yeltsin, President of Russia by direct contested election, Supreme Commander of the CIS nuclear arsenal, is a man beset by troubles but sure of himself. He rose to prominence supporting Gorbachev's reforms but was demoted in 1987 for criticizing the Communist Party leadership and pushing for faster reforms. In March 1989, he won election to the Congress of People's Deputies and later served in the USSR Supreme Soviet. In May 1990 he was elected president of Russia by the Russian Parliament; in July he resigned from the Communist Party following a hard-line challenge to Gorbachev's leadership. On June 12, 1991, Yeltsin won direct election for the presidency of Russia with 60 percent of the vote. He led the resistance to the failed August 1991 coup, rallying thousands to protect the Russian parliament from where he and his government were operating. When Gorbachev returned to Moscow, Yeltsin pushed him into resigning from the Communist Party. Yeltsin later joined with the leaders of Belarus and Ukraine to pronounce the end of the Soviet Union and form the Commonwealth of Independent States. He is facing vast challenges as he attempts to implement a free market, maintain control of nuclear weapons and the former Soviet army, and pull together the CIS.

Vladimir Zhirinovsky is a member of the Nashi coalition that supports the restoration of either the Soviet Union or its predecessor, the Russian Empire. Zhirinovsky ran in the June 1991 Russian presidential election that Yeltsin won; Zhirinovsky came in third. As chair of the misnamed Liberal-Democratic Party, he pushes xenophobia, cheap vodka, and expansion of territory through force.

GLOSSARY

"Brezhnev Doctrine". A policy enunciated by former Soviet premier Brezhnev in 1968 as justification for the invasion of Czechoslovakia. Brezhnev claimed that the Soviet Union had the right to protect socialism in member states of the Warsaw Pact.

Charter of Paris for a New Europe. One of five documents adopted at the November 1990 Paris CSCE summit meeting, the Charter lays out principles and agreements by the states to promote "a new era of democracy, peace and unity" in Europe.

Commonwealth of Independent States (CIS). Formed by the Presidents of Russia, Ukraine and Belarus, in Mensk in December, 1991 and subsequently joined by the Presidents of eight other republics (excluding the Baltic States and Georgia) at Alma Ata, Kazakhstan on December 12, 1991. The CIS is a loose body which has no central ministries, but appears to be serving as a transitional, coordinating structure as the Soviet Union breaks apart.

Conference on Security and Cooperation in Europe (CSCE). Also referred to as the "CSCE process," CSCE is a continuing series of meetings which began in Helsinki, Finland in 1972. The 1975 CSCE "Final Act" provides a set of guiding principles for peaceful relations and cooperation among the members. Because its membership (now 52 nations) includes all European countries plus the US, Canada, and all former republics of the USSR, it is the most inclusive European institution but also the most unwieldy.

Congress of People's Deputies of the former USSR was composed of 2,250 deputies directly elected by the people. Under Gorbachev's reforms, elections were contested for the first time in 1989. The Congress set basic guidelines for policy, could amend the Constitution, and elected the Supreme Soviet.

Conventional Forces in Europe (CFE) Treaty. The CFE talks among NATO and Warsaw Pact nations, which began in Vienna, Austria in 1987, produced a Treaty in November, 1990 setting limits on major items of military equipment from the Atlantic Ocean to the Ural mountains. The disintegration of the USSR has held up ratification and implementation of the Treaty.

European Bank for Reconstruction and Development (EBRD) began operations in London in April 1991, and is the first institution of post-Cold War Europe. The Bank is intended to foster the transition to democracy and free market economies in Eastern Europe and the former Soviet Union. The Bank must lend 60% of its funds to the private sector, and states receiving funds must maintain a multi-party democracy.

European Community (EC) is comprised of three distinct entities: the *European Coal and Steel Community* (ECSC) established in 1952, the *European Economic Community* (EEC), and the *European Energy Community* (Euratom) both established in 1958. The EC is the vehicle for West European economic and political integration. Its members are Belgium, Denmark, France, Germany, Greece, Ireland, Italy, Luxembourg, the Netherlands, Portugal, Spain and the United Kingdom.

General Agreement on Tariffs and Trade (GATT) is an international commercial agreement signed in 1947 by 96 nations (including the US). Four long-term goals of GATT: 1) non-discrimination in trade practices; 2) reduction of tariffs by negotiation; 3) elimination of import quotas (with some exceptions); and 4) resolution of differences through consultation. The GATT agreement is periodically reviewed and renewed. Russia and other successor states seek to join the GATT.

Glasnost or "Openness". A policy of greater freedom of speech and of the press initiated by former Soviet President Gorbachev. The policy opened the way for expressions of nationalism and criticisms of Gorbachev himself.

Gross National Product (GNP). The main market value of all goods and services bought for final use during a year. GNP is considered the most comprehensive measure of a nation's economic activity. *Real GNP* is GNP adjusted for inflation.

Group of Seven (G-7). Comprising the seven world monetary powers: the US, the United Kingdom, France, Germany, Japan, Italy, and Canada. Summits began in 1975 to devote attention to common economic problems.

Helsinki Declaration (or Helsinki Final Act). Adopted by the CSCE (see above) in 1975 as a statement of principles on human rights and also providing for confidence-building measures and disarmament. The statement of principles has provided the basis for judging progress toward genuine democracy, and a base for US policy toward the former Soviet Union.

Intercontinental ballistic missile (ICBM). A ballistic missile with a range of 5,500 kilometers or more. By custom, the term ICBM is used only for land-based systems, in order to differentiate them from submarine launched ballistic missiles (SLBM's) which can also be of intercontinental range.

International Atomic Energy Agency (IAEA). An autonomous agency of the United Nations, founded in 1957 charged with (a) promoting peaceful uses of atomic energy, and (b) ensuring that nuclear materials used for energy production and research are not diverted for military purposes. Nations that agree to the Non-Proliferation Treaty must conclude a "safeguards agreement" with the IAEA.

International Monetary Fund (IMF) was established at the end of World War II to promote international monetary cooperation and the expansion of trade, and provide mechanisms to stabilize international financial exchange. It also makes funds available to member states so that balance-of-payment needs can be corrected without measures that would threaten international prosperity. The IMF is likely to be the largest lender to the former Soviet Union. Its financial and technical aid is seen as critically important as the new states of the former Soviet Union seek to integrate their economies into world markets.

Marshall Plan. Named for then US Secretary of State George Marshall in 1947, was a massive American aid program to the war-devastated regions of Europe. The infusion of American aid and assistance provided by the Marshall Plan speeded European recovery from World War II. The US offered Marshall Plan assistance to Eastern Europe and the USSR, but Stalin refused.

Non-Proliferation Regime. A collection of treaties, agreements, voluntary guidelines, and international institutions that collectively work toward preventing the spread of nuclear weapons. The centerpiece is the Non-Proliferation Treaty (NPT), which came into force in 1970, and now has over 140 nations that are parties to the Treaty.

North Atlantic Treaty Organization (NATO). A collective defense organization based on the North Atlantic Treaty (Treaty of Washington) signed on April 4, 1949. It has been the main Western forum for coordination of policies and defense efforts toward the Soviet threat in Europe. Current members include Belgium, Canada, Denmark, France, Germany, Greece, Iceland, Italy, Luxembourg, the Netherlands, Norway, Portugal, Spain, Turkey, United Kingdom, and the United States.

Organization for Economic Co-operation and Development (OECD). Established in 1961 to replace the Organization for European Economic Co-operation (OEEC). The 24 nations that make up the OECD include the US, Canada, Australia, New Zealand, and Japan, as well as the nations of Western Europe. The purpose of the OECD is to promote economic and social welfare by coordinating policies of the member states.

Perestroika or "restructuring". A program initiated by former Soviet President Gorbachev to restructure and invigorate the stagnant Soviet economy. Perestroika was initially seen as a way to reform Communism, rather than to introduce a market economy.

The **Politburo** was the powerful policy-forming executive body of the ruling Communist Party in the former Soviet Union. Under Gorbachev, the monopoly power of the Communist Party was scaled back, and the Politburo became less important.

Strategic forces are designed for long-range attack on the territory of an adversary, in order to destroy its war-making potential. Strategic weapons include ICBM's, long-range bombers, and nuclear submarines.

Supreme Soviet, in the former Soviet Union, was technically the supreme state and legislative body but was essentially a ceremonial rubber stamp. Under Gorbachev's reforms implemented in 1989, the Supreme Soviet became more of a true legislature. The 542 deputies were elected from the popularly elected Congress of People's Deputies. Each republic had its own Surpreme Soviet, many remain in some form in the present republic governments.

Tactical weapons or forces are designed for short-range battlefield use. Tactical weapons include artillery, fighter planes, tanks, etc. Tactical weapons may be armed with conventional, nuclear, chemical or biological warheads.

Warsaw Treaty Organization (WTO, Warsaw Pact). Founded in 1955 as a response to West Germany's joining NATO. The USSR subsequently used the pact, however, to facilitate control over its East European "allies." The Warsaw Pact disbanded in 1991. It included Bulgaria, Czechoslovakia, East Germany, Hungary, Poland, Romania, and the Soviet Union. Albania, an original signatory, left in 1968. Yugoslavia never joined the Warsaw Pact.

World Bank. The single largest source of development assistance for developing countries (now including the countries of Eastern Europe and the former Soviet Union). The World Bank is composed of three related institutions — the *International Bank for Reconstruction and Development* founded at the end of World War II to facilitate investment and promote trade, the *International Development Administration*, and the *International Finance Corporation*, both aimed at the needs of very poor countries.

Sources: Congressional Quarterly, **Washington Information Directory 1991-1992**; Arms Control Association, **Arms Control and National Security: An Introduction** (1989); ACCESS Security Spectrum, *"Economic Dimensions of US National Security"* and *"The Future of NATO and US Interests;"* **SIPRI Yearbook 1991 World Armaments and Disarmament**.

THE NATIONS OF THE FORMER SOVIET UNION

Names and boundary representation
are not necessarily authoritative

1671 2-91 STATE (INR/GE)

Map courtesy of the State Department

Occupied by the Soviet Union
in 1945, administered by Russia,
claimed by Japan

Final boundaries of Estonia, Latvia and
Lithuania with the former Soviet Union are
expected to be confirmed by agreement.

THE BALTIC STATES, BELARUS, MOLDOVA, AND UKRAINE

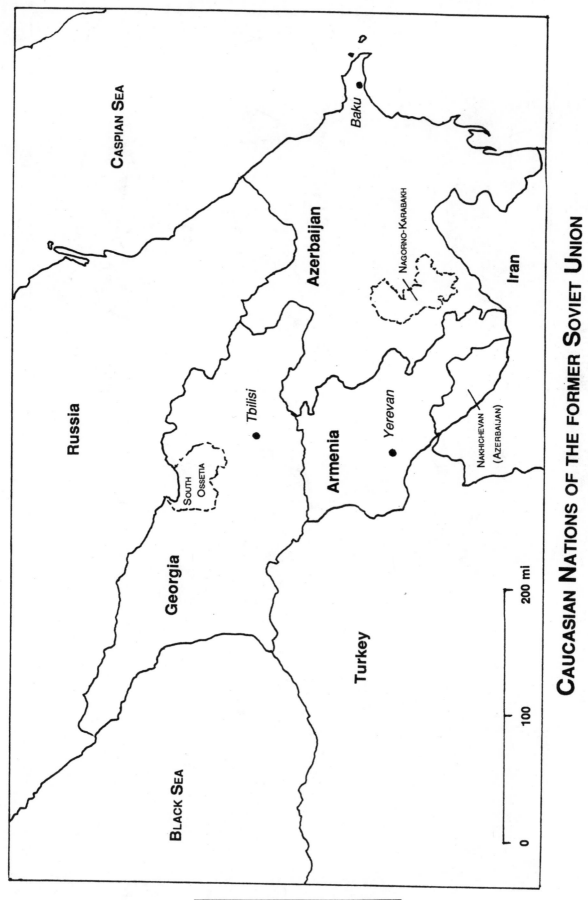

CAUCASIAN NATIONS OF THE FORMER SOVIET UNION

CASPIAN SEA

Baku

Azerbaijan

NAGORNO-KARABAKH

Iran

Russia

Tbilisi

Armenia

Yerevan

SOUTH OSSETIA

NAKHICHEVAN (AZERBAIJAN)

Georgia

Turkey

BLACK SEA

0   100   200 mi

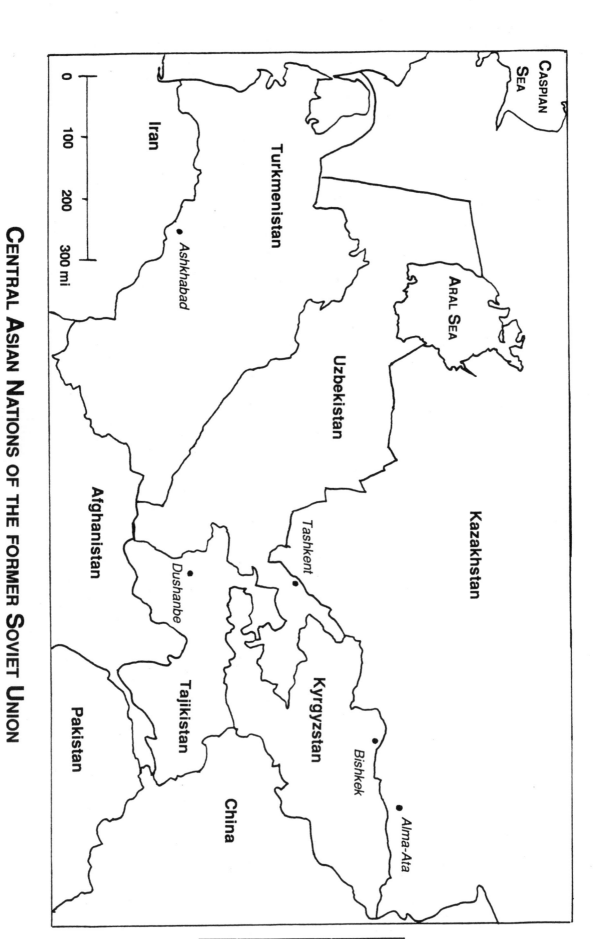

CENTRAL ASIAN NATIONS OF THE FORMER SOVIET UNION

CASPIAN SEA

Iran

Turkmenistan

• Ashkhabad

Uzbekistan

ARAL SEA

Kazakhstan

Afghanistan

Tashkent
•

Dushanbe
•

Tajikistan

Kyrgyzstan

Bishkek
•

Alma-Ata
•

Pakistan

China

0
100
200
300 mi

CHANGE AND CHALLENGE IN THE FORMER USSR
The End of the Cold War and the Dawn of a New Era
by Ronald J. Bee

On the morning of December 26, 1991, Mikhail Gorbachev left his dacha in the woods outside Moscow and climbed into his Zil limousine for his last trip to the Kremlin as President of the Soviet Union. When he arrived, his nameplate had already been replaced with "Yeltsin, Boris Nikolaevitch." Yeltsin, the first popularly elected President, now sat proudly at his desk. The Russian Tricolor flag flew over the Kremlin instead of the red and yellow hammer and sickle, a clear sign that Soviet rule and the Soviet empire had come to an end.

When Gorbachev came to power in March 1985, he did not seek this result. He envisioned a path of political and economic reform that could strengthen the USSR and reinvigorate the Communist Party. Instead, he fostered nothing less than a second Russian revolution that changed the course of history, a revolution that has not yet reached its endpoint.

Gorbachev initiated major political and economic reforms that sparked a revolution - the extent and pace of which often became as dizzying to the Soviet people as to Western experts. Gorbachev's reforms of *glasnost* (openness) and *perestroika* (economic restructuring) ultimately weakened the communist foundations of state secrecy and central government control that had existed since 1917.

Soviet communism had functioned through a repressive political system and a centrally planned economy. The USSR had built a first rate military of some five million soldiers under arms at the expense of its civilian economy; while it manufactured high quality armaments, it neither produced adequate consumer goods nor enough food to feed the Soviet population. For Gorbachev and other reformers, such "guns over butter" trade-offs could no longer be tolerated.

From 1945-89, during the Cold War, the Soviet Union dominated Eastern Europe. (The "East bloc" was comprised of Bulgaria, Czechoslovakia, East Germany, Hungary, Poland, Rumania, and the USSR.) Pro-Soviet governments imposed political controls by ensuring the "leading role" of the Communist Party, economic controls via the Council for Mutual Economic Assistance (CMEA or Comecon), and military controls through the Warsaw Treaty Organization (WTO or Warsaw Pact). When these controls were challenged, the USSR either threatened intervention (as in Poland in 1981) or actually invaded (as in Hungary in 1956 and Czechoslovakia in 1968). Following the 1968 invasion, then Soviet leader Leonid Brezhnev claimed the right to intervene in the internal affairs of allies when communist rule was threatened. This policy became known as the "Brezhnev Doctrine."

All this changed in 1989. In October, Mikhail Gorbachev said the USSR "had no right, moral or political right, to interfere in the events happening in Eastern Europe." This policy change permitted a political and largely peaceful revolution in Eastern Europe. In the process, the Brezhnev Doctrine died, COMECON dissolved, and the Warsaw Pact imploded.

The breakup of Soviet controls over Eastern Europe proved a harbinger of the breakup of the USSR. Gorbachev, however, still clung to the Communist Party as the best avenue for reform. He sought to transform the Soviet system from within, against great odds and many obstacles: among them, a society steeped in fear and inertia with no tradition of democratic government; a huge, ossified communist bureaucracy protecting its own interests; and a military and KGB (Committee on State Security) witnessing their privileges and influence dissolve before their very eyes.

Gorbachev intended to instill in the Soviet citizenry a belief that they had a stake in seeing the system succeed. His program of *glasnost* (openness) sought to open Soviet society so that it could and would participate in the decision-making process. *Glasnost* relaxed state secrecy and control over the news media, a move that created unprecedented candor and public criticism of the darker sides of Soviet history. It also opened a Pandora's box of ethnic problems as smoldering nationalities issues, repressed for decades, resurfaced with a vengance.

An historic turning point occurred in August 1991. Gorbachev had negotiated a Union Treaty that would have radically shifted power away from the Soviet central government to the republics. By August, six republics of Estonia, Latvia, Lithuania, Moldavia, Armenia, and Georgia had each formally announced its intention to leave the USSR and become independent nations. The other nine republics, at Gorbachev's coaxing, agreed to stay in the Union in exchange for virtual sovereignty over economic and social decisions. But on August 19, one day before the treaty's signing, communist hard-liners, fearing this devolution of power, seized control of the Soviet government.

An eight man committee, "The State Committee for the State of Emergency in the USSR," assumed Gorbachev's powers "with the aim of overcoming the profound and comprehensive crisis, political, ethnic and civil strife, chaos, and anarchy that threaten the lives and security of the Soviet Union's citizens." The Committee placed Gorbachev under house arrest and suspended the rights of all democratic political parties. Refusing to allow the clock to be turned back, thousands of citizens in Moscow and St. Petersburg went to the streets to protest the coup. They set up barricades and human shields to prevent tanks from approaching "The Russian White House," the Russian Parliament in Moscow.

Boris Yeltsin, the popularly-elected Russian president and reformer, stood on a tank and declared the coup "reactionary" and "unconstitutional". His pleas for democratic resistance were broadcast on news networks worldwide. President Bush called the coup illegal, and refused to recognize its leaders. The European Community cut off aid to the USSR. Meanwhile, key Red Army and KGB units defected to the protesters. Atop the tank, Yeltsin pleaded with the soldiers "not to shoot their mothers." The troops listened to him, and chose not to fire.

The coup collapsed in the face of mounting popular resistance and worldwide condemnation. By August 22, Gorbachev was restored to power, the coup leaders were arrested, and the entire Communist Party discredited. Yeltsin and other reformers gained new stature and quickly cleaned house to set the stage for accelerated reforms. Thirty of 34 central government ministers were fired immediately. The Communist Party's central administrative organs were dissolved, its assets and archives seized, and its activities suspended.

The failed coup proved to be a catalyst for the collapse of Soviet Communism. Central authority toppled in the wake of popular revulsion and growing nationalist sentiments. On September 6, 1991 full independence was granted to the Baltic States of Estonia, Latvia, and Lithuania. The breakup of the USSR became inevitable in early December when 90% of Ukraine voted for independence. Without Ukraine's rich farmland, heavy industry, and fifty-three million people, Gorbachev's hopes for a new union were doomed.

On the weekend of December 6-8, 1991, the Presidents of the republics of Russia, Ukraine and Belarus (formerly Belorussia) met at a hunting lodge near Brest in Belarus. These three leaders represented "The Slavic Heartland" of the USSR, some 70% of the population and 80% of its industry. On December 8, they proclaimed the creation of a Commonwealth of Independent States (CIS) and the death of the Soviet Union:

We the Republic of Belarussia, the Russian Federation and Ukraine, as founding members of the Union of Soviet Socialist Republics, having signed the Union Treaty of 1922 and hereafter referred to as the Agreeing Parties, state that the Union of Soviet Socialist Republics as a subject of international law and geopolitical reality has ceased to exist.

On December 21, at a meeting in Alma Ata, Kazakhstan, the CIS was expanded to eleven of the former Soviet republics: the Russian Federation, Ukraine, Belarus, Moldova (formerly Moldavia), Armenia, Azerbaijan, Kazakhstan, Uzbekistan, Turkmenistan, Tajikistan, and Kyrgyzstan (formerly Kirghrzia). The three Baltic States, proudly independent, and Georgia, sliding toward civil war, chose not to join. On December 25, 1991, Gorbachev resigned and handed over his presidential offices to Boris Yeltsin.

The USSR officially ceased to exist on December 26, 1991. Fifteen independent states took its place, eleven of which formed a loosely organized Commonwealth. In describing the CIS, the *Economist* commented, "The new structure is neither very common (its members argue all the time) nor very wealthy."

The CIS is not a nation, has no central government, and serves mostly as a forum for coordinating policies such as military issues, economic reform, banking, energy, transportation, and minority rights. The CIS has no central ministries. While often referred to as the Commonwealth, its last two words, *Independent States,* more clearly describe the political realities of the former Soviet Union. Most experts believe the CIS is more likely to fragment over time than to develop into a cohesive institution.

On February 2, 1992, at Camp David, President Bush proclaimed "the end of the Cold War and the dawn of a new era." Yeltsin, standing along side Bush, agreed, "From now on, we do not consider ourselves to be potential enemies."

PART I: ECONOMIC CHANGE AND CHALLENGE:
The Economic and Environmental Hazards of Post-Communism

Leonid Brezhnev, Soviet leader from 1964-82, bequeathed a dismal situation to his heirs. Economic decline, blatant corruption and nepotism, and worsening Soviet life-expectancies fostered a sense of political paralysis and economic stagnation. Brezhnev's death in 1982, followed by two infirm successors who died soon after taking office, Yuri Andropov and Konstantin Chernenko, heightened the Soviet malaise.

Mikhail Gorbachev came to power in 1985 with a mandate to improve the bleak performance of the Soviet economy. When Gorbachev arrived, at age 54, he was the youngest member of the Politburo. New blood was needed to address urgent problems. In the face of rising alcoholism and declining economic output, he introduced a policy of renewed discipline, anti-alcoholism, and accelerated output. By 1987, however, this approach had failed, indicating to Gorbachev that Soviet economic policy needed a complete overhaul. His answer was *perestroika* (restructuring).

Gorbachev argued that *perestroika* would revitalize the Soviet economy and eventually make it competitive with the West. He and his colleagues proposed a number of radical measures to make this possible. They included: reducing, at all levels, the size and role of the Communist Party bureaucracy; decentralizing economic management to enterprises in areas such as production, marketing, and wages; providing paid incentives to managers and workers to increase productivity; reforming prices and reducing government subsidies of goods and services to reflect market value; and a gradual opening of the economy to the outside world.

Perestroika led to a weakening of the Communist Party's grip on the "command economy" - state ownership of the means of production and central control over economic transactions and decision-making. But even after economic power was decentralized, meaningful economic change remained elusive. Increased budget deficits and spiraling inflation prevented progress. Debates intensified over whether to cut defense spending at a time when the USSR was embroiled in a war with Afghanistan. Moreover, many felt Gorbachev was "selling out" Marxism-Leninism. Extreme shortages of food and consumer items further reduced public confidence in the government's ability to "deliver the goods" of reform.

For all his good intentions, Gorbachev faced many difficult hurdles in implementing *perestroika*. First, his policies threatened the governing elite - and all the privileges that they had come to expect. His reforms fomented opposition in the communist party's central apparatus and regional organizations, in the military and the KGB, and in the entrenched bureaucracy, all of which resisted reform. Second, Gorbachev faced a skeptical and politically conservative general population, especially in rural areas where the urban intelligentsia were traditionally distrusted. Third, by opening the doors, *glasnost* permitted the re-emergence of unrest among nationalities whose ethnic violence and demands for independence detracted from Gorbachev's reforms. Fourth, the end of subsidized trade with Eastern Europe (following the revolutions of 1989) created further strains and shortages. Finally, Gorbachev had inherited a bevy of daunting, deep-seated economic problems that defied easy solutions. Food shortages threatened to provoke social disorder and violence; asking patience and support for reforms is most difficult when stomachs are empty. Despite its fine objectives, *perestroika* was failing. From the breadlines in Moscow to the frontlines in Afghanistan, the inefficient Soviet command economy was not producing enough goods. Gorbachev began to look to the West for help.

With the deteriorating Soviet economy in mind, leaders of the Group of Seven industrial nations (the G-7, comprised of the US, UK, France, Germany, Italy, Canada, and Japan) and the President of the European Community (EC) met in July 1990 in Houston. They asked the International Monetary Fund (IMF), the World Bank, the Organization for Economic Cooperation and Development (OECD), and the newly formed European Bank for Reconstruction and Development (EBRD) to prepare a study on the Soviet economy that could recommend specific reforms and set criteria for Western assistance.

When completed, the joint study stressed the need for four simultaneous reforms to enable the Soviets to make a rapid full scale transition to a market economy: decontrol prices to allow the ruble to reflect more realistically the value of goods and services; privatize industry, to permit competition that controls prices, improves consumer goods, and breaks state monopolies; cut government spending to reduce the USSR's budget deficit by slashing subsidies and defense spending; and stop printing rubles, to allow the government to absorb the excess money supply and control inflation. The study urged that once the USSR committed to these reforms, then, and only then, should the West contribute financial assistance. Without these criteria, it was argued, the

West would be investing large sums in the USSR with no guarantee of success. Food aid, however, could receive immediate priority, and Western technical assistance could help restructure companies, and design a banking and marketing system.

On August 8, 1990, Gorbachev and Yeltsin announced their support for a 500 day plan (called the Shatalin Plan) which called for moving beyond *perestroika* to a market economy and a pluralistic system of government. On September 24, Gorbachev was granted - but did not always use - extraordinary powers to implement the plan. Among his decrees was one that allowed 100% foreign ownership of enterprises and equal legal status for foreign investors, although most investors remain skeptical. Reformers believed that only radical change could win back public confidence and attract foreign investment. Conservatives, however, denounced it as a restoration of capitalism.

By June 1991, the failure of the economic reforms to produce results prompted worries about a right-wing coup and yet another proposal for change. Grigory Yavlinsky, co-author of the Shatalin plan, together with American economists at Harvard University's Kennedy School of Government, proposed extensive economic reforms to be implemented over a six year period. Called the "Grand Bargain," this plan linked the implementation of specific economic changes to the provision of Western financial assistance.

The plan stipulated that: basic economic rights, including private property and privatization of state enterprises, must be legalized; economic monopolies must end; budgetary and monetary imbalances must be stabilized by cutting defense spending and subsidies to state enterprises; prices must be liberalized to follow supply and demand; and the economy must be opened to the outside world, thus requiring a convertible currency.

If these stipulations could be met, the authors envisaged Western aid of up to $30 billion to be distributed over six years, a sum, they argued, that represented only a small percentage of the gross national product (GNP) of the industrialized world.

At the July 1991 G-7 meeting, Gorbachev proposed a plan similar to the Grand Bargain. He also surprised observers by seeking full membership for the USSR in the IMF and the World Bank. In response, the G-7 pledged associate membership to the IMF for the USSR, but not the massive aid that Gorbachev sought for the Soviet economy. While Gorbachev instigated some reforms sought by the West, he proved unable to introduce all of them. The Soviet economy steadily declined, causing panic, hoarding and consequently worsening shortages, particularly of consumer goods. One 1991 Soviet report cited that ninety-six per cent of 1,200 different basic consumer goods were not available for sale in state-run stores. As a result, the black market thrived and continues to be quite strong. One Russian

---

Yeltsin's Plan for the Russian Economy

Price and Wage Reform. Yeltsin lifted many price controls and proposes to base wages on productivity. Previously, prices reflected government decisions on the importance of a good or service, unrelated to the cost of producing it.

Balanced Budget. Yeltsin proposes to stop financing some 70 former Soviet ministries and other central government institutions in 1992, pressing them to bring wages in line with productivity. He also plans to increase revenues by charging market rates for energy and other natural resources.

Reforming the Banking System. Yeltsin would create a reserve banking system to coordinate monetary policy for Russia and other republics that agree to join in an economic community with one currency, the ruble.

Establishing a Social Safety Net. Economic reforms are bringing hardship to many, especially pensioners and others on fixed incomes. Yeltsin proposes non-cash benefits such as free meals, food coupons, and other basic necessities for those below a certain minimum income.

Privatize Assets and Break up Industrial Monopolies by selling smaller, less profitable state enterprises in the service and industrial sectors to private individuals, and privatizing state and collective farms that operate at a loss. State control would be maintained over many large enterprises and farms that operate on a profit-making basis. Large monopolistic state enterprises would be broken up into smaller competing ones.

Convert Defense Industries by switching plants that have produced military items into producing civilian goods. Military use absorbed much of the Soviet GNP and also received priority on fuel and other basic items.

Introduce Limited Hard Currency Convertibility. The ruble has not been traded on world money markets, sharply limiting investment and trade because it is difficult for foreign investors to bring their profits home. Yeltsin proposes permitting Russian citizens to purchase and sell hard currency (like US dollars, German marks and Japanese yen) through authorized banks, and allowing foreign investors to sell rubles for hard currency.

Liberalize Foreign Trade by permitting all entities in Russia, both private and state-owned, to conduct foreign trade but requiring entities earning hard currency foreign profits to sell a portion of the currency to the Russian Central Bank.

Source: Congressional Research Service

---

observer, commenting on the desperate situation, has said: "Today, Russians do not ask themselves what they can do for their country, but rather what can you do for me, and preferably in hard currency."

The Grand Bargain lost relevance after the August 1991 coup attempt, and after the subsequent breakup of the USSR. Some of its objectives were overtaken by events. Nonetheless, its economic prescriptions mirrored a growing consensus among Western economists on how to transform a command economy to a market-oriented one.

After the Soviet Breakup, Daunting Problems Remain

In the aftermath of the August 1991 coup attempt, it soon became apparent that the governments of the then still republics of the USSR, especially Russia, Ukraine, and Kazakhstan, were de facto asserting control over economic and political affairs in their respective territories. On October 28, 1991, Boris Yeltsin presented a radical reform program to the Russian legislature calling for tough monetary and financial credit policy, strengthening of the ruble, and liberalization of price controls. Yeltsin stated that if his program were implemented, improvements in the economy could begin as early as fall 1992. By mid-November, Yeltsin issued decrees to carry out these reforms, and to seize control of the Soviet government's production and sale of precious metals, diamonds, oil and petroleum products on Russian territory. These decrees placed much of the USSR's mineral wealth under Russian control.

Even after the breakup of the USSR in December 1991, Russian economic policy continued to have a strong impact on almost all successor state (former republic) economies. By virtue of its size and dominant economic position, Russia has for centuries maintained a dominant role in Eurasia. With 77% of the USSR's land area, 51% of the population, the largest industries and resource base, and control over major financial institutions, Russia still has a natural leadership role to play, whether other successor states like it or not. For example, on January 1, 1992, Russia lifted price controls on most items; a number of other republics, including Ukraine, followed suit, fearing that higher prices in Russia would result in flight of their scarce resources to Russian market-places, in the absence of export controls. Thus far, Yeltsin has remained steadfast in his commitment to change. In early April 1992, he asserted, "only one avenue of advance has the right to exist now - the continuation of radical reforms."

Optimists also believe Russia may be the locomotive of economic reform for other successor states of the former Soviet Union. Pessimists, however, point to the daunting list of economic woes facing Yeltsin. Most experts contend that the Russian economy has deteriorated to crisis levels. The leaders of the failed coup in August 1991 cited poor economic conditions as one of their motivations; the economic growth and inflation rates have only worsened since then (see charts). Despite hard times, the people of the former Soviet Union have been unwilling to go back to communist ways of doing business. How long their patience will last, or what alternatives they ultimately choose, however, remain open to question.

The Russian Congress of People's Deputies, from which the smaller standing parliament is drawn, contains many communists. A draft resolution, circulated by conservatives on April 8, 1992, sought to strip Yeltsin of many of his emergency powers as well as force him to step down as prime minister by the end of July 1992. The West worried that reform was sputtering. On April 11, the legislature passed the resolution to force Yeltsin

Annual Growth of GNP in Percent for the Soviet Union

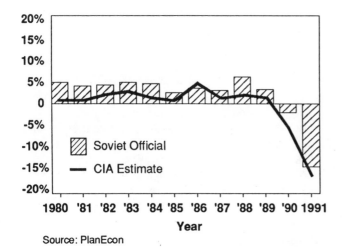

Source: PlanEcon

Annual Inflation Rate for the Soviet Union

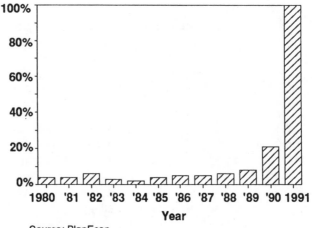

Source: PlanEcon

to step down as prime minister by a vote of 683 to 230. Yeltsin's Cabinet, citing frustration over the legislature's effort to weaken economic reform, offered to resign their posts on April 13, 1992. On April 14, a compromise was achieved that would allow Yeltsin's government to decide which congressional measures it will adopt and let Yeltsin remain acting prime minister. Yeltsin's struggles to implement reform not only indicate the scope of the problems, but also suggest the danger of a resurgence of hard-line rule if conditions do not improve soon.

Environmental and Health Problems

Against the backdrop of a failing economy, the former USSR also faces a crisis in environmental and health problems. In their 1992 study, *Ecocide in the USSR: Health and Nature under Siege* (NY: Basic Books, 1992), experts Murray Feshbach and Alfred Friendly, Jr. begin their study by stating, "when historians finally conduct an autopsy on Soviet Communism, they may reach the verdict of death by ecocide...no other great industrial civilization so systematically and so long poisoned its land, air, water, and people." The costs to clean up the environment alone, they say, can only be estimated, and will likely be many times the value of the current GNP of the former Soviet Union. At the same time, medical supplies are in critically short supply. Without remedial action, they argue, continued environmental neglect will only place more burdens on an already debilitated medical care system.

Many studies point out how Soviet industrialization and farming strategies aimed at "growth at any cost" severely polluted the air and water. The list of environmental ills is simply staggering. Some 70 million city dwellers breathe air that is contaminated with at least five times the allowed limit of dangerous chemicals. High levels of pesticides are found in most foods. Some 920,000 barrels of oil are spilled every day in Russian oil fields, roughly the equivalent of one Exxon Valdez spill every six hours. Lake Baikal, the deepest fresh water lake in the world, has been severely polluted by industrial waste. Likewise, some seventy percent of the fish in the Volga river contain mercury. The huge Aral Sea is evaporating because the rivers that fed it were diverted for agricultural purposes; immense salt and dust bowls have swirled into the earth's atmosphere, raising the level of global particulates by more than five per cent. Some six million acres of farmland have been lost to erosion.

A disturbing legacy of Soviet communism is that it has left Russia and the other successor states with massive environmental degradation, among the worst in the world. The "quality" and length of life of the general population has only suffered as a result. In 1987, according to a study by the IMF, the average life expectancy of a Soviet man was 64.2 years compared to 71.6 years in the OECD countries; the average life expectancy for a Soviet woman was 73.3 years compared to 78.0 years among Western industrial countries; and about 25 of every 1000 Soviet children died in infancy compared to about 8 in 1000 for the West.

The Effects of the Nuclear Age

Nuclear contamination, from weapons testing areas, nuclear waste sites, and nuclear power plant accidents have endangered public health and safety. For example, two kindergartens in Estonia were reportedly built on a radioactive waste dump. Officials in Ukraine have already buried some 400 tons of beef contaminated by the 1986 Chernobyl nuclear accident; another 920 tons is scheduled to be buried in June 1992. Scientists recently found another eleven areas contaminated by Chernobyl. Radiation levels are still high, and the extent of the damage to humans and livestock may not be known for years.

Experts warn that 16 nuclear reactors of the Chernobyl type and others with serious safety problems are "Chernobyls waiting to happen." Since Chernobyl, some 60 nuclear power projects have been abandoned, but the reactors that remain are working overtime to make up for decreasing fuel and electric energy supplies. On March 24, 1992, radioactive gases leaked from a reactor at Sosnovy Bor, sixty miles west of St. Petersburg. It was a small accident, but served as a reminder of possible future nuclear disasters.

In Armenia, now suffering an energy blockade from Azerbaijan, the atomic energy minister wants to reopen a Chernobyl-type reactor to meet Armenian energy needs, even though the reactor lies in a dangerous earthquake zone. In March 1992, Yelena Bonner, wife of the late physicist Andrei Sakharov, appealed to the World Bank for funds to reopen the plant and bring it up to standards. Some Western experts have called for an international commission and the International Atomic Energy Agency to evaluate the most dangerous reactor safety problems and seek ways to alleviate the risks. By one estimate, refitting reactors throughout Eastern Europe and the former USSR would cost some $7.5 billion.

US and Western Assistance to the former USSR

As noted earlier, many observers hold that the fate of democracy in the former USSR is directly linked to the success of market reforms. Many also think that the nations of the former Soviet Union are too poor to simultaneously rebuild their economies, repair its ecological damage and health care systems, and make the transition to market-oriented economies alone. Western assistance is viewed as key in this regard.

Apart from selling large amounts of grain on occasion, the US did not provide economic grants, loans, or trade concessions to its chief adversary, the Soviet Union, through most of the Cold War. After Mikhail Gorbachev introduced sweeping reforms, however, bilateral relations improved steadily. Since December 1990, the US has proposed over $5 billion in US assistance and credits for the republics of the former Soviet Union. Over two-thirds of that amount is in agricultural credit guarantees toward the purchase of American farm products, grant food aid, and Defense Department surplus food donations (mostly left over from Operation Desert Storm). Additional aid has been proposed in humanitarian/technical assistance, Economic Support Funds (ESF), Agency for International Development (AID) medical assistance, and development assistance, Farmer-to-Farmer programs, and US Agriculture Department technical assistance. The US Congress also authorized that $400 million be spent to help transport, safeguard and destroy Soviet nuclear weapons (see **Part II: Military Change and Challenge**).

On December 12, 1991, Secretary of State Baker outlined further plans to help the former Soviet Union. An international coordinating conference would be held in Washington January 22-23, 1992 to divide the duties among 47 donor countries and seven international organizations. At the meeting, working groups were established in five areas: food, shelter, energy, medicine, and technical assistance. A follow-up conference will take place in Lisbon, Portugal, most likely in May.

In opening the conference, President Bush pledged $645 million in US aid: $500 million for humanitarian/technical assistance; $85 million in Economic Support Funds; $25 million for medical assistance; $20 million for the Farmer-to-Farmer program, and $15 million in AID development assistance. Bush said "Operation Desert Hope," a major short-term airlift of 54 flights to carry food and medical supplies to the former Soviet Union is to begin on February 10, 1992.

In addition to US efforts, other major bilateral pledges have been made by West European nations, especially Germany, as well as Japan and Canada. The US, UK and Japan were initially more cautious and conditional in deciding on multilateral aid to the Soviet Union; whereas Germany, France and Italy pushed for higher amounts of assistance with less strings.

Germany has provided by far the largest amount of assistance. Since 1989, Germany has spent or committed more than $45 billion to help the former Soviet Union. A part of this is free grants and subsidies with a large share relating to an agreement regarding the withdrawal of Soviet troops from the former East Germany, including building housing in the former Soviet Union for Soviet soldiers returning home. The largest portion involves credits and direct grants. Germany not only has an interest in making German unification as smooth as possible, but also in seeing that economic reforms succeed in the former Soviet Union. Should reforms fail, hundreds of thousands of refugees from the former Soviet republics are likely to cross the German border; putting additional strains on a German economy already strapped by the need to rebuild eastern Germany.

On March 21, 1992 German Chancellor Helmut Kohl went to Washington to discuss, among other topics, multilateral plans for additional aid to the former Soviet Union, and topics for the next G-7 meeting to take place in Munich in July 1992. "A solid program of help for self-help" was discussed, a program subsequently announced by President Bush on April 1, 1992.

On that date, Bush declared US support for a multilateral assistance package to help Russia and the other new states transform their economies. There are three elements to the multilateral program: about $18 billion in 1992 to help Russia stabilize and restructure its economy; a $6 billion currency stabilization fund to bolster confidence in the Russian ruble; and membership for Russia and other new states in the IMF by early May 1992. The total package calls for about $24 billion to be coordinated by the G-7 for delivery. The American share of the cost will be between 20 and 25 percent.

Before this pledge, US assistance amounted to only a fraction of the aid provided by the European Community as a whole (some $32.5 billion). This caused irritation in Europe, where the US is widely thought to be assuming too little of the aid burden. Observers point out, however, that dramatic increases in US aid are unlikely for at least three reasons: America's own economic difficulties and, in particular, a large budget deficit, limits its ability to commit resources to foreign assistance; American public hostility to foreign aid has grown as a result of the recession, making it harder to see a potential benefit to US security over the long term; and US banks are not as commercially entrenched in the former Soviet Union as their European competitors. Moreover, the US is less exposed geographically since any refugees fleeing economic collapse, potential anarchy or civil conflict in the former Soviet Union are more likely to migrate toward the European Community.

The April 1 aid package proposal was undoubtedly timed to try to show support for a beleaguered Yeltsin and to influence the April 11 Russian legislature vote on whether to slow the pace of economic reform. Western support gave Yeltsin leverage to end the brief government crisis, but others may surface if Yeltsin cannot halt a precipitous decline in living standards and stabilize the Russian economy.

PART II. MILITARY CHANGE AND CHALLENGE:
NEW OPPORTUNITIES, NEW DANGERS

The end of the Cold War affords unprecedented opportunities for cooperation. With the Warsaw Pact dissolved and NATO redefining its purpose, prospects are good for establishing new security relationships between East and West. Significant cuts in both military budgets and force structures are underway, and further reduction of nuclear and conventional arsenals seems promising. Many Americans are enthusiastic about cashing in on a "peace dividend," where resources once spent on superpower competition can now be applied to non-military needs.

Others caution, however, that as we promote peaceful democratic evolution after the dissolution of the Soviet Union, our optimism should be tempered by the fact that the breakup has ushered in new dangers. They point out that Ukraine alone may field military forces as large as any in Europe, while Russia retains much of the former Soviet Union's military force, the largest in the world. Active duty personnel are estimated at more than 3 million; reserve personnel are even greater than this. Although Western military leaders admit that the threat has been greatly reduced, and more force reductions are likely, they are less certain about assessing the long-term status of Soviet nuclear and conventional forces.

One thing is clear: the future size, composition, and deployment of these forces will strongly influence the military balance in Europe and the potential for a stable security system. It is possible that the successor states to the USSR will all be inclined to reduce their military forces. On the other hand, depending on the degree to which the new states wish to emphasize and protect their sovereignty, new arms races could result from the uncertainties, fears, and potential threats seen by leaders of the new states. Ethnic unrest, exacerbated by dire economic straits, represents another wild-card. Although the August 1991 coup attempt failed, there is no guarantee that reformers intent on establishing democracy and a free market system will prevail everywhere in the former Soviet Union. New dictators could emerge out of political turmoil and economic hardship, creating new security challenges.

In any case, a number of concerns have emerged about the future military forces in the region. Among the most important:

◇ *Nuclear Forces*: concerns about who will have the finger on the nuclear button for some 27,000 Soviet strategic and tactical nuclear weapons; and about the status of the Strategic Arms Reduction Treaty (START);

◇ *Nuclear Proliferation*: concerns about new nuclear nations appearing in the wake of the Soviet breakup, and how the spread of nuclear weapons materials, tech-

nology and expertise to developing countries can be stopped;

◇ *Conventional Forces*: concerns about unemployed soldiers and their allegiances, about what will happen to the vast array of conventional weapons; and about the status of the Conventional Armed Forces in Europe (CFE) Treaty; and

◇ *Conversion of Soviet Military Industries*: concerns about how to convert the huge military industry infrastructure into a viable civilian one.

WHO CONTROLS THE NUCLEAR FORCES?

The former Soviet Union has a vast array of nuclear weapons: some 27,000 warheads are deployed on about sixty different types of delivery systems, ranging from artillery shells to intercontinental ballistic missiles (ICBMs). About 12,000 are strategic, long-range nuclear warheads, many of which remain targeted on the US; they are carried on land-based ICBMs, submarine launched ballistic missiles (SLBMs), and weapons on bombers with the range needed to attack the continental US. The other 15,000 are tactical, short-range nuclear warheads intended for battlefield use; they are mounted on delivery systems such as artillery shells, short-range missiles, nuclear air defense and ballistic missile interceptors, nuclear torpedoes, sea-launched cruise missiles (SLCMs), and bombs for shorter-range aircraft.

The vast majority of Soviet nuclear weapons are deployed or stored in Russia. About 25% are in Kazakhstan, Ukraine, and Belarus (formerly Byelorussia). The command and control system for all Soviet nuclear weapons is located in Moscow. A central command authority is responsible for authorizing their use. The breakup of the USSR has generated much Western concern about who controls this large number of strategic weapons aimed primarily at the United States and its allies.

STRATEGIC NUCLEAR WEAPONS

On December 25, 1991, Mikhail Gorbachev resigned the presidency, handing over the nuclear weapons launch codes to Russian Federation President Boris Yeltsin. Five days later, an important meeting took place in Mensk, Belarus. On December 30, the leaders of Belarus, Kazakhstan, Russia and Ukraine - the only Commonwealth states with strategic long-range nuclear missiles on their soil - agreed that nuclear weapons would remain under central command and control. Any decision to use nuclear weapons would be "made by the president of the Russian Federation in agreement with

Nuclear Weapons in the Commonwealth of Independent States (Estimate as of January 1992)						
State	Strategic Offensive	Ground Forces	Air Def. Forces	Air Force	Navy	Total
Russia	8,750	4,200	2,675	2,375	2,750	20,750
Ukraine	1,750	600	125	1,050	500	4,025
Kazakhstan	1,400	0	0	0	0	1,400
Belarus	100	0	0	575	150	825
TOTAL	12,000	4,800	2,800	4,000	3,400	27,000
Source: Arms Control Association						

the heads of the Republic of Belarus, the Republic of Kazakhstan, and Ukraine, and in consultation with the heads of other member states of the Commonwealth."

Currently, only Yeltsin and the commander-in-chief of the CIS military forces, Marshal Yevgeny Shaposhnikov, have briefcases with the nuclear launch codes. According to US CIA Director Robert Gates, a third briefcase, once controlled by the chief of the Soviet General Staff, is now "apparently in reserve." In January 1992, a hotline communications system was installed to permit all four leaders from the nuclear republics to consult simultaneously. Presently, however, no non-Russian states have the technical ability to either initiate or block a launch.

Another important issue involves the safety and security of nuclear weapons - preventing their unauthorized release and use. A variety of elaborate human and technical mechanisms are employed in this regard. Soviet nuclear weapons sites and storage depots are heavily guarded. Each tactical and strategic nuclear warhead has its own serial number for tracking purposes. Tactical nuclear warheads are often stored separately from their launchers, and those guarding them cannot arm them. Soviet strategic nuclear weapons - like American systems - apparently use "permissive action links" (PALs), electronic locks that require two sets of codes to unlock and launch the weapons (also known as "strategic nuclear weapons authorization and enabling codes"). Experts believe that when the codes are entered incorrectly, the locks automatically freeze, and the weapons can neither be released nor launched.

Only the central command authority can release the correct codes. Boris Yeltsin, as President of the Russian Federation, is at the apex of that chain of command. As yet, no republic has suggested that this system be replaced. Ukraine and Kazakhstan, however, have periodically intimated they may keep some weapons as diplomatic leverage against the larger Russian Federation; Ukrainian President Kravchuk stopped withdrawal of tactical nuclear weapons to Russia, arguing that Kiev could not verify that they would be destroyed. But the 1991 Alma Ata and Mensk accords call for full withdrawal of tactical nuclear weapons from Belarus, Kazakhstan, and Ukraine to Russia by July 1, 1992. Ukraine has committed to withdraw its strategic nuclear

warheads by the end of 1994. If all goes according to plan, Russia would at that time be the only remaining nuclear nation among the successor states to the USSR.

STATUS OF THE STRATEGIC ARMS REDUCTION TREATY (START)

After over nine years of negotiation, the US and the Soviet Union signed a START Agreement on July 31, 1991. President Bush submitted the agreement to the Senate for ratification on November 25, 1991. With the breakup of the USSR and the subsequent pledge of the Russian Federation to assume obligations for START, however, strategic arms reductions proposals have become more frequent and unilateral, going beyond START reductions. Many believe that, under current circumstances, START does not go far enough. Presidents Bush and Yeltsin seem to agree.

On January 28, 1992, President Bush, in his State of the Union Address, proposed cutting the US strategic nuclear arsenal to 4,700 warheads - about 50% less than authorized by START. Bush announced a number of unilateral cuts in strategic programs, including: cutting production of the B-2 Stealth Bomber at twenty planes, cancelling production of new warheads for the Trident II SLBM, killing the Midgetman missile program, ending production of MX test missiles, stopping the advanced cruise missile program at the 520 missiles already paid for (instead of the planned 1000), and shifting a large portion of strategic nuclear bombers to conventional use.

On January 29, 1992, President Yeltsin responded positively to Bush's proposals, suggesting that both sides cut their forces even further, to between 2,000 - 2,500 strategic warheads. Yeltsin announced that 600 ICBMs and SLBMs carrying nearly 1,250 nuclear warheads had been taken off alert, that 130 missile silos and six missile-carrying submarines had been liquidated, that further production of Bear and Blackjack bombers was cancelled, and that both air and sea launched cruise missile production lines were being shut down. President Yeltsin further proposed that all remaining weapons in Russia and the United States "should not be aimed at American or Russian targets."

Other strategic arms reduction proposals have called for as few as 600 weapons (see chart on page 46).

TACTICAL NUCLEAR WEAPONS

The command, control, safety, and security of tactical nuclear weapons generate more concern than strategic weapons because their warheads are smaller, more numerous, easier to conceal and transport, more widely dispersed, and more likely to fall into the hands of a third party. As the USSR dissolved, worries mounted

Selected Proposals for Strategic Arms Reductions below Warhead Levels in START

Number of Warheads	Proposal
600	Andrei Kokoshin, *Bulletin of the Atomic Scientists,* September 1988
1,000	Carl Kaysen, Robert S. McNamara, and George W. Rathjens, *Foreign Affairs,* Fall 1991
1,000-2,000	Committee on International Security & Arms Control, National Academy of Sciences, 1991 (second-stage cuts)
1,000-2,000	Jonathan Dean and Kurt Gottfried, Union of Concerned Scientists, 1991
Below 2,000	Harold A. Feiveson and Frank N. von Hippel, *International Security,* Summer 1991
2,000-2,500	Boris Yeltsin, United Nations, 1992
Below 3,000	Harold Brown, *Arms Control Today,* May 1990
3,000	John D. Steinbruner, Michael M. May, and George F. Bing, *International Security,* Summer 1988*
3,000-4,000	Committee on International Security & Arms Control, National Academy of Sciences, 1991 (first-stage cuts)
4,700	George Bush, State of the Union Speech, 1992
4,000-6,000	Reed Report, Strategic Air Command, 1991
6,000	START Treaty, 1991**

*Most proposals consider 3,000 warheads to be the level beneath which current targeting strategy must be revised and 2,000 to the level beneath which third-country forces (United Kingdom, France, China) must become involved in negotiations.

** START permits 6,000 "accountable" strategic warheads on each side. Because of lenient counting rules on air-launched weapons, each side may in reality deploy several thousand additional warheads.

Source: "Dismantling the Arsenals: Arms Control and the New World Agenda," by Jack Mendelsohn, *Brookings Review,* Spring 1992.

that some of the 15,000 tactical nuclear weapons might be claimed by successor states, or fall into the hands of terrorists, nationalist zealots, or developing nations seeking a nuclear capacity. Questions were also raised about the reliability of safeguards on these weapons, and about possible breaches in security at warhead storage facilities.

On September 27, 1991, responding primarily to these concerns, President Bush announced a set of unilateral decisions, including one to remove and destroy all US ground-based short-range nuclear forces. The President did, however, reserve the right of the US to keep a residual, air-mounted nuclear capability for NATO. He invited President Gorbachev to reciprocate. In response, on October 5, 1991, President Gorbachev reciprocated, further proposing US-Soviet limitations on air-delivered tactical nuclear weapons as well.

After the demise of the USSR, on December 21 at Alma Ata, the four republics with weapons on their soil pledged by July 1, 1992 to "insure the withdrawal of

tactical nuclear weapons to central factory premises for dismantling under joint supervision [in Russia]." On March 12, 1992, however, Ukrainian President Leonid Kravchuk announced he had stopped withdrawing Ukrainian-based tactical nuclear weapons to Russia, citing a lack of guarantees that Russia would destroy them. Days later, Boris Yeltsin said that Kravchuk called him to assure that the transfer would continue. But on March 20, at a CIS summit in Kiev, Kravchuk vehemently denied he had called Yeltsin.

Kravchuk's stance may have been politically motivated. In December 1991, 90% of Ukrainian voters opted for independence; since then, many Ukrainians feel strongly that Russia has consistently undermined Ukraine's sovereignty, has done so in a heavy-handed manner, and should not be allowed to gain a military advantage. Some have also speculated that Kravchuck is sending a signal to Washington that he wants a slice of US aid - seen by Ukrainians to be focused too narrowly on Russia. Whatever his motives, Kravchuk's actions have undermined Western confidence in the ability of the CIS to meet its July 1 deadline for withdrawal of all tactical nuclear weapons outside of Russia, and have raised questions about Ukraine's longer term willingness to become a non-nuclear state. On April 7, 1992, Secretary of State James Baker warned that the US's ability to provide economic aid "will depend upon the fulfillment of those commitments regarding nuclear safety and responsibility" - a statement seen by many to be directed at Ukraine.

The US Congress authorized President Bush to spend $400 million from the FY1992 defense budget to assist the storage, disablement, and dismantling of Soviet tactical nuclear warheads. The bill was signed into law on December 12, 1991. The US established a delegation on Safety, Security, and Dismantlement (SSD) to formulate a specific package of assistance. In meetings held in Moscow from March 5-13, 1992, the US proposed seven areas of potential assistance: fissile material containers, protective blankets, special railway cars, nuclear materials storage facilities, accident response, accounting and control for nuclear material, and conversion of uranium and plutonium into fuel for power reactors.

Russian officials believe they can dismantle about 1,500 warheads per year - a rate that will require 10 years to dismantle the 15,000 tactical nuclear warheads. The process was reported to be ahead of schedule by the end of February, 1992 before the Ukrainian disagreement flared up.

NUCLEAR PROLIFERATION

A vast Soviet nuclear industry stood behind the 27,000 weapons, including uranium mines, plutonium reactors, stockpiles of fissile material, laboratories, test sites, components factories, assembly plants, and transport and storage facilities. According to various CIA reports, nearly a million Soviets were involved in the nuclear weapons program; some 3,000-5,000 worked on producing plutonium or enriching uranium; another 2,000-3,000 had critical nuclear weapons design skills. It is estimated that about 100-150 tons of weapons-grade plutonium, and 500-700 tons of highly enriched uranium have been produced by the Soviet nuclear weapons industry over the last 40 years. Unknown amounts of plutonium have been separated from civilian nuclear reactor wastes as well.

The potential sale or transfer of nuclear weapons materials, technology, and know-how remains a serious concern. With a deteriorating economy, declining defense spending, job insecurity, a need for hard currency, and a surplus of nuclear materials and expertise, the incentives for unemployed Soviet nuclear engineers or strapped successor states to sell abroad might prove compelling. (One Soviet scientist described the dismal situation as warranting "survival before science.") While no hard evidence exists to suggest that nuclear weapons, nuclear components, or weapons-grade materials are being smuggled out of the former USSR, some experts believe that conditions are ripe for a "nuclear black market."

There are two proliferation dangers: one is that Ukraine, Kazakhstan or other republics will emerge as new nuclear weapons states; the second is that existing nuclear states (Russia) will export nuclear materials, technology and know-how abroad to those seeking a nuclear capacity. US efforts to keep Soviet nuclear weapons under the unified control of Russia, and encouragement of non-nuclear successor states to sign the Nuclear Nonproliferation Treaty (NPT) are aimed at preventing successor states from developing their own nuclear forces. Attempts to set up a system of nuclear export controls are designed to stem the sale of nuclear materials and technology abroad.

Currently, one other successor state could claim a need to develop an indigenous nuclear weapons program out of legitimate security concerns. Some experts have suggested that Armenia, currently fighting with Azerbaijan, parallels Israel for motives to build a bomb. Both nations are small, are surrounded by Muslims, share a legacy of persecution and genocide (Jews in Germany during World War II and Armenians at the hands of the Turks in 1915-16), have experienced a diaspora (dispersal) of their peoples, and possess the proud commitment to building national identity as a way of remembering the past. Armenia, however, while perhaps having the motives, does not currently have the means to build its own bomb.

Most experts agree that the risks of nuclear exports from the former USSR are greater than the development of new nuclear weapons programs. "Nuclear entrepreneurs" have emerged from the two former Soviet nuclear weapons laboratories to sell their services abroad. One company, the international CHETEK Corporation, has advertised "peaceful nuclear explosives" (PNE) as a means of disposing of highly toxic chemical and industrial waste, decommissioned nuclear reactors, and retired nuclear and chemical weapons.

US efforts to stop nuclear exports have focused on: 1) stemming the Soviet "nuclear brain drain;" 2) promoting the acceptance of a system of nuclear export controls; and 3) encouraging adherence to and compliance with the Nuclear Nonproliferation Treaty (NPT). First, to stem the brain-drain, President Bush pledged $25 million to establish an institute in Russia where former nuclear scientists could pursue peaceful research. Plans for the center were finalized in Moscow on April 1, 1992; participants will include Russia, the US, the European Community, Japan, and Canada. Furthermore, the US Department of Energy (DOE) has agreed to hire 116 scientists at a Moscow laboratory to work on fusion energy research. Expansion of US-Russian cooperation in space technology has also been proposed. President Yeltsin further suggested that US-Russian research be conducted on creating a joint global ballistic missile defense system.

Second, under strong US pressure, Yeltsin announced that Russia will establish nuclear export control laws. Some observers worry that declarations of intent are much easier than ensuring that controls will be implemented. Others assert that a control regime must not just include Russia, but all successor states to be effective. In a climate of economic and social chaos, they say, nuclear nonproliferation may be at best secondary to more pressing concerns.

Third, the US has pressed successor states to sign on to the Nuclear Nonproliferation Treaty (NPT). In the US view, the Russian Federation has inherited the USSR's obligation under the Treaty. On December 21, 1991 at Alma Ata, Belarus and Ukraine committed to joining the Nuclear Nonproliferation Treaty. Kazakh President Nursultan Nazarbayev has made conflicting statements to Western statesmen about whether Kazakhstan intends to sign as a non-nuclear or nuclear state. Concerns still exist about whether Ukraine and

Kazakhstan intend to retain some nuclear weapons for leverage against Russia.

CONVENTIONAL FORCES

Among the thorniest issues is how and whether to divide the armed forces of the former Soviet Union. While Russia argued initially for maintaining unified military forces for a "common strategic space," Ukraine, Moldova, and Azerbaijan declared they wanted their own national armies. On February 14, 1992 in Mensk, Russia and several other republics agreed to a unified conventional force for a two-year transitional period. This agreement, however, risks being overtaken by events.

Troubles both between and inside successor states have complicated the military question. In conflicts *between* successor states - as in Armenia and Azerbaijan - some CIS soldiers have defected to join the ranks of local militias. CIS munition dumps have also been commandeered. In another region, Ukraine claimed the entire Black Sea fleet, based in the Ukrainian port of Sevastopol, even though most of the fleet's officers and sailors are Russian.

Troubles *inside* successor states - such as the Georgian civil war and ethnic strife within Moldova - raise further questions about what armed forces belong to whom. For example, on March 20, 1992, Moldova's President Mircea Snegur ordered the seizure of former Soviet military property in a move to create its own army. Snegur ordered the takeover of all equipment, arms, and buildings of the former Red Army. In turn, Boris Yeltsin issued a decree transferring jurisdiction over the 14th Guards Army (based in Moldova) from the CIS to Russia. The dangers of army involvement in Moldova are increasing, and troops have been drawn into the fighting in the eastern Trans-Dnestrian region between ethnic Russians and Moldovan police.

On March 16, 1992, The Russian Federation issued an eight-part decree that provided for a Russian ministry of defense, setting the groundwork for the creation of a separate Russian army. The decree made clear that the new Russian army will be part of the CIS joint command, thus separating the decision from Ukraine's move to establish a completely independent army. However, the uncertain future of the CIS may mean that the Russian army will end up just as "independent" in practice as the Ukrainian army will be.

Reaction to the Russian decree from non-Russian states was relatively muted, but many responded by announcing their own military plans. Ukraine had already announced in November 1991 that it intended to develop its own army of up to 700,000 soldiers, and was not surprised by the Russian move. On March 19, the Belarussian Parliament voted to create an independent army, reportedly between 90,000 and 100,000 troops. Kazakhstan, which had been among the strongest supporters for a unified military structure, reluctantly began to establish its own "national guard" units.

When the Russian army takes shape, it will still be by far the largest in Europe and one of the largest in the world. In late March, 1992, at a meeting in Brussels, Colonel General Pavel Grachev, Yeltsin's top defense aide, told US Secretary of Defense Richard Cheney that Russia intends to reduce its forces from more than 3 million troops to between 1.2 and 1.3 million. Several hundred thousand troops due to be withdrawn from eastern Germany, Poland, the Baltic States, and Mongolia will fall under the auspices of the Russian Federation. Assuming the CFE is implemented, the Russian army will have some 21,500 main battle tanks, 33,500 armored personnel carriers, 15,500 artillery systems, 1,215 helicopters, and 2,750 combat aircraft. While revised distribution of forces will permit a more "defensive" posture, such large numbers of weapons will ensure that a considerable offensive potential remains.

In terms of weaponry and a military industrial base, Russia will dwarf all other former Soviet republics. Roughly 80-85% of the USSR's military plants were concentrated in Russia. In certain sectors, such as military aviation and nuclear weapons production, all relevant factories were situated in Russia.

Regarding the navy, the Russian Federation already controls the Baltic, Northern and Pacific fleets, leaving only the status of the Black Sea fleet in doubt. On April 6, 1992, President Kravchuk claimed formal legal authority over all armed forces on Ukrainian territory, including the Black Sea naval forces. The next day, Marshal Shaposhnikov, commander of the CIS armed forces, read Yeltsin's decree asserting that the Black Sea fleet is under Russian jurisdiction and CIS command. Moreover, the decree stated that Russia would finance the fleet and that it would fly under the flag of St. Andrew, as was customary during the days of the Russian czars. Negotiations between Ukraine and Russia to divide the fleet are reportedly slated for mid-April 1992.

Over the next couple years, the Russian Defense Ministry will have to confront two delicate issues: how to develop a new military doctrine and how to treat the Russians who live outside the Russian Federation but who may wish to join the Russian army. Questions of doctrine will not only be important for determining the potential uses of Russian military power, but will also be key to the development of civil-military relations. The treatment of Russians in other states - such as Moldova and Ukraine - will raise problems about broader relations and potential conflicts between CIS states.

A major problem is that soldiers, without a job or the Soviet Union, do not know to whom or what they should pledge allegiance. Desperate for hard currency, they have sold their weapons to civilians, militias, tourists - anyone willing to buy them. The dissolution of the Warsaw Pact on April 1, 1991 and the consequent exodus of Soviet soldiers returning home from Eastern Europe only make this problem worse. Some 245,000

Red Army soldiers have already left Eastern Europe; the remaining 39,000 in Poland are scheduled to leave by the end of 1993, and some 225,000 in Germany are due home by 1994. As demobilization continues, Russia has encountered severe housing problems. While Germany has pledged five billion deutschmarks to build housing, Russians complain that German construction projects are mostly in Ukraine, leaving large numbers of returning Russian soldiers facing the prospect of homelessness.

STATUS OF THE CONVENTIONAL ARMED FORCES IN EUROPE (CFE) TREATY

The Conventional Armed Forces in Europe (CFE) Treaty was signed before the dissolution of the Warsaw Pact and the USSR on November 19, 1990. Twenty-two members of the Warsaw Pact and NATO then set equal ceilings on conventional forces from the Atlantic Ocean in the West to the Ural Mountains in the East. Under the treaty, each side (NATO and Warsaw Pact) may not have more than 20,000 tanks (16,500 with active units), 20,000 artillery pieces (17,000 with active units), 30,000 armored combat vehicles (27,300 with active units), 6,800 combat aircraft, and 2,000 attack helicopters.

Implementation of the CFE Treaty has been sidetracked because of the breakup of the USSR. While the Commonwealth of Independent States has agreed to

Soviet CFE Forces by Republic*

Republic	Tanks	ACVs	Arty.	Helo.	Aircraft
Armenia	258	641	357	7	0
Azerbaijan	391	1265	463	24	124
Belarus	2263	2776	1384	82	650
Estonia	184	201	29	10	153
Georgia	850	1054	383	48	245
Latvia	138	100	81	23	103
Lithuania	184	1591	253	0	46
Moldova	155	402	248	0	0
Russia	5017	6279	3480	570	2750
Ukraine	6204	6394	3062	285	1431

*As declared in February 1991

Source: Arms Control Today

adhere to the treaty, individual states have not yet agreed on how to reapportion the limits set for two bodies that no longer exist: the Warsaw Pact and the Soviet Union. Some states disagree on what forces are "formerly Soviet" or "newly national." Moreover, the CIS has limited authority over the successor states - several of which, such as Azerbaijan, Georgia and Moldova, are not interested in setting limits on their armed forces at a time when they are enmeshed in their own conflicts. Others, such as Ukraine, Kazakhstan, Russia, and the Baltic States, are establishing their own armies as an expression of sovereignty.

CONVERSION OF SOVIET MILITARY INDUSTRIES: BREAKING UP IS HARD TO DO

The successful conversion of Soviet military industries to civilian use is considered key to economic recovery in the former USSR. About 70% of all Soviet research and development personnel worked for or in the military. By some estimates, Soviet military industries accounted for between 60-80% of the entire Soviet economy. The Soviet military and its industries employed over 11 million citizens - and with dependents, this figure jumped to more than 40 million. What will these people do now? How and when can they be employed in productive economic activity?

Several different approaches have been attempted or discussed to meet this massive problem. As part of his *perestroika* reforms, Gorbachev adopted an economic conversion program which relied on the traditional "top-down" Soviet command approach. He made the Military Industrial Commission, the key planning body that oversaw Soviet military production and related industries, responsible for shifting resources from military goods to consumer products. Reputedly, conversion plans drafted in Moscow often failed to take account of factory skills and equipment or problems of securing supplies for production. Yeltsin's conversion program focuses more on urging factories to produce consumer or commercial goods related to their previous defense work. For example, a factory that produced fighter planes might be urged to make civilian aircraft. Yeltsin has also recognized, however, that some factories cannot be converted and need to be closed to reduce the drain on the Russian treasury.

In January 1992, the Russian parliament appropriated some 12 billion rubles just to pay unemployed defense workers. Adequate investment and technical help from the West to restructure and retool key industries, however, still is needed. One plant director commented, "the drowning man has to save himself." Long-term plans for conversion do not meet short term needs for food and subsistence. Accordingly, President Yeltsin has been pressured by conservatives to build conventional weaponry for export. Experts worry about sales of Russian tanks and combat aircraft to unstable areas such as the Middle East.

Western industrialized nations have recognized that promoting Soviet conversion is in their interests. The Group of Seven has declared a readiness to provide investment and technological assistance for this purpose. Most efforts will be concentrated on the Russian Federation where the bulk of military might and industry resides. On April 1, 1992, President Bush announced a $24 billion multilateral aid package for the Russian Federation and the other successor states to be coordinated by the G-7. Some of this money, yet to be determined, will be allocated for Soviet defense conversion.

PART III: ETHNIC UNREST AND NATIONALISM:
HOT SPOTS TO WATCH

Concerns about soldiers and their equipment are particularly relevant to the conflicts and tensions that have emerged in the wake of the Soviet breakup. In several cases, ethnic unrest has erupted into open warfare, which has claimed perhaps 4,000 lives since 1985. In others, tensions driven by nationalist aspirations could eventually provoke violence.

The reasons for these and other potential conflicts are steeped in the history of the Russian and Soviet empire. Although many in the West viewed the country as a monolith, the USSR was really a multi-nation state comprised of over a hundred different nationalities. Through a variety of means and ruses, states were acquired over four centuries — first by tsars, and then by communists.

When Vladimir Lenin reached power he promised, but did not deliver, independence for Ukraine, Georgia and other regions. Joseph Stalin only continued to forcibly add land to the Soviet empire. Via the Hitler-Stalin Pact of 1939, he took what is now Moldova from Romania, and the Baltic states of Estonia, Latvia, and Lithuania. Internally, Stalin repressed nationalities, forcibly moved specific ethnic groups from one region to another, and installed Russian culture and language to unify the USSR through "Russification." And these are but a few examples.

With *glasnost* came an avalanche of ethnic grievances, national aspirations and increasing violence. With the end of the USSR, these problems did not subside. One expert calculates that over 80 conflicts are currently underway in the former Soviet Union. While space does not permit treatment of all of them, a number of the more important ones permit the reader to grasp a sense of the complexities.

Hot spots discussed here include: the Transcaucasus region, where Armenians and Azeris are fighting over the enclave of Nagorno-Karabakh, and where Georgia is in the midst of civil war; Moldova, where the eastern region of Dnestr, predominantly Russian, has declared independence from the rest of Moldova; Ukrainian-Russian tensions, where disputes over dividing up Soviet military forces mask deeper nationalist sentiments; tensions within multi-ethnic Russia itself; and Central Asia, where poverty and disputes over land and water rights could trigger local conflicts.

Nagorno-Karabakh: Battleground for National Identity

Armenians and Azeris are presently fighting an undeclared war for possession of the disputed enclave of Nagorno-Karabakh ("Mountainous Karabakh"). Armenians and Azeris now fight over borders created by their old Communist rulers. Yet the animosity between the two nations pre-dates the USSR by centuries.

Armenia once stretched over a large area from the Mediterranean to the Black and Caspian Seas. In 314 A.D., Armenia became the first state to adopt Christianity. Over many centuries, it was invaded by Arabs, Persians, and Turks. Muslim conquerors often ruthlessly persecuted their Armenian subjects. Since the Turkish invasion of the 16th century, Armenians have generally considered Turks their greatest enemies. Armenians see Azeris as Turks because they are a Turkic people that identified themselves as Turks until 1938. Tensions between Muslim Azeris and Christian Armenians stem in large part from memories of violence done to forebears.

The Russian empire expanded in the 19th century, taking control of Eastern Armenia. In 1915, when Turkey was at war with Russia, Armenians were caught in the cross-fire. The Turks not only deported Armenians from the front lines but massacred them in huge numbers. Turkey still insists that the deaths resulted from the fog of war, but for Armenians, it amounted to genocide. Up to 1.5 million Armenians were killed. The Armenian Holocaust has served as a rallying cry for nationhood and cultural independence.

By 1920, Turkey and Russia had invaded Armenia again. The Soviets annexed Eastern Armenia, eventually creating the republic of Azerbaijan. Nagorno-Karabakh, located in Azerbaijan, is the easternmost area of historic Armenia. Stalin carved out the borders so as to exclude Karabakh; and, for over 60 years, the Soviets also stifled disputes. The advent of *glasnost* in the 1980s, however, brought with it an Armenian movement to reclaim Karabakh; Azeris countered with their own movement to retain it. Violence broke out in 1988, and has increased in intensity. More than one thousand people have died to date. Since the start of the violence, Azerbaijan has imposed an economic blockade against Armenia and Nagorno-Karabakh, preventing railway lines from delivering food and fuel.

Nagorno-Karabakh voted overwhelmingly for independence last fall; in response Azerbaijan declared that the region no longer had a special autonomous status. Two days later, the Karabakh Executive Council, the locally elected legislature, appealed for membership in the CIS. Clashes between Armenians and Azeris have intensified. CIS munitions have been commandeered by both sides, and the bloodshed continues.

No one has been able to resolve the conflict. Turkey is under domestic political pressure to aid Azerbaijan. Several appeals have been made by Armenian and CIS leaders to the United Nations for peacekeeping troops. On March 17, 1992, United Nations envoy Cyrus Vance traveled to Karabakh on a fact-finding tour. Gorbachev, Yeltsin, and Kazakh President Nazarbayev each made efforts to stabilize the situation, but no solution has yet emerged.

Georgia: Nationalism and Civil War

Georgia, the birthplace of Joseph Stalin and former foreign minister Eduard Shevardnadze, is the only republic of the original Soviet Union that has refused to join the CIS, and has not applied for membership in the United Nations. To the north of Georgia are the Caucuses, Europe's highest mountains. To the west is the Black Sea, where legend has it that Jason and the Argonauts sailed to find the mythical Golden Fleece. Georgia's Black Sea resorts were heavily visited by Muscovites on holiday, at least before April 9, 1989, also known as "Bloody Sunday." On that night, Georgians gathered in the main square of Tbilisi, Georgia's capital, to demand independence. Soviet troops quashed the demonstration, clubbing twenty people to death in the latest chapter of revolts, invasions, and struggles for cultural independence.

Georgia converted to Christianity in the fourth century, and existed as a kingdom for nearly 1500 years. The nation was conquered by Arabs in the 7th century, by Mongols in the 13th century, and by various Turkish and Persian empires. In the 18th century, Georgia suffered several invasions from Persia, and Georgian Kings petitioned the Russian tsars for protection, which was granted in 1783. Under Russia's wing, Georgian culture - language, literature, and art - developed, producing a national identity that remains until today. From 1918-21, Georgia was an independent social democratic republic with ties to Western democracies.

In February 1921, the experiment ended with the invasion of the Red Army. Lenin eventually tolerated more Georgian cultural expression. In 1924, however, Joseph Stalin gained power, and repressed any nationalist expressions with an iron fist. After Stalin died in 1953, Georgian nationalism reemerged. In the 1970s, protests took place over forced use of the Russian language. Communist rule maintained order and suppressed opposition.

Georgia declared its independence from the USSR on April 9, 1991, exactly 2 years after Bloody Sunday, but its transition to democracy fell quickly to civil war. The leader of the Georgian nationalist movement, Zviad Gamsakhurdia, won 87% of the vote in a free election, but proceeded to act like a dictator. Freedom of the press, political opposition, and non-Georgian minorities were repressed.

In December 1991, anti-government rebels attacked the Georgian parliament building, eventually forcing Gamsakhurdia to flee. Since then, his supporters have been fighting a civil war against the rebels. No resolution is yet in sight.

Ukrainian-Russian Tensions
A "Landmine Under the Future of Mankind"?

Ukraine, the size of France with a population of 53 million, borders the Russian Federation, which is almost twice the size of the United States with about 150 million people. Kiev, the capital city of Ukraine, was once the cultural and political capital of the Eastern Slavic lands. The 9th century Kiev Rus ruled Moscow until Russia and Ukraine were separated by invading Mongols. From the 13th century, when Kiev itself fell to the Mongols until the present, Ukraine has been ruled by Mongols, Lithuanians, Poles, and Russians with only brief periods of independence. But the 9th century Kiev Rus is still proudly remembered.

More recent events explain the suspicion and bitterness Ukrainians feel toward their giant neighbor. At the time of the Russian Revolution in 1918, the Russian Bolsheviks were forced to sign a separate treaty with Germany to end Russia's role in World War I. An independent Ukraine as a buffer state was part of the price Germany extracted. As soon as Germany was defeated, Lenin reneged on the treaty, and the Ukraine was reconquered in 1919-20 after bloody civil war.

Stalin's rise to power in the Soviet Union after Lenin's death was a catastrophe for Ukraine, as for other lands. He forcibly collectivized agriculture in the 1930's. Stalin's policies created a man-made famine, which combined with his purges claimed the lives of at least 3-5 million Ukrainians. Stalin also introduced forced cultural "Russification" as a way to unify the Soviet Union, replacing Ukraine's language and culture with Russia's. The land, churches, and property of Ukrainian Catholic and Ukrainian Autocephalus Orthodox churches were given to the Russian Orthodox Church and their clergy purged or persecuted. Some Ukrainians were forcibly dispersed to other parts of the USSR. Not surprisingly, in World War II, some Ukrainians at first viewed the invading German Nazi army as liberators. Although subsequently Ukraine resisted Nazi rule, it also resisted the reimposition of Soviet rule at the end of World War II.

Finally, in 1986, the accident at the Chernobyl nuclear power plant heightened Ukraine awareness of serious ecological problems resulting from Soviet economic systems. The Chernobyl disaster contaminated large areas of Ukraine farmland, and many fear the effects of radiation exposure on the population. There are eight nuclear power plants operating in Ukraine.

These memories fuel the disagreements between Russia and the Ukraine on the distribution of the military and other assets of the former Soviet Union. Disagreements have already surfaced between Ukraine and Russia over who controls military assets. Ukraine is home to an army of more than a million soldiers, only 40% of which are ethnically Ukrainian, and which has an officer corps that is overwhelmingly ethnically Russian. Ukraine is also home to the Black Sea Fleet, comprised of some 97,000 sailors and 350 ships.

At a meeting in Mensk in December 1991, after much debate, the CIS agreed that individual states could control "nonstrategic forces" such as ground troops. By January 1992, Ukraine came to interpret this to mean Ukrainian control over the Black Sea Fleet, based in the Ukrainian city of Sevastopol, which is largely made up of ethnic Russians. Ukrainian President Kravchuk not only declared the fleet under his control, but also ordered all military personnel based in Ukraine (reportedly 75% Russian) to take an oath of loyalty to Kiev or to leave. In response, Boris Yeltsin proclaimed the Black Sea Fleet "was, is, and will be Russia's." Tempers subsided by January 12, 1992 when negotiators agreed that part of the fleet would be assigned to Ukraine, but to date, the details for this allocation of forces have not been finalized. Both sides have committed not to take any unilateral actions, and to seek solutions through negotiations.

Long distrustful of Russian intentions, Ukrainians are seeking to build a new state. They have created a new currency to undermine the ruble, declared their intention to create a Ukrainian army, vacillated over nuclear disarmament (see section on tactical nuclear weapons), and remained intransigent over who gets the Black Sea Fleet. Kravchuk's policies irked Russian conservatives and reformers alike. Conservative Russian Federation Vice-President Alexandr Rutskoi joined other legislators in drafting a sharply worded letter to the Ukrainian parliament warning that Ukraine's move to seize the Black Sea Fleet had created an "explosive situation." Anatolii Sobchak, the reformist mayor of St. Petersburg, went further, charging that the Ukrainian army constituted a "landmine under the future of all mankind."

Tensions Within the Russian Federation

At least thirty-one autonomous regions exist within the Russian Federation, a system dating from the Bolshevik revolution that created these areas in the name of self-determination. The autonomous regions in Russia represent a variety of Muslim nationalities, minorities of the North Caucasus, and Siberian peoples that closely resemble the Eskimos of North America. Since *glasnost* and the subsequent demise of the USSR, these areas have either declared independence or called for greater autonomy.

In November 1991, Chechen-Inguish, with about 1.3 million people in the North Caucasus, declared its independence from Russia. The majority of the Chechen are Sunni Muslims. The economy is based largely on oil. After the August coup, the Chechen-Inguish republic's National Congress of the Chechen People (founded in 1990) dismissed its communist leadership, formed its own parliament, elected a president (General Dzhokar Dudaev), and declared itself a sovereign state. In November 1991, Russian President Yeltsin called a state of emergency and sent troops to Grozny, the Chechen capital. On the same day, Dudaev declared a general mobilization and the creation of a Chechen national guard, appealing to all Muslims to turn Moscow into a disaster zone. Some 70,000 volunteers were ready to protect Chechen.

On November 10, the Russian parliament, in emergency session, rejected Yeltsin's decision and called for a peaceful solution. Russian troops retreated in confusion. To date, there is no settlement between Russia and the Chechen Republic. Russia refuses to acknowledge Chechen independence but has made no additional military overtures.

Tatarstan is an oil-rich republic the size of West Virginia with 3.6 million people. Turkic descendants of invaders who swept across Russia in the 13th century, the Tatars produce some 30 million tons of oil annually and its economy is equal to the size of all three Baltic states combined. On March 21, 1992, the most populous autonomous area, Tatarstan, voted 61% for independence. Russia failed to block the referendum. On March 24, 1992, however, Tatarstan's president, Mintimer Shaimiyev, said he wished to develop a practical relationship with Russia that would permit economic autonomy while counting on Russia to ensure the country's defenses. In view of Tatarstan's size and importance, Russia may elect to cut a special deal that gives it the status of a "freely associated state."

On March 31, Yeltsin persuaded 18 formations and regions in Russia to sign a federal treaty that lays out the basic division of powers between Russia and the local governments. Both Chechen-Inguish and Tatarstan refused to initial the document. If Yeltsin agrees to a special status for Tatarstan, however, other republics may back out of the treaty to negotiate a better deal.

Moldova: Ethnic Romanians versus Russians

Present day Moldova is the eastern part of old Moldavia, one of two Romanian principalities formed during the thirteenth and fourteenth centuries. It was originally known as the Roman province of Dacia. In 1812, after a war between Russia and Turkey, Turkey ceded the eastern part of Moldova, then known as

Bessarabia, to Russia. Karl Marx later denied the legality of the ill-gotten gain since it was not part of the Ottoman Empire. Although annexed in 1924, the area returned back to Romanian control.

On August 2, 1939, as part of the Hitler-Stalin Pact, Bessarbia was annexed as the Moldavian republic of the USSR. Moldovans, as they are now called, ethnically Romanian, are proud of their cultural heritage. However, the Moldovan language, a Latin script, was replaced by the Russian Cyrillic alphabet under Stalin's Russification program. Sixty-four percent of the population has its cultural heart in Romania, and at the very least sought free contacts with Romanians. By March 1989, as many as 80,000 demonstrators took to the streets, often meeting violent Soviet crackdowns. Ethnic Moldovans made the Moldovan language the focus of a broad-based movement of dissent.

Twelve percent of the population is ethnic Russian that mostly live east of the Dnestr River. With the breakup of the USSR, tensions between Moldovans and Russians intensified. In eastern Moldova, Russians declared their independence and created a self-proclaimed "Dnestr Republic," neither recognized by Moldovans nor the Russian Federation. Russian soldiers stationed there, however, began choosing sides, and armed detachments of the Dnestr Republic began extending their control from Russified cities to the Moldovan countryside. Moldova, in turn, declared a state of emergency, and nationalized all military assets of the former USSR on its territory. Clashes continue to occur between the forces. Although the Russian Federation has not stepped into aid the Russian separatists, political pressures have mounted to send in the cavalry. Yeltsin has proposed setting up CIS "peacekeeping forces" between the combatants, but it is unclear whether this action would help or exacerbate the problem.

Central Asia: Nationalism, Land & Water

Central Asia stretches from the Caspian Sea to the Gobi Desert. Both Alexander the Great and Genghis Khan came here as conquerors. Its cities were once linked to the silk trade; Marco Polo crossed through Central Asian hills on his way to China. To its inhabitants, this region is central in a geographic sense because it is between the great powers of China, India, Russia, and the Middle East, and central in an intellectual sense, for these peoples see themselves as at the crossroads of East and West.

Central Asian civilization peaked in the ninth and tenth centuries during the Iranian Samanid Dynasty. Mausoleums from that period are still standing. Achievements in astronomy, mathematics and literature are proudly remembered.

Not so proudly remembered, however, was the 19th century Russian invasion that pushed southward. By 1886, the Russians, in competition with the British, had conquered the entire region, and tried to put their stamp on it. Around 1924, Stalin created five different republics, somewhat artificially: Uzbekistan, Khirghizia, Kazakhstan, Turkistan and Tajikistan. Mosques and religious schools were closed and the Arabic alphabet replaced with the Russian cyrillic. Kazakhstan turned into a place for Stalin's labor camps, prisons, and nuclear weapons testing grounds. Compared to the southern parts of Central Asia, however, Kazakhstan was an environmental paradise.

The Aral Sea, once the fourth largest lake in the world, has decreased in size by 40% over the last thirty years. Since 1960, farm irrigation projects have reduced its volume by two-thirds. If the current rate of use continues, the Aral Sea will disappear by the year 2000. In Uzbekistan, where farms once grew many crops, the Soviets created one huge cotton plantation on heavily irrigated land. While some fruit and grain are still produced, the cotton mono-culture has destroyed the fertility of much of the soil.

The old communist leadership has remained in control of the five central Asian republics since they gained full independence in January 1992. Kazakhstan and Kyrgyzstan will probably liberalize their politics at the same rate as the Russian Federation, but others have made only cosmetic moves toward political and economic reforms.

Inter-ethnic violence has erupted throughout the region over economic problems, and land and water rights - especially between Tajiks and Uzbeks, and Kyrgyz and Turkmen. The Uzbeks, 25 million strong, have the strongest sense of nationalism, and many do not recognize Tajikistan as a separate state.

In 1989 all Central Asian states ousted Russian as their official language, adopting their own native tongues. Since then, the number of Central Asian mosques has reportedly grown from 160 to more than 5000. Some have worried about violence sprouting from a resurgent Islam in the area tied to Muslim fundamentalism. However, some experts believe this threat to be exaggerated since violence between Muslims is contrary to their principles of "no nationalities under Islam." Others point to the on-going conflicts between Sunnis and Shiites as an example of what could happen.

Given the terrible state of the environment, economic infrastructure, and irrigation problems, billions of dollars are needed to build new bridges, roads, and waterways. Many experts believe that economic problems are more likely to cause regional conflicts than Islamic fundamentalism.

PART IV: THE VIEW FROM THE WEST
US POLICY OPTIONS

For more than forty years, competition with the Soviet Union, and the specter of the nuclear arms race dominated Americans view of the world. Now the Soviet Union has disintegrated, leaving a welter of difficult and unanticipated problems and opportunities. Yeltsin, like Gorbachev before him, has captivated the West by his commitment to political and economic change. Resistance to his reforms at home, however, remains formidable, especially as economic conditions worsen. Conservatives in Russia seek to slow the pace of change at a time when it is most needed and linked to Western financial assistance. Some warn we may witness a situation similar to Weimar Germany before World War II. (At that time, economic chaos overwhelmed Germany's fledgling democracy and paved the way for the rise of authoritarian rule under Adolph Hitler). In any case, the transformation of the Soviet economy and the establishment of stable democratic regimes is important to the West as well as to the people of the Commonwealth of Independent States.

The United States and its allies have had to confront a variety of policy questions. How should we best respond to these dramatic changes? To what degree should the West stand by or actively engage in influencing the ultimate outcome of the changes underway? What political, economic, and military changes and challenges exist for the former Soviet Union? What issues do they raise for the United States and its allies?

US Policy Principles

US government spokespersons have enunciated five general US policy principles regarding the political changes in the former USSR. These principles seek to nurture peaceful democratic evolution and to reenforce international agreements on human rights -such as the Helsinki Final Act:

1. *Self-Determination* - The future of the former USSR is for the peoples themselves to decide, peacefully and consistent with democratic values and practices. The Helsinki Final Act should set the standard in this regard;
2. *Respecting Borders* - Both internal and external borders should be respected. Any change of borders should occur only through legitimate, consensus-building, and peaceful processes, consistent with the Helsinki Final Act;
3. *Supporting Democracy* - Democracy and the rule of

law should govern the transformation. Peaceful change can and should only occur via orderly democratic processes, especially through the process of elections;
4. *Safeguarding Human Rights* - Human rights should be safeguarded, based upon full respect for the individual and including equal treatment of minorities; and
5. *Respecting International Law* - Respect must be paid to international law and obligations, especially adherence to the Helsinki Final Act.

A Spectrum of US Views Regarding the Former USSR

Today, beyond setting general principles, the new era of change and challenge also presents important US foreign policy choices. For over forty years, the US based much of its foreign and military policies on containing the expansion of Soviet power and influence. With the Cold War over, and the strategic environment changing, the US must adjust longstanding assumptions regarding security threats and priorities. The US policy debate involves determining the breadth and scope of that adjustment.

At Issue: The US public debate over the former USSR is linked to determining the US role in the post Cold War era, and prompts the following questions: To what degree should the US lead, defer, or step back from efforts to assist the former USSR? What political, economic and military policy priorities are in the national interest now that the Cold War is over? What can the US realistically afford to do? What should US policy be toward Soviet nuclear weapons, proliferation, conventional weapons, and regional conflicts? How should the end of the Cold War affect the US military posture and budget?

While far from exhaustive, the following "schools of thought" summarize the viewpoints on these complex issues. The spectrum of US views includes materials adapted from ACCESS Security Spectrum on "Economic Dimensions of US National Security" and "The Future of NATO and US interests," and from the Foreign Policy Association's "Breakup of the Soviet Union" Great Decisions 1992 (see entries pp.80, 92). The Political Priorities positions were presented in the Center for Foreign Policy Development at Brown University's "Facing A Disintegrated Soviet Union." (see entries pp. 80, 85). Readers are encouraged to consult the Suggested Readings (pp. 67-68) for these and other formulations.

Position One
US, World Leader

Now that Soviet Communism has collapsed, America is the only remaining superpower. The US must continue its global leadership role because no one else can effectively fill its shoes. American power to influence events militarily and economically must adjust to the growing strength of other nations, while actively aiding democratic and economic reforms in Eastern Europe and the former USSR. Without resolute US leadership and a strong US military posture, the processes of economic and political evolution could falter and fall back to tyranny and repression. The US cannot afford to let this happen. Retrenchment and isolationism are short-sighted policies that resulted in two world wars in this century; the US must now seize this moment of history and promote policies that safeguard our - and the former USSR's - future interests; otherwise, we will only have to get involved later, and at far greater cost.

Political Priorities: *Support a Stable Russia*. The collapse of the Soviet Union marks a victory for US foreign policy. In the current atmosphere of uncertainty, America must act as the anchor of international order. That means ensuring the stability of Russia as our top priority. Only Russia has the power to maintain stability in this potentially explosive region that includes over one hundred national groups, deep ethnic divisions, and some 27,000 nuclear warheads. The US must actively help Russia adopt democratic and market-oriented reforms. Anything less cannot ensure the peace. Just as we organized an alliance against communism during the Cold War, today we must organize a coalition in support of freedom. After struggling so long and spending so much to defeat our Cold War enemy, we would now be foolish not to lend a hand to our new-found friend.

Position Two
US, Partner in an Interdependent World

As economic wealth and resources have become more equally distributed among the advanced industrial countries, the management of peace and security should be sought through multilateral cooperation and greater policy coordination. The US will remain a leading player, but it cannot and need not solve all of the world's problems by itself. The post Cold War era requires a collective approach that strengthens and uses existing international institutions to ensure global security and stability. The emerging political-economic centers of power - Europe, Japan and North America - should coordinate policy through existing multilateral institutions such as the Group of Seven (G-7), the Organization for Economic Cooperation and Development (OECD), the World Bank, the International Monetary Fund (IMF), the International Atomic Energy Agency (IAEA), the European Bank for Reconstruction and Development (EBRD), the United Nations (UN), the European Community (EC), NATO, and the Conference on Security and Cooperation in Europe, (CSCE).

Political Priorities: *Strengthen Democracy in All Newly Independent Republics*. Each of the newly independent republics has the right to determine its own future and the international community has the responsibility to treat each of them as equal members. Efforts must be made to make each republic a viable partner of the international community, with a stake in abiding by internationally accepted norms and responsibilities. A multilateral approach that includes US participation is the best way to accomplish this goal.

Position Three
Come Home, America

The US is undergoing a serious economic and technological decline. A realistic sense of the strengths and limits of our power compels an American withdrawal from overextended international commitments. Now that the Cold War is over, the US should first and foremost get its own house in order. We should not allow artificial military needs to jeopardize our real economic interests. *Variation One:* The US must revitalize its schools, health care system, economic infrastructure, and industries to become more competitive in the 21st century. This will require investment at home and not abroad. *Variation Two:* Government has drained resources from the American economy for decades. In a time of unprecedented political and economic opportunity, our policy should be to draw back from Europe and Asia and avoid forming new alliances with other countries. America's priority is a foreign policy aimed exclusively at the welfare of American citizens. Our economic destiny, entrepreneurism, and continental security should guide our interests, not any European or Asian balance of power.

Political Priorities: *America First: Mind Our Own Business*. For nearly forty-five years since World War II, we have deployed troops in Europe and around the world, and spent trillions to contain the Soviet threat. Now that the USSR is gone, America must focus on America first. The United States will serve as a terrible role model for emerging democracies if it continues to fall apart at the seams. If we want other nations to look to us for moral leadership, we must first get our own house in order. Who are we to tell the new republics what to do and how to do it, anyway? They know best what they must do to reform their own society. If Europeans contend it is so vitally important to support the former USSR, let them take on the responsibility themselves.

Position One Continued
US, World Leader

Economic Priorities: *Create a New Marshall Plan*. At this historic time, the US should increase aid to the successor states of the USSR to help rebuild their economic and social infrastructures. A new Marshall plan is needed to help prevent economic chaos and despair from plummeting 280 million people into another version of authoritarian rule. Just like the original Marshall Plan, which only temporarily raised the burden on the US taxpayer, benefits will accrue to US farmers, who will have more markets for their commodities, and to US workers, who will have more jobs and job security. Moreover, US taxpayers will spend less on defense budgets over the longer term. Immediate, substantial, and sustained US aid and technical assistance is the best way to demonstrate to the peoples of the former USSR that the West wants to help them succeed in their historic efforts at political and economic reform.

Military Priorities:

Nuclear Weapons: As the only remaining nuclear superpower, the US must ensure that nuclear arms reductions agreements are adhered to, and that no new nuclear threats emerge from the former Soviet Union. That means only Russia should retain a nuclear capability. The US should do all it can to guarantee that the destruction of existing Soviet strategic and tactical arsenals is done as quickly and safely as possible. The US can afford to eliminate all but its air-delivered nuclear weapons from Europe. Maintaining some US nuclear weapons in Europe remains important for at least several years for two reasons: first, since large numbers of Soviet nuclear weapons still exist, they are needed for purposes of deterrence; and second, they form a buffer against any regional instabilities that crop up in the former Soviet Union.

Position Two Continued
US, Partner in an Interdependent World

Economic Priorities: *Provide Limited US Assistance*. The US can only provide limited assistance to the former Soviet Union because of US budget considerations and because it is more appropriate for existing multilateral financial institutions like the World Bank and the IMF to shoulder the responsibility. While the West can help, the successor states to the former USSR must commit themselves to market-oriented reforms in accordance with accepted Western economic practices. The US can take measures to encourage businesses to invest in the former USSR, and should cooperate with multilateral institutions such as the World Bank, the IMF, the G-7 (US, Germany, UK, France, Canada, Italy, and Japan), the EBRD, and the EC to help. While the US cannot afford to finance another Marshall Plan, it can, with other industrial nations, provide its fair share toward getting the job done.

Military Priorities:

Nuclear Weapons: NATO remains the most appropriate multilateral organization to coordinate European nuclear weapons policy. A limited yet important US nuclear presence is still needed to deter threats to European security, and to reassure Europeans of our commitment to stability both as Russia reduces its nuclear forces and as it confronts a variety of nationalities problems. Cooperation with the UK and France - Europe's independent nuclear powers - may grow more important in post Cold War Europe.

Position Three Continued
Come Home, America

Economics Priorities: *America First: Let Them Sink or Swim on Their Own.* The US cannot afford to make Russia or the other new republics into welfare states. After footing most of the defense bill for Europe and Asia during the Cold War, US taxpayers should somehow reap the benefits of their investment. Now that the Cold War is won, let those who benefitted most from that protection step forward to shoulder future defense burdens. Why should Americans now pay to support unemployed former Soviets when Americans are out of work at home? Why should Americans pay to retool Soviet industries when American industries are sorely in need of revamping? Revitalizing American industry, improving American education, and lowering health care costs must take top priority if we wish to compete economically in the 21st century. The US should spend whatever savings it reaps from cutting the defense budget only to benefit American citizens.

Military Priorities:

Nuclear Weapons: While it is in the US interest to see Soviet nuclear weapons destroyed, US taxpayers should not have to pay for their destruction. It is ironic that Americans who paid to defend against Soviet nuclear weapons for so long are now being asked to pay for their destruction. The United States need no longer provide a nuclear commitment to Europe and should withdraw all its nuclear weapons from Europe (and Asia) as soon as possible.

Position One Continued
US, World Leader

Proliferation: America should ensure that all successor states to the former USSR become parties to the Nuclear Nonproliferation Treaty. The US must lead the way in monitoring and organizing international efforts to keep nuclear materials and technology from being exported to terrorists and nations like Iraq and Libya seeking a nuclear capability. The US has the technological monitoring capacity to ensure that this is done. Russian nuclear scientists should either be employed at a joint research institute in Moscow financed by US funds, or directly by US government agencies such as the Department of Energy.

Conventional Weapons and Regional Conflicts: Reductions in conventional armed forces agreed to under the Conventional Armed Forces in Europe (CFE) Treaty should be implemented as quickly as possible, whether the former Soviet troops remain under a CIS command or in national military forces. If it is the latter, then the smaller the forces, the less likely they are to pose a threat to the West or to one another. The US should assist efforts to convert Soviet military industries to civilian use. To the extent possible, the US should encourage peaceful and democratic solutions to ethnic and nationalist problems.

Implications for the US Military: Even though the Cold War is over, the world remains a dangerous place. It would be a mistake to reduce US military forces too quickly or too deeply. US forces will be reduced in Europe, but will remain strong enough to act as a stabilizing factor during uncertain times. While some cuts in defense spending are necessary and appropriate, it would be unwise to reduce the defense budget by more than $50 billion dollars in the next five years.

Position Two Continued
US, Partner in an Interdependent World

Proliferation: Multilateral organizations such as the IAEA need to work with the former USSR to monitor nuclear arms reductions and prevent nuclear technology and materials from falling into the wrong hands. A nuclear export control regime should be made a priority, perhaps building on existing agreements of the "London Suppliers Group." Efforts should be made to employ Soviet nuclear engineers and technicians. Successor states must be encouraged to sign the Nuclear Nonproliferation Treaty (NPT). Nuclear reactor safety should also receive attention, since 16 of the former Soviet Union's 46 reactors are of the Chernobyl type, and risk similar international catastrophes.

Conventional Weapons and Regional Conflicts: Multilateral institutions must ensure compliance with the Conventional Armed Forces in Europe (CFE) Treaty and with the Helsinki Final Act. The US can best use its influence through NATO, but will also have to play a constructive role in the CSCE. The EC, to the extent that it develops a common military policy, will have its own role and influence in European affairs. Until these structures define their missions, regional conflicts in the former USSR may have to be addressed by the UN Security Council - much like what has happened in Yugoslavia .

Implications for the US Military: The collapse of Soviet communism has increased the need for multilateral approaches to security. There is no alternative given America's economic problems at home. The US will remain a superpower, but it must cut its military budget by at least $100 billion, reduce forces overseas, and rely more on reserve forces. The US will remain a military superpower, but our allies in Europe and Asia can pick up more of the tab and responsibility for their own defense.

Position Three Continued
Come Home, America

Proliferation: The US cannot afford to act as the world's policeman for nuclear or would-be nuclear powers. There is insufficient evidence to suggest that the US will be directly threatened by the proliferation of nuclear weapons. These weapons are most likely to be aimed at neighboring enemies, not at North America. Until this situation changes, we should not worry about it. We should be more concerned with the proliferation of domestic economic ills besetting the United States.

Conventional Weapons and Regional Conflicts: While it is in the US interest to see the Soviet conventional weapons destroyed, it is not in the US interest to maintain any US forces overseas to ensure that this happens. The US should pull back from its international military commitments to enable more investment in domestic needs. Regional conflicts are best addressed by the involved parties, not US soldiers. American workers and business now deserve to be paid back for providing the post World War II security umbrella that allowed formidable competitors like Japan and Germany to emerge.

Implications for the US Military: In the next century, real American security will be directly linked to its economic competitiveness abroad. If we neglect our own industries, we will continue to fall behind and weaken our standard of living. A cut in the US defense budget of at least $200 billion in the next five years would be the best way to advertise the value of converting Soviet military industries to civilian production.

SUGGESTED READINGS

The End of the Cold War

Armstrong, David & Erik Goldstein, eds. *The End of the Cold War*, (Portland, Oregon: Frank Cass, 1991).

Avinieri, Shlomo. "The Return to History: The Breakup of the Soviet Union," *The Brookings Review*, Vol. 10, No. 2, Spring 1992.

Bialer, Seweryn. "The Death of Soviet Communism," *Foreign Affairs*, Vol. 70, No.5, Winter 1991/92.

Borovik, Artyom. "Waiting for Democracy," *Foreign Policy*, No. 84, Fall 1991.

Brzezinski, Zbigniew K. *The Grand Failure: The Birth and Death of Communism in the Twentieth Century.* (New York: Scribner, 1989).

Deudny, Daniel & John Ikenberry. "The International Sources of Soviet Change,"*International Security*, Vol. 16, No. 3, Winter 91-92.

Gaddis, John L. *The Long Peace* (NY: Oxford, 1987).

Horelick, Arnold L. *US-Soviet Relations: From a "Post-Cold War" to a "Post-Communism" Era?* (Santa Monica, CA: Rand Corp., 1991).

Hyland, William G. *The Cold War: Fifty Years of Conflict*, (New York: Random House, 1991).

"International Security Toward the New Century," The Center for American-Eurasian Studies and Relations, *The Eurasian Report*, Special Issue, Vol. 2, No. 1, Winter 1992.

Kanet, Roger E. & Edward A. Kolodziej. *The Cold War as Cooperation*, (Baltimore: Johns Hopkins, 1991).

Kegley, Charles W. Jr., ed. *The Long Post War Peace*, (New York: HarperCollins, 1991).

Kegley, Charles W. Jr. & Kenneth L. Schwab. *After the Cold War*, (Boulder, CO: Westview Press, 1991).

Kennan, George F. "Communism in Russian History," *Foreign Affairs*, Vol. 69, No. 5, Winter 1990/91.

Kirkpatrick, Jeane J. *The Withering Away of the Totalitarian State...and Other Surprises.* (Washington, DC: The American Enterprise Institute Press, 1990).

Lynn-Jones, Sean M., ed. *The Cold War and After*, (Cambridge, Mass.: MIT Press, 1991).

Maier, Charles S. *The Cold War in Europe*, (New York: Markus Wiener Publishing, 1991).

Mandelbaum, Michael. "The End of the Soviet Union," *Foreign Affairs*, Vol. 71, No. 1, January 1992.

Naylor, Thomas. *The Cold War Legacy*, (Lexington, MA: Lexington Press, 1991).

Nye, Jr., Joseph S., Kurt Biedenkopf and Motoo Shina. *Global Cooperation After the Cold War: A Reassessment of Trilateralism,* Triangle Papers: 41, The Trilateral Commission, July 1991.

Oberdorfer, Don. *The Turn: From the Cold War to a New Era. The United States and the Soviet Union, 1983-1990.* (New York: Poseidon Books, 1991).

Ralston, Richard E., ed. *Communism: Its Rise and Fall in the 20th Century* (Christian Science Monitor, 1991).

Ulam, Adam. *The Communists: The Story of Power and Lost Illusions 1948-1991*, (NY: Scribners, 1992).

Glasnost, Perestroika, and Economic Reforms

Aganbegyan, Abel. "The Economics of Perestroika," *International Affairs* (London), Vol. 64, Spring 1988.

Allison, Graham & Grigory Yavlinsky. *Window of Opportunity: The Grand Bargain for Democracy in the Soviet Union.* (New York: Pantheon Press, 1991).

Aslund, Anders. *Gorbachev's Struggle for Economic Reform: the Soviet Reform Process, 1985-1988*, (Ithaca, NY: Cornell University Press, 1989).

Baker, James A., III. "Points of Mutual Advantage: Perestroika and American Foreign Policy," *Vital Speeches of the Day,* Vol. 56, Nov. 115, 1989.

Balzer, Harley D. *Five Years That Shook the World.* (Boulder, CO: 1991).

Bialer, Seweryn. "Gorbachev's Program of Change: Sources, Significance, Prospects," *Political Science Quarterly*, Vol. 103, Fall 1988.

Blank, Stephen J. et al. *Economic Perestroika: The Consequences of Success.* Occasional Paper. (Carlisle Barracks, PA: Strategic Studies Institute, US Army War College, April 1990).

Cohen, Stephen F. & Katrina vanden Heuvel. *Voices of Glasnost: Interviews with Gorbachev's Reformers*, (New York: W.W. Norton, 1989).

Desai, Padma. *Perestroika in Perspective: The Design and Dilemmas of Soviet Reform.* (Princeton, NJ: Princeton University Press, 1989).

Eisen, Jonathan, ed. *The Glasnost Reader* (New York: Plume Books, 1990).

Feifer, George. "The New God Will Fail: Moscow: Skeptical Voices on Perestroika," *Harper's*, Vol. 277, No. 1661, Oct. 1988.

Franklin, Daniel. "The Soviet Economy: A Survey," *Economist*, Vol. 307, April 9, 1988.

Furtado, Charles F., Jr. & Andrea Chandler, eds. *Perestroika in the Soviet Republics*, (CO: Westview, 1991).

Goldman, Marshall I. "Perestroika in the Soviet Union," *Current History*, Vol. 87, No. 531, Oct. 1988.

Gorbachev, Mikhail. *The Coming Century of Peace*, (Richardson & Sherman, 1986).

—*Peace Has No Alternative: Articles and Interviews*, (Advent, NY: Patriot Publishers, 1987).

—*Perestroika and Soviet-American Relations*, (Madison, Conn.: Sphinx Press, 1990).

—*Perestroika: New Thinking for Our Country and the World*, (New York: Harper and Row, 1987).

Gregory, Paul R. *Restructuring the Soviet Economic Bureaucracy.* (New York: Cambridge University Press, 1990).

Hanke, Steve H. & Kurt Schuler. *Currency Convertibility: A Self-Help Blueprint for the Commonwealth of Independent States.* (Washington: CATO Institute, 1992).

Hardt, John P. & Sheila N. Heslin. *Perestroika: A Sustainable Process for Change.* (NY: Group of Thirty, 1989).

Herlihy, Michael G. "Gorbachev, Glasnost and God," *America*, Vol. 158, No. 1, Jan. 2-9, 1988.

Hewett Ed A. & Victor H. Winston, eds. *Milestones in Glasnost and Perestroika* (DC: Brookings Institution, 1991).

Holloway, David. "Gorbachev's New Thinking," *Foreign Affairs*, Vol. 68, No. 1, Winter 1988.

Hosking, Geoffrey A. *The Awakening of the Soviet Union.* (London: Heinemann, 1990).

Hough, Jerry. *Russia and the West: Gorbachev and the Politics of Reform.* (New York: Touchstone, 1990).

International Monetary Fund. *A Study of the Soviet Economy.* (Washington: IMF Publications, Jan. 1991).

Kaiser, Robert G. *Why Gorbachev Happened: His Triumph and His Failure.* (NY: Simon & Schuster, 1991).

Kull, Steven. *Burying Lenin: The Revolution of Soviet Ideology and Foreign Policy.* (Boulder, CO: Westview, 1992).

Laptev, Ivan. "Glasnost, A Reliable Instrument of Perestroika," *International Affairs*, (Moscow), No. 6, June 1988.

Laquer, Walter. *The Long Road to Freedom: Russia and Glasnost.* (New York: Charles Scribner's Sons, 1989).

McCauley, Martin. *Gorbachev and Perestroika.* (New York: St. Martin's Press, 1990).

Naylor, Thomas H. *The Gorbachev Strategy: Opening the Closed Society* (Lexington, MA: Lexington Books, 1988).

Nove, Alec. "The Problems of Perestroika," *Dissent*, Vol. 36, Fall 1989.

Parker, Richard. "Assessing Perestroika," *World Policy Journal*, Vol. VI, No. 2, Spring 1989.

Peck, Merton J. & Thomas Richardson, eds. *What Is to Be Done? Proposals for the Soviet Transition to the Market.* (New Haven: Yale Univ. Press, 1991).

Powell, David E. "Soviet Glasnost: Definitions and Dimensions," *Current History*, Vol. 87, Oct. 1988.

Richardson, Thomas. "The Grand Bargain Plan and Economic Recovery," *Nuclear Times*, Vol. 9, No. 4, Winter 1991-92.

Shevardnadze, Eduard. *The Future Belongs to Freedom.* (New York: The Free Press, 1991).

Sobchak, Anatoly. *For a New Russia: The Mayor of St. Petersburg's Own Story of the Struggle for Justice and Democracy.* (New York: The Free Press, 1991).

Solovyov, Viktor. *Boris Yeltsin.* (New York: Putnam, March 1992).

Taarasulo, Isaac J., ed., *Perils of Perestroika: Viewpoints from the Soviet Press, 1989-91* (Wilmington, DE: SR Books, 1992).

Takayuki, Ito, ed. *Facing Up to the Past: Soviet Historiography Under Perestroika.* (Sapporo: Slavic Research Center, Hokkaido University, 1989).

Taubman, William & Jane. *Moscow Spring* (New York: Summit Books, 1989).

US Congress. House. Committee on Small Business. *Perestroika and its Implications for the United States.* Hearings, 100th Congress, 2nd session. Sept. 23 and 30. 1988. (Washington, DC: G.P.O., 1989).

US Congress. Joint Economic Committee. Subcommittee on National Security Economics. *Economic Reforms in the USSR.* Hearings, 100th Congress, 1st session. (Washington, DC: G.P.O., 1988).

USSR Supreme Soviet, Mikhail Gorbachev's Address. 1st Session. Moscow, Kremlin, 1 August 1989.

Woll, Josephine. "Fruits of Glasnost: A Sampling from the Soviet Press," *Dissent*, Vol. 36, Winter 1989.

World Bank. *The Economy of the USSR: Summary and Recommendations.* (DC: World Bank, Jan. 1991).

Yeltsin, Boris. *Against the Grain.* (New York: Simon & Schuster, 1990).

Z, Pseud. "To the Stalin Mausoleum," *Daedalus*, Vol. 119, No. 1, Winter 1990.

Zwick, Peter. "New Thinking and New Foreign Policy Under Gorbachev," *PS: Political Science & Politics*, Vol. 22, June 1989.

Environmental and Health Problems

Androshin, Alexandr. "Free Medical Services: The End of the Myth," *Business in the USSR*, No. 7, December 1990.

Bonner, Elena, "Health Care in the Soviet Union," *Freedom at Issue,* Nov.-Dec., 1990.

Feshbach, Murray & Alfred Friendly, Jr. *Ecocide in the USSR: Health and Nature Under Seige.* (NY: Basic, 1992).

Fishbein, David Joel. "Do DNA: Alchoholism in the Soviet Union," *JAMA: The Journal of the American Medical Association,* Vol. 266, No. 9, 4 September 1991.

French, Hillary. "Environmental Problems & Politics in the Soviet Union," *Current History*, Vol. 90, No. 558, Oct. 1991.

Gale, Robert P. & Thomas Hauser. *Final Warning: The Legacy of Chernobyl.* (NY: Warner Books, 1988).

"Glasnost and Ecology: Three Reports from the Soviet Union," *Environment,* Vol. 30, Dec. 1988.

Jankin, Elizabeth Darby. "Green Cries from Red Square," *Buzzworm*, Vol. 2, No. 2, March-April 1990.

Kotlyakov, V.M. "The Aral Sea Basin: A Critical Environmental Zone," *Environment*, Vol. 3, No. 1, Jan.-Feb, 1991.

"The Legacy of Soviet Communism: Poisoning Russia," *US News & World Report*, Vol. 112, No. 14, 13 April 1992.

Levi, Barbara Goss. "International Team Examines Health in Zones Contaminated by Chernobyl," *Physics Today,* Vol. 44, No. 8, August 1991.

Loukjanenko, V. "Water Crisis in the USSR," *World Health*, Jan.-Feb. 1990.

Medvedev, Zhores, *The Legacy of Chernobyl.* (NY: W.W. Norton, 1990).

"Moscow's Dirty Secrets," *US News & World Report*, Vol. 112, No. 5, 10 February 1992.

Nichols, Mark. "Deadly Shortages: Decay Sabotages Care in the Soviet Union," *McLean's,* Vol. 104, No. 32, 12 August 1991.

"The Perils of Ex-Soviet Nuclear Power," *The Economist,* Vol. 322, No. 7752, 28 March 1992.

"No Place for Babies," *The Economist,* Vol. 310, No. 7588, 4 February 1989.

Schoenfeld, Gabriel. "A Dosimeter for Every Dacha," *Bulletin of Atomic Scientists,* Vol. 31, No. 6, July-August 1989.

"The Sick Man of Eurasia," *The Economist,* Vol. 316, No. 7673, 22 September 1990.

"Soviet Medicine," *U.S. News & World Report,* Vol. 109, No. 14, 8 October 1990.

Strong, Maurice. "40 Chernobyls Waiting to Happen," *New York Times,* 22 March 1992.

Yegorov, Alexander. "The Lessons of Baikal," *Soviet Life,* No. 2, February 1989.

The Soviet Coup (August 19 - 21, 1991)

Baker, James. "Conflict in the Soviet Union," *Dispatch*, US Department of State, 26 August 1991.

Bush, George. "The Crisis in the Soviet Union," *Dispatch*, US Department of State, 19 August 1991.

Colton, Timothy J. "The Resignation of Mikhail Gorbachev," *Soviet Economy*, Vol. 7, Oct. 1991.

"Coup and Aftermath," *National Review*, 23 September 1991.

Frangulov, Vladimir G., Kent D. Lee & Yuri Usachev. *The Coup: Underground Moscow Newspapers from Monday, August 19 to Wednesday, August 21, 1991.* (Minneapolis: East View Publications, 1991).

Goldman, Marshall I. "Three Days That Shook My World," *World Monitor*, 30 October 1991.

Gorbachev, Mikhail. *The August Coup.* (New York: Harper Collins, 1991).

Holden, Gerard. *The Road to the Coup: Civil-Military Relations in the Soviet Crisis.* (Frankfurt: Peace Research Institute Frankfurt, 1991).

Malia, Martin. "The August Revolution," *The New York Review of Books,* 26 September 1991.

McAuley, Alastair. "The Economic Consequences of Soviet Disintegration," *Soviet Economy,* Vol. 7, July-Sept. 1991.

Meyer, Stephen M. "How The Threat (and the Coup) Collapsed: The Politicization of the Soviet Military," *International Security*, Vol. 16, No. 3, Winter 1991/92.

Miller, Stephen. "The Soviet Coup and the Benefits of Breakdown," *Orbis,* Vol. 36, No. 1, Winter 1992.

Pozner, Vladimir. *Eyewitness: A Personal Account of the Unraveling of the Soviet Union.* (Random House, 1992).

Reddaway, Peter. "The Threat to Gorbachev," *New York Review of Books,* Vol. 36, Aug. 17, 1989.

Shevtsova, Lilia. "The August Coup and the Soviet Collapse," *Survival*, Spring 1992.

Shipler, David K. "Report from Moscow: After the Coup," *The New Yorker*, Vol. 67, No. 38, 11 November 1991.

"Soviet Coup," *Vital Speeches of the Day,* Vol. 57, No. 23, 15 Sept. 1991. (Series of speeches by key leaders)

Sturua, Melor. "The Real Coup," *Foreign Policy*, No. 85, Winter 1991-92.

Trimble, Jeff & Peter Vassiliev. "Three Days That Shook the World," *US News & World Report*, Vol. 111, No. 21, 18 November 1991.

Nuclear Weapons, Proliferation, & Arms Control:

Adelman, Kenneth et al, "On Proliferation," *The National Interest,* No. 27, Spring 1992.

Allison, Graham, Ashton B. Carter, and Philip Zelikow, "The Soviet Arsenal and the Mistaken Calculus of Caution," *The Washington Post,* March 29, 1992.

Aspin, Les. "A New Kind of Threat: Nuclear Weapons in an Uncertain Soviet Union," House Armed Services Committee, 12 September 1991.

Baker, James. "Supporting Scientists of the Former Soviet Union," US Dept. of State, *Dispatch,* Vol. 3, No. 8, 12 February 1992.

Bartholomew, Reginald. "US Effort to Halt Weapons Proliferation in the Former Soviet Republics," *US Department of State Dispatch,* Vol. 3, No. 6, 10 February 1992.

Blair, Bruce. Testimony Before the US Senate Committee on Foreign Relations, Subcommittee on European Affairs, on Soviet Nuclear Safeguards. 24 September 1991.

Bohlen, Celestine. "A Soviet (Russian)Academy is Adrift," *New York Times,* 14 December 1991.

Broad, William. "Soviet Company Offers Nuclear Blasts to Anyone With the Cash," *New York Times,* 7 November 1991.

---. "US Plans to Hire Russian Scientists in Fusion Research," *New York Times,* 6 March 1992.

Brown University, Center for Foreign Policy Development, "Nuclear Weapons in the Former Soviet Union," in *Facing a Disintegrated Soviet Union.* (Providence: Choices for the 21st Century Education Project, January 1992).

Burns, William F. "Testimony Before the House Armed Services Committee on US Efforts to Facilitate Dismantlement of Nuclear Weapons in the Former USSR," House Armed Services Committee, 26 March 1992.

Calingaert, Daniel. *Soviet Nuclear Policy Under Gorbachev.* (Westport, CT: Greenwood Publishing Group, 1991).

Campbell, Kurt M., Ashton B. Carter, Steven E. Miller, & Charles A. Zraket. *Soviet Nuclear Fission: Control of the Nuclear Arsenal in a Disintegrating Soviet Union* (Cambridge: Harvard Center for Science and International Affairs, 1991).

Cochran, Thomas B., William M. Arkin, Robert S. Norris, & Jeffrey I. Sands. *Soviet Nuclear Weapons.* (New York: Harper & Row, 1989).

Committee on International Security and Arms Control. *The Future of the US-Soviet Nuclear Relationship* (Washington, DC: National Academy Press, 1991).

Cox, David. "Thinking About Nuclear Weapons After the Coup," *Peace & Security,* Winter 1991/92.

Dean, Jonathan. *Nuclear Security in a Transformed World.* (DC: Union of Concerned Scientists, Feb. 1992).

Ellsberg, Daniel. "Nuclear Security and the Soviet Collapse," *World Policy Journal,* Winter 1991-92.

Feduschak, Natalia A., "Ukraine Seeks to Get Control of Nuclear Arms," *Wall Street Journal,* 26 March 1992.

Feldbaum, Carl & Ronald J. Bee. *Looking the Tiger in the Eye: Confronting the Nuclear Threat.* (NY: Vintage, 1990).

Fesperman, Dan. "Soviet Nuclear Scientists Ripe for Offers from Highest Bidder," *Baltimore Sun,* 17 Nov. 1991.

Fialka, John J. "The Risk Now Posed by the Soviet 'Nukes' is One of Management," *Wall Street Journal,* 20 November 1991.

Gates, Robert. Testimony before the Senate Governmental Affairs Committee, 15 January 1992.

Hiatt, Fred. "A-Arms Chief Says Russia Needs Help," *Washington Post,* 5 Feb. 1992.

Hiatt, Fred. "Possible Moves to Third World Seen for Soviet A-Arms Experts," *Washington Post,* 28 Nov. 1991.

Hibbs, Mark. "Vulnerable Soviet Nuclear Experts Could Aid Clandestine Weapons Aims," *Nuclear Fuel,* 28 Oct 1991.

"How Steady are the Trigger Fingers of the `Central Eurasian Arsenal'?" *National Journal,* 11 January 1992.

Kaysen, Carl, Robert S. McNamara, & George W. Rathjens. "Nuclear Weapons After the Cold War," *Foreign Affairs,* Vol. 70, No. 4, Fall 1991.

Ksanfomality, Leonid. "Survival Before Science," *Bulletin of Atomic Scientists,* Vol. 47, No. 10, December 1991.

Lockwood, Dunbar. "After START: Bidding Down," *Bulletin of the Atomic Scientists,* Vol. 48, No. 3, April 1992.

Makhijani, Arjun and Katherine Yih. "What to Do at Doomsday's End: How the World Can Step Back from Nuclear Brinkmanship," *Washington Post,* 29 March 1992.

Mendelsohn, Jack. "Dismantling the Arsenals: Arms Control and the New World Agenda," *The Brookings Review,* Vol. 10, No. 2, Spring 1992.

Milhollin, Gary & Gerard White. "Explosive Disunion: The Trade in Soviet Nuclear Know-How," *Washington Post,* 8 December 1991.

Morrocco, John D. "Soviet Military Breakdown Worries US as Control Over Nuclear Arms Splinters," *Aviation Week and Space Technology,* Vol. 135, No. 24-25, 16 December 1991.

Norris, Robert S. & William Arkin. "Where the Weapons Are," *Bulletin of the Atomic Scientists*, Vol. 47, No. 9, November 1991.

"The Nuclear Epidemic," *U.S. News & World Report*, Vol. 112, No. 10, 16 March 1992.

"Nuclear Weapons in the Former Soviet Union," *Arms Control Today* (Special Issue), Vol. 22, No. 1, Jan./Feb. 1992.

Pavlov, Gennadi A. Testimony Before the US Senate Committee on Foreign Relations, Subcommittee on European Affairs, on the command and control of Soviet Nuclear Weapons, 24 September 1991.

Potter, William C. "The New Suppliers," *Orbis*, Vol. 36, No. 2 Spring 1992.

——"Russia's Nuclear Entrepeneurs," *New York Times,* 7 November 1991.

Rauf, Tariq. "New Soviet Nuclear Challenge," *Defense News*, 25 Nov. 1991.

Rauf, Tariq. "Who Controls Soviet Nuclear Weapons?" *Barometer*, Fall 1991.

Scarlott, Jennifer. "Nuclear Proliferation After the Cold War," *World Policy Journal*, Vol VIII, No. 4, Fall 1991.

Schmitt, Eric. "Soviet Nuclear Move Ahead of Schedule," *New York Times*, 28 February 1992.

Sharansky, Natan. "The Greatest Exodus," *New York Times Magazine,* 2 February 1992.

Sheinman, Lawrence & David A.V. Fisher, "Managing the Coming Glut of Nuclear Weapon Materials," *Arms Control Today,* Vol 22, No. 2, March 1992.

US Congress. Senate. Committee on Foreign Relations. Subcommittee on European Affairs. "Command and Control of Soviet Nuclear Weapons: Dangers and Opportunities Arising from the August Revolution," Hearing, 102nd Congress, 1st Session, S. Hrg. 102-402, 24 Sept. 1991.

US Congress. Senate. Committee on Foreign Relations. "The START Treaty in a Changed World," Hearing, 102nd Congress, 1st Session, S. Hrg. 102-406, Sept. 19-Nov. 7, 1991.

Warnke, Paul C. & John Parachini. "More Nuclear Reductions Possible," *Council on Economic Priorities Research Report,* December 1991.

Conventional Weapons: Red Army, Arms Transfers, & Arms Control

Bacarrere-Becane, Catherine. "The Soviet Army in Search of a New Identity," *European Viewpoint Series,* Aug. 1991.

Baker, James. "CFE: Foundation for Enduring European Security," US Dept. of State, *Dispatch,* Vol. 2, No. 28, 15 July 1991.

Bluth, Christopher. *New Thinking in Soviet Military Power.* (New York: Council on Foreign Relations, 1990).

Brumberg, Abraham. "The Road to Minsk," *New York Review of Books,* Vol. 39, 30 Jan. 1992.

"CFE: Foundation for Enduring European Security," *US Department of State Dispatch*, 15 July 1991.

Dunay, Pal. *The CFE Treaty: History, Achievements and Shortcomings.* (Frankfurt: Peace Research Institute Frankfurt, October 1991)

"Former Soviet Republics Announce Intention to Honor CFE," *BASIC Reports on European Arms Control*, No. 19, 21 January 1992.

Glantz, David M. *Soviet Military Strategy in the 1990s: Alternative Futures.* Occasional Paper. (Carlisle Barracks, PA: Strategic Studies Institute, US Army War College, 1991).

Goldring, Natalie, Sandra J. Ionno and Colleen Logan, *Trends and Issues in Third World Arms Transfers.* (Wash., DC: British American Security Information Council, April, 1992).

Hiatt, Fred. "Commonwealth Splits on Unified Military," *Washington Post,* 15 February 1992.

Ionno, Sandra J. and Colleen Logan, *Summary of Recent Initiatives to Control the Arms Trade.* (Wash., DC: British American Security Information Council, March 1992).

Izyumov, Alexei. "16th Republic: Armed and Dangerous," *Washington Post*, 22 January 1992.

Kaufman, Richard F. "Economic Reform and the Soviet Military," *Washington Quarterly,* Vol. 11, No. 3, Summer 1988.

Lepingwell, John W.R. "Towards a Post-Soviet Army," *Orbis,* Vol 36, No. 1, Winter 1992.

Plater-Zyberk, Henry. "The Red Army's Blues," *National Review*, September 23, 1991.

Riveles, Stanley. "The Soviet Breakup: Peace and Stability After the Putsch," *Nuclear Times*, Vol. 9, No. 4, Winter 1991-92.

Rogov, Serrgey. "The End of the Cold War and Soviet Military Spending," *Disarmament,* (UN Quarterly), XIII: 3, 1990.

Schmemann, Serge. "Yeltsin Makes a Surprise Visit to the Black Sea Fleet," *New York Times*, 29 January 1992.

US Congress. Senate. Committee on Armed Services. "Conventional Forces in Europe Treaty," Hearing, 102nd Congress, 1st Session, Senate Hearing 102-421. Nov. 4-13, 1991.

Warner, Edward L., III. *The Decline of the Soviet Military: Downsizing, Fragmentation, and Possible Disintegration.* (Santa Monica, CA: Rand Corp., 1992).

Conversion

ACCESS. "From Guns to Butter?: USA & USSR," *ACCESS Resource Brief,* Vol. IV, No. 3, Aug. 1990.

Adelman, Kenneth L. & Norman R. Augustine. "Defense Conversion," *Foreign Affairs*, Vol. 71, No. 2, Spring 1992.

Almquist, Peter & Kevin O'Prey. "Beating Swords into Agricultural Complexes: Soviet Economic Conversion," *Arms Control Today,* Vol. 20, No. 10, Dec. 1990.

CIA, *The Soviet Weapons Industries: An Overview.* Washington, DC: Directorate of Intelligence, Report # DI 86-10016, September 1986.

Cooper, Julian. *The Soviet Defence Industry: Conversion and Economic Reform.* (New York: Council on Foreign Relations, 1991).

Deutsche Bank Economics Department. *The Peace Dividend - How to Pin it Down?* (DC: Transatlantic Futures, February, 1990).

Faltsman, Vladimir. "What Do We Expect of Conversion?" *Business Contact,* No. 2, Mar.-Apr. 1990.

Hardt, John P. "Conversion or Chaos?" *Bulletin of the Atomic Scientists,* Vol. 46, No. 1, Jan.-Feb. 1990.

Izyumov, Alexi. "The Other Side of Disarmament," *International Affairs* (Moscow), May, 1988.

Kincade, William & Keith Thomson, "Economic Conversion in the USSR: Its Role in Perestroika," *Problems of Communism*, Jan.-Feb., 1990.

Maggs, Peter. "Beating Swords into Washing Machines," Council on Economic Priorities Report, 1990.

Marlin, John Tepper & Paul Grenier, eds., *Soviet Conversion 1991* (New York: Council on Economic Priorities, 1991).

O'Prey, Kevin. "The Soviet Peace Dividend? Trends and Prospects...," *Soviet Defense Notes,* Vol. 2, #3, June 1990.

Rosefielde, Steven. "Assessing Soviet Reforms in the Defense Industry," *Global Affairs*, Vol. IV, No. 4, Fall 1989.

Rumer, Boris. "Beating Swords Into...Refrigerators?" *World Monitor,* January 1992.

US Congress. Senate. Committee on Armed Services. "Soviet Military Conversion," Hearing, 102nd Congress, 1st Session, Senate Hearing 102-320, 19 Sept. 1991.

White, Gregory L. "Retooling Soviet Defense Sector Proves Difficult," *Wall Street Journal,* 6 Sept. 1990.

Wolf, Charles, Jr. *Defense and the Macroeconomics in the Soviet Union.* (Santa Monica, CA: Rand Corp. 1990).

Ethnic Unrest & Nationalism in the former USSR

Ethnic Unrest/Nationalism/General

Alexeyeva, Ludmilla. "Unrest in the Soviet Union," *Washington Quarterly*, Vol. 13, No. 1, Winter 1990.

Bialer, Seweryn, ed. *Politics, Society and Nationality Inside Gorbachev's Russia.* (Boulder, CO: Westview Press, 1989).

Bozzo, Robert. "Gorbachev and the Nationalities Problem," *Global Affairs*, Vol. 5, No. 3, Summer-Fall 1990.

Brezinski, Zbigniew. "Post-Communist Nationalism," *Foreign Affairs*, Vol. 68, No. 5, Winter 1989-90.

Conquest, Robert, ed. *The Last Empire.* (Stanford, CA: Hoover Institution Press, 1986).

Denber, Rachel. *The Soviet Nationality Reader: The Crisis in Context.* (Boulder, CO: Westview Press, 1991).

Derry, Christina & Ronald J. Bee. "The Nationalities Question in the USSR," *ACCESS Resource Brief,* Vol. IV., No. 5, Sept. 1990.

Diuk, Nadia & Adrian Karatnycky. "Nationalism—Part of the Solution," *Orbis*, Vol. 34, No. 4, Fall 1990.

Dobbs, Michael. "Russian Troops Caught in Growing Ethnic Strife," *Washington Post*, 4 March 1992.

Fuller, Graham E. "The Breaking of Nations," *The National Interest,* No. 26, Winter 1991/92.

Furtado, Charles F., Jr. & Andrea Chandler. *Perestroika in the Soviet Republics: Documents on the National Question.* (Boulder, CO: Westview Press, 1992).

Goble, Paul. "Ethnic Politics in the USSR," *Problems in Communism*, Vol. 38, July-Aug. 1989.

———"Forget the Soviet Union," *Foreign Policy*, No. 86, Spring 1992.

Hajda, Lubomyr. "The Nationalities Problem in the Soviet Union," *Current History*, Vol. 87, Oct. 1988.

Hajda, Lubomyr & Mark Beissinger, eds. *The Nationalities Factor in Soviet Politics and Society.* (Boulder, CO: Westview Press, 1990).

"The Ingathering Storm of Nationalism," *New Perspective Quarterly,* Vol. 8, Fall 1991.

Kingkade, W. Ward. *Estimate and Projections of the Population of the USSR by Major Nationality: 1979 to 2050.* (Washington: Center for International Research, Bureau of the Census, 1988).

Lee, Gary. "Multiple Ethnic Conflicts Challenging Gorbachev," *Washington Post,* 29 Feb. 1988.

Mandelbaum, Michael, ed. *The Rise of Nations in the Soviet Union.* (New York: Council on Foreign Relations, 1991).

Motyl, Alexandr J., ed. Forthcoming. *Westview Series on the Post-Soviet Republics.* (Boulder, CO: Westview Press, 1992): Paul Goble, *Russia.* Jan Zaprudnik, *Belorussia.* Gregory Gleason, *Central Asia/Kazakhstan.* Rein Taagepera, *Estonia.* Janis J. Penikis, *Latvia.* V. Stanley Vardys, *Lithuania.* Roman Szporluk, *Russia.* Victor L. Mote, *Siberia.* Henry R. Huttenbach, *Transcaucasus.* Yaroslav Bilinsky, *Ukraine.*

Nahaylo, Bohdan & Victor Swoboda. *Soviet Disunion: A History of the Nationalities Problem in the USSR.* (New York: The Free Press, 1989).

Nelson, Daniel N. "Europe's Unstable East," *Foreign Policy,* No. 82, Spring 1991.

Olcott, Martha Brill. "The Soviet Disunion," *Foreign Policy,* No. 82, Spring 1991.

Seay, Douglas. *Promoting the Peaceful Decolonization of the Soviet Union.* (DC: Heritage Foundation, 1990).

Simon, Gerhard. *Nationalism and Policy toward the Nationalities in the Soviet Union: From Totalitarian Dictatorship to Post-Stalinist Society.* (Boulder, CO: Westview Press, 1991).

Smith, Graham. "Gorbachev's Greatest Challenge: Perestroika and the National Question," *Political Geography Quarterly,* Vol. 8, Jan. 1989.

The Soviet Multinational State: Readings and Documents. Edited by Martha B. Olcott with Lubomyr Hajdda and Anthony Olcott. (Armonk, NY: M.E. Sharpe, 1990).

"Soviet Nationalities," *Journal of Soviet Nationalities,* Vol. 1, Spring 1990: Whole Issue.

"Successor States to the USSR," *RFE/RL Daily Report,* 10 February 1992.

Tishkov, Valerii. "Glasnost and the Nationalities Within the Soviet Union," *Third World Quarterly,* Vol. 11, Oct. 1989.

Glynn, Patrick, ed. *Unrest in the Soviet Union.* (DC: American Enterprise Institute for Public Policy Research, 1989).

U.S. Congress. Senate. Committee on Foreign Relations. Subcommittee on Eur. Affairs. "Soviet Disunion: Creating a Nationalities Policy," Hearing, 101st Congress, 2nd Session. July 24, 1990. Washington, G.P.O., 1990.

"USSR and Successor States," *RFE/RL Research Report,* 3 January 1992.

Transcaucasus Region: Georgia, Armenia, Azerbaijan

Altstadt, Audrey L., *The Azerbaijani Turks: Power and Identity Under Russian Rule.* (Stanford, CA: Hoover Institution Press, 1992).

Altstadt, Audrey L. "Nagorno-Karabakh—"Apple of Discord" in the Azerbaijan SSR," *Central Asian Survey,* Vol. 7, No. 4, 1988.

Armenian National Committee of America, "Transcaucasus: A Chronology," Vol. I, No. 4, 1 April 1992.

"A Conflict Analysis of the Armenian-Azerbaijani Dispute,"' *Journal of Conflict Resolution,* Vol. 34, Dec. 1990.

Avilishvili, Zourab. *The Independence of Georgia in International Politics 1918-21* (London, 1940).

Fuller, Elizabeth. "Nagorno-Karabakh: The Death and Casualty Toll to Date," New York: Radio Liberty Research, RL531/88, Dec. 2, 1988.

—*Whither the Nagorno-Karabakh Campaign?* (New York: Radio Liberty Research, 1988).

Goltz, Thomas. "Survivors Describe Armenian Attack," *Washington Post,* 4 March 1992.

Hovannisian, Richard G. "Nationalist Ferment in Armenia," *Freedom at Issue,* No. 105, Nov.-Dec. 1988.

"The Nagorno-Karabakh Dispute," (New York: Radio Liberty Research, 1988).

Saroyan, Mark. "The 'Karabakh Syndrome' and Azerbaijani Politics," *Problems of Communism,* Vol. 39, Sept.-Oct. 1990.

Sobhani, Sohrab C. "Azerbaijan: A People in Search of Independence," *Global Affairs,* Vol. VI, No. 1, Winter 1991.

Suny, Ronald Grigor. *The Making of the Georgian Nation.* (Bloomington, IN: Indiana University Press, 1988).

Moldova

Nahaylo, Bohdan. *National Ferment in Moldavia.* (New York: Radio Liberty Research, 1988).

Socor, Vladimir. "Creeping Putsch in Eastern Moldova," *RFE/RL Research Report,* Vol. 1, 12 Jan. 1992.

—"Why Moldova Does Not Seek Reunification With Romania," *RFE/RL Research Report,* Vol. 1, Jan. 31, 1992.

Ukraine and Byelarus

Brzezinski, Ian. "The Geopolitical Dimension," *The National Interest,* No. 27, Spring 1992.

Carynnyk, Marco et al., eds. *The Foreign Office and the Famine: British Documents on Ukraine and the Great Famine of 1932-33* (Kingston, Ontario, 1988).

Clarke, Douglas L. "The Battle for the Black Sea Fleet," *RFE/RL Research Report,* Vol. 1, Jan. 31, 1992.

Gross, Jan T. *Revolution from Abroad: The Soviet Conquest of Poland's Western Ukraine and Western Belorussia* (Princeton, 1988).

Korotich, Vitaly. "The Ukraine Rising," *Foreign Policy,* No. 85, Winter 1991-92.

Krawchenko, Bohdan. *Social Change and National Consciousness in 20th Century Ukraine* (London, 1985).

Kuzio, Taras. "Non-Russian Nationalism in the USSR and Soviet Nationality Policy," *Ukrainian Review,* Vol. 32, Spring 1984.

Little, David. *Ukraine: The Legacy of Intolerance.* (Washington, DC: United States Institute of Peace, 1991).

Lubachko, Ivan S. *Belorussia under Soviet Rule: 1917-1957* (Lexington, Kentucky, 1972).

Marples, David. *Ukraine Under Perestroika.* (New York: St. Martin's Press, 1991).

Mihalisko, Kathleen. "Ukraine Asserts Control Over Nonstrategic Forces," *RFE/RL Research Report,* Vol. 1, 24 January 1992.

Schulte, Heinz. "Break-Up Looms for the Baltic Fleet," *Jane's Defence Weekly,* Vol. 17, 18 January 1992.

Solchanyk, Roman. *Literature, History, and Nationalities Policy in the Ukraine.* (NY: Radio Liberty Research, 1982).

Stone, Norman. "The Mark of History," *The National Interest,* No. 27, Spring 1992.

United States Institute of Peace. "Religion, Nationalism, and Intolerance - Ukraine's Millenium of Strife," *In Brief,* No. 32, June 1991.

Urban, George. "The Awakening," *The National Interest,* No. 27, Spring 1992.

Vakar, Nicolas P. *Belorussia: The Making of a Nation* (Cambridge, MA, 1956).

The Baltic States: Estonia, Latvia, Lithuania

Beinikis, Vineta & Ronald J. Bee. "Independence for the Baltic States," *ACCESS Resource Brief,* Vol. V, No. 3, Sept. 1991.

Clemens, Walter C., Jr. *Baltic Independence and Russian Empire.* (New York: St. Martins, 1991).

Loeber, Andre D. et al. *Regional Identity Under Soviet Rule: The Case of the Baltic States.* (Kiel, Germany: Univ. of Kiel, 1990).

Misiunas, Romuald J. & Rein Taagepera. *The Baltic States: Years of Dependence 1940-1980* (London, 1983).

Pajanjis-Javis, J. *Soviet Genocide in Lithuania* (NY, 1980).

Rauch, Georg von. *The Baltic States: The Years of Independence 1917-1940* (London, 1974).

Raun, Toivo U. *Estonia and the Estonians.* (Stanford, CA: Hoover Institution Press, 1991).

Trapans, Jan Arveds, ed. *Toward Independence: The Baltic Popular Movements.* (Boulder: Westview, 1991).

Vesilind, Pritt. "The Baltic Nations: Estonia, Latvia, and Lithuania Struggle Toward Independence," *National Geographic,* Vol. 178, No. 5, Nov. 1990.

Russia (including autonomous regions)

Allworth, Edward, *Ethnic Russia: The Dilemma of Dominance* (NY, 1980).

Aron, Leon. "The Russians Are Coming: Millions of Soviet Refugees Will Be Fleeing to the West," *Policy Review,* No. 58, Fall 1991.

Balzer, Marjorie Mandelstam. "Ethnicity Without Power: the Siberian Khanty in Soviet Society," *Slavic Review,* Vol. 42, Winter 1983.

Carter, Stephen K. *Russian Nationalism: Yesterday, Today and Tomorrow.* (New York: St. Martin's Press, 1990)

Dunlop, John B. *The New Russian Nationalism* (Washington, 1985).

Fisher, Alan W. *The Crimean Tatars.* (Stanford, CA: Hoover Institution Press, 1978).

—— "The Crimean Tatars: A Struggle for Survival," *Inquiry* (San Francisco), Vol. 3, Jan. 7 & 21, 1980.

Goble, Paul A. "Misreading Russia: The Costs to America," *Washington Post,* Outlook Section, 19 January 1992.

"Government, Nationalities and the Jews of Russia, 1772-1990," *Soviet Jewish Affairs,* Vol. 21, Summer 1991.

Kozyrev, Andrei. "Russia: A Chance for Survival," *Foreign Affairs,* Vol. 71, No. 2, Spring 1992.

Krasnov, Vladislav. *Russia Beyond Communism: A Chronicle of National Rebirth.* (Boulder, CO: Westview, 1991).

Likhachev, Dmitrii Sergeyevich. "The National Nature of Russian History," The 2nd Annual W. Averell Harriman Lecture, Nov. 13, 1990. New York Columbia Univ.

Moro, David A. "The National Rebirth of Russia: A US Strategy for Lifting the Soviet Siege," *Policy Review,* No. 43, Winter 1988.

Motyl, Alexander J. "Russian Hegemony and Non-Russian Insecurity: Foreign Policy Dilemmas of the USSR's Successor States," *Harriman Institute Forum,* Vol. 5, Dec. 1991.

"Nationalism and Self-Determination in the Republics: The Russian Revival," Conference Report, 1st Session, *Report on the USSR,* Vol. 3, 1 Oct.1991.

Pipes, Richard. "Russia's Chance," *Commentary,* Vol. 93, Mar. 1992.

Pospielovsky, Dimitry. "Russian Nationalism: An Update," *Report on the USSR,* Vol. 2, 9 Feb. 1990.

Rorlich, Azade-Ayse. *The Volga Tatars.* (Stanford, CA: Hoover Institution Press, 1986).

"Russia and Ukraine: A New Crimean War," *Economist,* Vol. 322, No. 7744, 1 Feb. 1992.

Sheehy, Ann and Bohdan Nahaylo. *The Crimean Tatars, Volga Germans and Meskhetians: Soviet Treatment of Some National Minorities*, 3rd edition, Minority Rights Group Report #6, (London, 1980).

Simes, Dimitri. "Russia Reborn," *Foreign Policy,* No. 85, Winter 1991-92.

Tolz, Vera & Elizabeth Teague. "Is Russia Likely to Turn to Authoritarian Rule?" *RFE/RL Research Report,* Vol. 1, 24 Jan. 1992.

Tsipko, Aleksandr. "Ukraine, Russia, and the National Question: An Interview with Aleksandr Tsipko," *Report on the USSR,* Vol. 2, 17 Aug. 1990.

Williamson, John. "The Prospects for Russian Reform," *International Economic Insights,* Vol. 3, Jan.-Feb. 1992.

Central Asia: Kazakhstan, Turkmenistan, Uzbekistan, Tajikistan, Kyrgyzstan

Akiner, Shirin. *Islamic Peoples of the Soviet Union,* 2nd edition (London, 1987).

Allworth, Edward A. *The Modern Uzbeks: From the Fourteenth Century to the Present, A Cultural History.* (Stanford, CA: Hoover Institution Press, 1990).

Bennigsen, Alexandre. "Unrest in the World of Soviet Islam," *Third World Quarterly,* Vol. 10, April 1988.

Bennigsen, Alexandre & Enders Wimbush. *Muslims of the Soviet Empire.* (Bloomington, IN: Indiana Univ., 1986).

Carrere d'Encausse, Helen. *Islam and the Russian Empire: Reform and Revolution in Central Asia.* (Berkeley: California Press, c. 1988).

Critchlow, James. "Kazakhstan: The Outlook for Ethnic Relations," *RFE/RL Research Report,* Vol. 1, 31 Jan. 1992.

—*Nationalism in Uzbekistan: A Soviet Republic's Road to Sovereignty.* (Boulder, CO: Westview Press, 1991).

Fierman, William, ed. *Soviet Central Asia: The Failed Transformation.* (Boulder, CO: Westview Press, 1991).

Kaplan, Robert D. "Central Asia: Shattered Zone," *Atlantic,* April 1992, Vol. 269, No. 4.

Olcott, Martha Brill. "Central Asia's Post-Empire Politics," *Orbis,* Vol. 36, No. 2, Spring 1992.

—*The Kazakhs.* (Stanford, CA: Hoover Institution Press,1987).

Wimbush, S. Enders. "The Muslim Ferment in Soviet Central Asia," *Global Affairs,* Vol. II, No. 3, Summer 1987.

U.S. Policy Deliberations

ACCESS. "The Economic Dimensions of US National Security," *ACCESS Security Spectrum,* Vol. V, No. 1, Jan. 1991.

— "The Future of NATO and US Interests," *ACCESS Security Spectrum,* Vol. V, No. 3, December 1991.

Aslund, Anders & Richard Layard. "Help Russia Now," *New York Times,* 5 December 1991.

Baker, James. "America and the Collapse of the Soviet Union: What has to be Done," US Dept. of State, *Dispatch,* Vol. 2, No. 50, 16 December 1991.

— "The Euro-Atlantic Architecture: From West to East," US Dept. of State, *Dispatch,* Vol. 2, No. 25, 24 June 1991.

Ball, Nicole & Robert S. McNamara. "Link Economic Aid to Military Limits," *New York Times,* 11 January 1992.

Brown University, Center for Foreign Policy Development. *Facing A Disintegrated Soviet Union.* (Providence: Choices for the 21st Century Education Project, January 1992).

Brzezinski, Zbigniew. "Selective Global Commitment," *Foreign Affairs,* Vol. 70, No. 4, Fall 1991.

Bush, George. *National Security Strategy of the United States.* The White House, August 1991.

— "Coordinating Assistance to the New Independent States," US Dept. of State, *Dispatch,* Vol. 3, No. 4, 27 Jan. 1992.

--"The Need for an Active Foreign Policy," US Dept. of State, *Dispatch,* Vol. 3, No. 11, March 16, 1992.

Calleo, David P. *The Bankrupting of America: How the Federal Budget is Impoverishing the Nation,* (New York, Morrow, 1992).

Center for Defense Information. "A New Military Budget for a New World," The Defense Monitor, Vol XX, No. 2, 1991.

De Santis, Hugh, "The Graying of NATO," *Washington Quarterly,* Vol. 14, No. 4, Autumn 1991.

Feldman, Linda. "US Envoy Strauss: Help Russia," *Christian Science Monitor,* 16 March 1992.

Foreign Policy Association. "The Breakup of the Soviet Union: US Dilemmas," *Great Decisions,* 1992.

Haglund, David G. & Olaf Mager, eds. *Homeward Bound? Allied Forces in the New Germany.* (CO: Westview, 1992).

Heuser, Beatrice. "What Strategy for Post-Cold War Europe?" *Orbis,* Vol. 36, No. 2, Spring 1992.

Hoagland, Jim. "The Russia Debate: Nixon vs. Brzezinski," *Washington Post,* 26 March 1992.

Holmes, Kim & Jay Kosminsky. *Reshaping Europe: Strategies for a Post-Cold War Europe* (DC: Heritage Foundation, 1990).

Holt, Pat M. "America's Feeble Aid to Russia," *Christian Science Monitor,* 12 March 1992.

Hyland, William. "Downgrade Foreign Policy," *New York Times,* 20 May 1991.

Ikle, Fred Charles. "Comrades in Arms: The Case for a Russian-American Defense Community," *The National Interest,* Number 26, Winter 1991.

Kissinger, Henry, "The Question of Aid," *Washington Post,* 31 March 1992.

Kopper, Hilmar, "Why the West Must Help Save the Soviet Economy," *Financial Times,* 10 July 1991.

Krauthammer, Charles. "Bless Our Pax Americana," *Washington Post,* 22 March 1991.

La Follette, Karen. "Government Loans for the Soviet Union: A Disservice to US Taxpayers and Soviets Alike," Cato Institute Foreign Policy Briefing, No. 8, 26 April 1991.

Lall, Betty G. & John Tepper Marlin, eds. *Building A Peace Economy: Opportunities and Problems of Post-Cold War Defense Cuts.* (Boulder, CO: Westview Press in cooperation with the Council on Economic Priorities, 1992).

Levgold, Robert, "While We Sleep," *New York Times,* 10 December 1991.

Livingston, Robert G. "Let Germany Do It," *New York Times,* 21 March 1992.

Mead, Walter R. "On the Road to Ruin: Winning the Cold War, Losing the Economic Peace," *Harper's,* March 1990.

Melloan, George. "Will State Ever Get Ukraine's Message," *Wall Street Journal,* 23 March 1992.

Morrison, David C. "Bringing Them Home," *National Journal,* December 7, 1991.

Nelson, Daniel N. "NATO - Means, but no Ends," *Bulletin of Atomic Scientists,* Vol. 48, No. 1, Jan./Feb. 1992.

Nixon, Richard. *Seize the Moment: America's Challenge in a One Superpower World.* (NY: Simon & Schuster, 1992).

Perkovich, George. "Counting the Costs of the Arms Race," *Foreign Policy,* Number 85, Winter 1991-92.

Randolph, Eleanor, "Ex-Soviet Aid: How, What and to Whom?" *Washington Post,* 19 January 1992.

Ravenal, Earl. Designing Defense for a New World Order (DC: Cato Institute, 1991).

Sachs, Jeffrey D. "Saving a Prostrate Russia," *Washington Post,* 24 November 1991.

Schlessinger, James. "New Instabilities, New Priorities," *Foreign Policy,* No. 85, Winter 1991-92.

Snyder, Jed. "NATO: What Now?" *The American Enterprise,* Sept./Oct. 1991.

Spechler, Martin C. "No Marshall Plan for Russia," *Christian Science Monitor,* 25 March 1992.

Steinbruner, John D. "The Prospect of Cooperative Security," in J. Steinbruner, ed., *Restructuring American Foreign Policy,* (Washington, DC: Brookings, 1989).

Tonelson, Alan. "What is the National Interest?" *The Atlantic Monthly,* July 1991.

Ullman, Richard H. *Securing Europe* (Princeton, NJ: Princeton U. Press, 1991).

Van Evera, Stephen. *Managing the Eastern Crisis: Preventing War in the Former Soviet Union,* Defense and Arms Control Studies Program Working Paper, Center for International Studies, MIT (Cambridge, MA 02139, January 1992).

Walker, Jenonne. "Keeping America in Europe," *Foreign Policy,* No. 83, Summer 1991.

Annotated Bibliography and Other Resources

The following is a list of reports, studies, articles, and books focusing on the former Soviet Union. Entries contain publication title, author, date, organization that produced the material, and a brief description of the work. **The vast majority of publications listed here are available from organizations listed in the "Guide to Organizations" section; refer there for telephone number or address. Publications by organizations not in that section are listed here with a telephone number to assist in obtaining material.** This list includes recent articles from the major foreign policy journals, reports and studies by organizations, a diverse collection of books, directories, and databases.

BALTIC STATES

AABS Newsletter
Periodical: Quarterly
Association for the Advancement of Baltic Studies
The purpose of the Association is the promotion of research and education in Baltic studies.
To obtain, call: (908) 852-5258.

Baltic Weekly
Periodical: Weekly
Radio Free Europe/Radio Liberty
This periodical contains extracts from the Daily Report based on Radio Liberty broadcasts on political, economic and social issues in the Baltic states.
To obtain, call: (202) 457-6912.

Documentation: Averting Moscow's Baltic Coup
Article
Orbis: A Journal of World Affairs, Summer 1991, Vol. 35, No. 3
Foreign Policy Research Institute
Statements and documents from the Baltic crisis. The reaction from Baltic leaders, Yeltsin, and the West may have helped dissuade Gorbachev from using force.

Independence for the Baltic States
Periodical by Vineta Beinikis and Ronald J. Bee
Resource Brief, September 1991, Vol. V, No. 3
ACCESS
Summarizes the Baltic states' independence initiatives. Includes a listing of organizations that can provide additional information and background readings.

Latvian News Digest
Periodical: 5 per year
American Latvian Association in the United States
News and views on Latvian issues culled from the world press.

BUSINESS & ECONOMICS

Commersant: The Russian Business Weekly
Periodical: Weekly
Refco Group
Written in Moscow, includes articles on politics, money, business, and law. To obtain, call: (312) 930-6500.

Currency Convertibility: A Self-Help Blueprint for the Commonwealth of Independent States
Report by Steve H. Hanke and Kurt Schuler
Foreign Policy Briefing, January 22, 1992, No. 17
Cato Institute
Discusses the issue of currency convertibility and its effect on the economic and political situation in the former Soviet Union. Provides recommendations on how to set up a Currency Board. To obtain, call: (202) 546-0200.

Delovie Lyudi: Business in the Ex-USSR
Periodical: Monthly
Formerly known as **Business in the USSR**
A French-Soviet joint venture published in translation containing articles by leading Soviet economists and specialists on many aspects of the Soviet economy.
To obtain, call: (212) 629-4460.

Economic Newsletter of the Russian Research Center at Harvard University
Periodical: Monthly
Russian Research Center, Harvard University
Provides updates on Russian economic issues.

Eye on the East: A Review of Events in Eastern Europe and the CIS
Periodical: 26 per year
Pacific-Sierra Research Corporation
Information on business, foreign trade, investment, prices, privatization, and budgets of countries in Eastern Europe and the CIS. To obtain, call (703) 527-4975.

From Guns to Butter?: USA and USSR
Resource Brief, August 1990, Vol. IV, No. 3
ACCESS
This one-sheet brief summarizes the issues in economic conversion/adjustment after the Cold War. Includes listings of organizations focusing on these issues and additional readings.

The Future of Russian Capitalism
Article by Jude Wanniski
Foreign Affairs, Spring 1992, Vol. 71, No. 2
Council on Foreign Relations
Explores the incredible potential for the explosion of capitalism and free markets in Russia.

Globalizing the GATT: The Soviet Union's Successor, Eastern Europe, and the International Trading System

Book by Leah A. Haus
Brookings Institution, February 1992

The book analyzes the origins and evolution of Soviet and East European relations with the GATT and assesses alternative policies for bringing the Soviet successor states into the international trade institution.

The Grand Bargain

Article by Steven Rosefielde
Global Affairs, Winter 1992, Vol VII, No. 1
International Security Council

The author argues against making significant financial investments in the republics of the former Soviet Union. To obtain, call: (202) 828-0802.

Growing Soviet Food Shortages: A Result of Economy-Wide Monetary Imbalance

Report by William Liefert
Geonomics Institute, September 1991

This paper discusses the breakdown of the monetary system during the economic restructuring, and the rise of barter trade, black markets, and food hoarding.

International Joint Ventures: Soviet and Western Perspectives

Book edited by Alan B. Sherr, Ivan S. Korolev, et al
Center for Foreign Policy Development, 1991

Soviet and Western trade experts and economists contributed alternating chapters, developing viewpoints on issues of negotiating and operating joint ventures in the former Soviet Union. Includes a list of all US-Soviet joint ventures as of June 1990.

Investing in Reform: Doing Business in a Changing Soviet Union

Seminar report
Geonomics Series, May 1991
Geonomics Institute

Essays from a "gateways" seminar addressing the effects of recent changes in banking, currency, and foreign investment laws, the role of local governments, and factors for Western companies to consider before moving into the Soviet market.

Milestones in Glasnost and Perestroyka: The Economy

Book, edited by Ed A. Hewett and Victor H. Winston
Brookings Institution, 1991

Selected articles from *Soviet Economy*, an academic journal by 19 Soviet, American and European scholars. Charts the changes that are moving the new Soviet republics from a centrally planned economy to a more integrated and localized system of exchange.

A Peace Dividend in the Former Soviet Union?

Report by Otto Storf and Andreas Gummich
Focus Eastern Europe, January 1992
Deutsche Bank Economics Department
Distributed by Transatlantic Futures

Provides a one-sheet summary of the difficulties in the conversion process from military to civilian production that the former Soviet Union is attempting. The prospects, according to the authors, are bleak.
To obtain, call: (202) 462-1222.

PlanEcon Consumer Markets Report, PlanEcon Energy Report, PlanEcon Chemical Report

Periodicals: Quarterly
PlanEcon

These three reports provide information on retail trade markets; energy production, trade, and consumption; and production, trade, investment and the privatization of the chemical industries in the former Soviet Union and Eastern Europe. To obtain, call: (202) 898-0471.

PlanEcon Report

Periodical: Weekly
PlanEcon

Contains information on the economies in Eastern Europe and the former Soviet Union, including statistics and tables. To obtain, call: (202) 898-0471.

Practical Information: Trade and Investment - Russia, Ukraine, Byelarus, Moldova, Georgia, Armenia, Azerbaijan, Uzbekistan, Turkmenistan, Tajikistan, Kazakhstan, Kyrgystan

Report
Russia and Independent States Division, U.S. Department of Commerce, March 1992

This report provides information on business and investment in the former Soviet Union. It includes travel tips, trade events, U.S. government contacts for information and advice, and a list of business directories and periodicals. To obtain, call: (202) 377-4655

The Return of Individual Farming in the Soviet Union

Report by Don Van Atta
Geonomics Institute, September 1991

Examines the failures of the large collective and state farms that have dominated Soviet agriculture for the past 60 years and explores the prospects for returning at least part of this system to small, independent farms.

Russia, Commonwealth Business Law Report

Periodical: Monthly
Buraff Publications

Contains recent Soviet legislation in translation, and analysis of the legislation. To order, call: (202) 862-0990.

The Significance of the Soviet Economy
Report
Deutsche Bank Economics Department, September 91
Distributed by TransAtlantic Futures.

Information to provide a basis for assessing the significance of the Soviet economy for the world. To obtain, call: (202) 462-1222.

Russian Business Reports
Periodical: Weekly
Russian Information Services

Reports business, economic, trade, and legal developments from Russia and the other republics. To obtain, call: (802) 223-4955.

Soviet Aerospace & Technology
Periodical: Twenty-six issues per year
Phillips Publishing

Contains reports on developments in the Soviet military and space industries. To order, call: (800) 722-9120.

Soviet Business & Trade
Periodical: Twice monthly
Welt Publishing

Articles on trade issues and recent developments in industry sectors. To order, call: (202) 371-0555.

Soviet Conversion 1991
Report edited by John Tepper Marlin and Paul Grenier
Council on Economic Priorities, February 10, 1991

Summarizes a conference between Soviet government officials, industry heads, and scholars, and US scholars and conversion experts. Includes a directory of Soviet and American specialists and information on Soviet conversion efforts. To order, call (212) 420-1133.

Soviet Economic Reform: Perestroika or 'Catastroika'?
Article by Philip Hanson
World Policy Journal, Spring 1991, Vol 8, No. 2
World Policy Institute

The only real hope for a successful economic transformation is that the central authorities will ultimately choose- or be forced to accept- a process of peaceful decentralization that will allow reform to grow from the bottom up. To order, call: (212) 490-0010.

The Soviet Union at the Crossroads: Facts and Figures on the Soviet Republics
Report
Deutsche Bank, June 1991
Distributed by TransAtlantic Futures.

Offers economic prognoses for, as well as facts and figures on, each republic. To obtain, call: (202) 462-1222.

A Study of the Soviet Economy
Report
International Monetary Fund, March 1991

Three volumes of background papers providing a comprehensive overview of the Soviet economy's structure, recent history, and wide-ranging problems. Presents proposals and discusses implementation in specific sectors. To obtain, call: (202) 623-7430.

CENTRAL ASIA

Central Asia Monitor
Periodical: 6 per year
Central Asia Monitor

To provide scholars, corporations and politicians with the impartial information on events and tendencies in the region. To obtain, fax to: (802) 537-4362.

Central Asia's Post-Empire Politics
Article by Martha Brill Olcott
Spring 1992
Orbis: A Journal of World Affairs, Vol. 36, No. 2
Foreign Policy Research Institute

Explores the difficulties of the 5 Central Asian republics of the former Soviet Union. They face economic and environmental problems and growing nationalism.

Report on Turkmenistan's Referendum on Independence: October 26, 1991
Report
Commission on Security and Cooperation in Europe, November 27, 1991

Discusses the results and implications of the vote on independence in Turkmenistan, as witnessed firsthand by Commission staff members.

MILITARY & ARMS CONTROL

Counting the Costs of the Arms Race
Article by George Perkovich
Foreign Policy, Winter 1991-92. No. 85
Carnegie Endowment for International Peace

Argues for moving toward cooperative security and a radical reduction of the nuclear threat, to about 3,000 warheads on each side.

Defense Conversion: Bulldozing the Management
Article by Kenneth Adelman and Norman Augustine
Foreign Affairs, Spring 1992, Vol. 71, No. 2
Council on Foreign Relations

Makes recommendations for achieving conversion of the defense industries in the former Soviet Union.

Did "Peace Through Strength" End the Cold War?
Article by Thomas Risse-Kappen
International Security, Summer 1991, Vol. 16., No. 1
Center for Science and International Affairs, Harvard University

Argues that the INF Treaty was not simply a result of Western bargaining from strength. Instead, it has to be explained in terms of domestic coalition-building dynamics, particularly in Western Europe and the Soviet Union.

Former Soviet Republics Announce Intention to Honor CFE
Article
Basic Reports on European Arms Control, January 21, 1992, No. 19
British American Security Information Council

Discusses the future of the CFE Treaty after the breakup of the Soviet Union. Includes data on equipment in the former Republics.

The Future of Collective Security: Reflections on the Aftermath of the Persian Gulf War and the Breakup of the Soviet Union
Report by Edward C. Luck, Toby Trister Gati, Jeffrey Laurenti, Kathryn G. Sessions
United Nations Association of the USA, Oct. 10, 1991

This paper highlights some recent developments which are critical to prospects for collective security, particularly changes in the Soviet Union.

The Future of NATO and US Interests
Security Spectrum, December 1991, Vol V, No. 3
ACCESS

Provides a description of five possible futures for NATO in a world where the Soviet Union has collapsed. Includes listings of organizations supporting each position, a glossary, and a selection of additional readings.

The Harder Line inside the Soviet Union: What does it mean for Western Security?
Report by Andrew J. Goodpaster
Atlantic Council of the United States, March 11, 1991

This four page report looks at Gorbachev's turn toward more conservative internal policies and makes recommendations for US policy in response.

How the Threat (and the Coup) Collapsed: The Politicization of the Soviet Military
Article by Stephen M. Meyer
International Security, Winter 1991/92, Vol. 16, No. 3
Center for Science and International Affairs, Harvard University

The author argues that Soviet military had become a mirror of Soviet society, rent by political, economic and social turmoil. Solutions would involve creating an all-volunteer force, and banning the armed forces from holding political office or being active in political parties.

International Security and the Collapse of the Soviet Union
Article by Sergei Rogov
The Washington Quarterly, Spring 92, Vol. 15, No. 2
Center for Strategic and International Studies

Argues that the likely outcome of the breakup of the Soviet Union is a chaotic fragmentation of military power and competition among new states, raising grave dangers of new nuclear-armed powers. The West must focus on these issues and attempt to keep nuclear weapons in as few hands as possible.

NATO and Soviet Security Reform
Article by Stephen R. Covington
The Washington Quarterly, Winter 91, Vol. 14, No. 1
The Center for Strategic and International Studies

Although Soviet security policy has changed, European security depends on the implementation and institutionalization of security policy reform in the Soviet Union. A common definition of security must be followed by steps to build a mutual approach to security that will fortify the war prevention aims of all European nations.

A New Kind of Threat: Nuclear Weapons in an Uncertain Soviet Union
Report by US Congressman Les Aspin
White Paper, September 12, 1991
House Armed Services Committee

Examines the dangers of nuclear weapons in the disintegrating Soviet Union, including accidental launches, sale by military officials, and civil war. Discusses recommended US responses. To obtain, call: (202) 225-2191.

Non-Offensive Defense: Toward a Soviet-German Security Partnership
Article by Marian Leighton and Robert Rudney
Orbis: A Journal of World Affairs, Summer 1991, Vol. 35. No. 3

The collapse of the Warsaw Pact and weakening of NATO raise the question of whether the Soviet Union and Germany might form a security partnership in Europe. Such a peace order would herald the demise of NATO and a greatly diminished US security role in Europe.

Nuclear Notebook
Fact Sheet
The Bulletin of the Atomic Scientists, January/February 1992, Vol. 48, No. 1
Educational Foundation for Nuclear Science, Inc.

Fact Sheet and brief discussion of the current status of strategic nuclear forces in the US and former Soviet Union. To obtain, call (312) 702-2555.

Nuclear Proliferation Status Report
Report
Nuclear Non-Proliferation Project, March 1992
Carnegie Endowment for International Peace
This report highlights the latest developments in nonproliferation, including the CIS nuclear states.

Nuclear Security and the Soviet Collapse
Article by Daniel Ellsberg
Interviewed by Jerry Sanders and Richard Caplan
World Policy Journal, Winter 1991-92, Vol. 9, No. 1
World Policy Institute
Discusses the prospects for the end of the era of nuclear threats in light of the Soviet collapse, and how to work towards the elimination of these threats by the year 2000. To obtain, call (212) 490-0010.

A Program for World Nuclear Security
Report by Jonathan Dean and Kurt Gottfried
Union of Concerned Scientists, February 1992
Describes the current nuclear risks, with a focus on nuclear weapons of the former Soviet Union. A proposed plan for comprehensive control of nuclear weapons is then put forth. To obtain, call: (617) 547-5552.

Reversing the Arms Race: The Bush-Gorbachev Initiatives on Nuclear Weapons
Articles
CISSM Commentaries, November 1991, No. 4
Center for International Security Studies at Maryland
Eight articles by eight experts discussing the nuclear weapons initiatives agreed upon by Gorbachev and Bush in September and October of 1991.
To obtain, call: (301) 403-8174.

Russia and the Commonwealth States: Changes in Security Policies
Periodical: Bi-Monthly
Bulletin
The Atlantic Council of the United States
Four page summary of changes in Russian and other Commonwealth states' policies on defense, the military, arms control, and international security issues.

Russia's Post Revolution Challenge: Reform of the Soviet Superpower Paradigm
Article by Stephen R. Covington and John Lough
The Washington Quarterly, Winter 92, Vol. 15, No. 1.
The Center for Strategic and International Studies
Much of European security depends on how Russia handles the enormous military complex it has inherited from the Soviet Union. Its security will likely be based on its large nuclear arsenal, although major reductions are likely. The West must see how this situation is resolved before making long term security policy decisions.

The Soviet Army In Search Of a New Identity
Report by Catherine Bacarrere-Becane
European Viewpoint Series, August 1991, No. 1
US Crest
The breakup of the former Soviet Union has left the future of the military unclear. Confusion over the role and authority of a central governmental structure and the end of the Cold War have forced the army to reevaluate itself and its goals. Its future on the structure of a new union among the republics. To obtain, call: (703) 243-6908.

Soviet Intelligence & Active Measures
Periodical
Roy Godson, Ed.
Four issues per year
Institute for International Studies
Contains articles on current Soviet intelligence and security issues. To order, call: (202) 429-0129.

Soviet Military Policy: Continuity and Change
Article by William R. Van Cleave, et al
Global Affairs, Winter 1991, Vol. VII, No. 1
International Security Council
Summarizes a conference held in Washington that included numerous Soviet military officials and former US military officials. To obtain, call: (202) 828-0802.

The Soviet Military Today
Articles
Orbis: A Journal of World Affairs, Spring 1991, Vol. 35, No. 2
Foreign Policy Research Institute
Four articles on the changing Soviet military: "Does the Soviet Military Oppose Perestroika?", by Paula J. Dobriansky and David B. Rivkin, Jr.; "The Soviet Military Reshapes in Response to Malaise", by Dale R. Herspring; "The Soviet Military Goes High Tech", by Peter Schweizer; "The Soviet Military: Countering the West in New Ways", by Mikhail Tsypkin.

Soviet Nuclear Fission
Report by Kurt M. Campbell, Ashton B. Carter, Steven E. Miller, Charles A. Zraket
CSIA Studies in International Security, November 1991, No. 1
Center for Science and International Affairs, Harvard University
Discusses the dangers of nuclear weapons in the disintegrated Soviet Union. Recommends policy options for the US in dealing with potential problems. Dangerous issues include the future control of nuclear weapons, the breakdown of safety systems and the spread of nuclear weapons to other countries through the sale of weapons or scientific knowledge. To obtain, call: (617) 495-1400.

Soviet Nuclear Weapons: What, Where, and How Secure?
Fact Sheet
Center For Defense Information, August 30, 1991
   Two pages of information on the location, amount, and security of nuclear weapons in the Soviet Union. To order, call (202) 862-0700.

Soviet Swords of Damocles
Article by Marc J. Berkowitz
Global Affairs, Summer 1991, Vol. 6, No. 3
International Security Council
   The possibility of a Soviet offensive space weapons system is cause for alarm in the West.
To obtain, call (202) 828-0802.

Towards a Post-Soviet Army
Article by John W. R. Lepingwell
Orbis: A Journal of World Affairs, Winter 1991, Vol. 36, No. 1
Foreign Policy Research Institute
   The Soviet army is on the brink of a far-reaching transformation. Where will the process end? Will the Soviet army remain a unified military force? Or will it splinter into a number of new national armies being formed in the former Soviet republics? The answer has significant implications for Western policymakers.

NATIONALITIES

Glasnost, Perestroika, and Antisemitism
Article by Zvi Gitelman
Foreign Affairs, Spring 1991, Vol. 70, No. 2
Council on Foreign Relations
   Antisemitism in the Soviet Union is more visible and blatant today than at any time in the past forty years.

Journal of Soviet Nationalities
Periodical: Monthly
Center on East-West Trade, Investment, and Communications at Duke University
   This journal contains articles on nationality issues in the former Soviet Union. To obtain, call: (919) 684-5551.

Minority Rights: Problems, Parameters, and Patterns in the CSCE Context
Report, Fall 1991
Commission on Security and Cooperation in Europe
   Helsinki Commission staff report on national minorities, especially in the former Soviet Union.

Religion, Nationalism, and Intolerance - Ukraine's Millennium of Strife
Report
In Brief, June 1991, Number 32

United States Institute of Peace
   Will the diminution of centralized control in the Soviet Union contribute to a revival of conflict and intolerance based on matters of belief? In Ukraine, intolerance plays a significant role in conflict. Discusses the applicability of human rights standards and legal and political initiatives.

Soviet Disunion: A History of the Nationalities Problem in the USSR
Book by Bohdan Nahaylo and Victor Swoboda
Free Press, 1990
   This book is a chronological examination of the Soviet nationalities from the time of Lenin to the 1980's.

Soviet Disunion: Creating a Nationalities Policy
Report
Hearing before the Subcommittee on European Affairs of the Committee on Foreign Relations, US Senate
100th Congress, 2nd Session, July 24, 1990
   Senators and experts discuss the difficulties in aiding the people of the Soviet Union as the role of a central authority becomes increasingly nebulous. The implications of dealing with many new nations instead of one are considered. To obtain, call: (202) 224-4651

Report on the Armenian Referendum of Independence: September 21, 1991
Report, October 1, 1991
Commission on Security and Cooperation in Europe
   This report provides a brief summary of the Armenian referendum on independence. Includes a discussion of the process, the results, and the implications.

POLITICAL & WORLD AFFAIRS

America's Stake in the Soviet Future
Article by Graham Allison and Robert Blackwill
Foreign Affairs, Summer 1991, Vol. 70, No. 3
Council on Foreign Relations
   Argues it is in the US's best interest to attempt a version of the Marshall Plan to help the Soviet Union.

Challenges to the Post-Cold War Balance of Power
Article by Andrew C. Goldberg
The Washington Quarterly, Winter 91, Vol. 14, No. 1
The Center for Strategic and International Studies
   Examines the decline of the Soviet empire, the future role for the Soviets in the post-Cold War balance of power, and what this means to the US and other nations.

Civil Resistance in the East European and Soviet Revolutions
Report by Adam Roberts
Monograph Series, No. 4, 1991
Albert Einstein Institution

Examines the role played by "people power" in the undermining of communist regimes in East-Central Europe, independence by the Baltic States, and the defeat of the coup in the Soviet Union. To obtain, call: (617) 876-0311.

The Commonwealth & The Third World
Report by Mark N. Katz
Washington Strategy Paper, January 29, 1992
Washington Strategy Seminar
Examines policies of CIS members, especially Russia, toward the developing world. Concludes that Russia will focus on those countries it perceives as a threat. Thus, nations opposing China may still be allies. Russia may also support Arab causes because of the large Muslim population in the CIS.

Coup de Grace: The End of the Soviet Union
Article by Michael Mandelbaum
Foreign Affairs, America and the World, 1991/92, Vol. 71, No. 1
Council on Foreign Relations
August 1991 may become for Russians what 1688 is for British, 1776 for Americans, and 1789 for French: they broke with the old habits and asserted their rights.

The Death of Soviet Communism
Article by Seweryn Bialer
Foreign Affairs, Winter 1991-92, Vol. 70, No. 5
Council on Foreign Relations
The Soviet coup plotters badly misjudged the reaction of the people to their operation. Those who acted against Gorbachev believed that intimidation would still be decisive, as it had been for decades. They failed to see that much of the Soviet population had overcome its fear.

Documentation: The USSR in Turmoil: Views from the Right, Center, and Left
Article by Alvin Z. Rubenstein
Spring 1991
Orbis: A Journal of World Affairs, Vol. 35, No. 2
Foreign Policy Research Institute
Statements from all sides of the debate regarding Gorbachev's implementation (or lack thereof) of perestroika and glasnost.

Empire or Stability? The Case For Soviet Dissolution
Article by Alexander J. Motyl
World Policy Journal, Summer 1991, Vol 8, No. 3
World Policy Institute
The breakdown of the Soviet system has produced instability in Europe and Asia. Many feel that central control should be maintained at all cost to insure stability. If US policy in the event of a crackdown is threatening enough to dissuade the use of force, the likelihood of a peaceful disintegration of the Union would increase.
To obtain, call (212) 490-0010.

The Eurasian Report
Journal: 4 per year
The Center for American-Eurasian Studies & Relations
This journal includes articles, interviews, documents and speeches, and opinion essays, many focused on the former Soviet Union. To obtain, call: (202) 966-8651.

Face to Face with Freedom: A Glimpse of the Russian Soul During the August Coup
Book by Nancy Seifer
Freedom Press, 1991
The journal of an American writer during the coup.

Forget the Soviet Union
Article by Paul A. Goble
Foreign Policy, Spring 1992, No. 86
Carnegie Endowment for International Peace
The author argues that the Soviet Union is gone and that the Commonwealth of Independent States is only of passing importance. The United States should deal with each of the new nations independently.

From New Thinking to the Fragmentation of Consensus in Soviet Foreign Policy: The USSR and the Developing World
Report by Roger E. Kanet
Occasional Paper, June 1991
Program in Arms Control, Disarmament, and International Security, Univ. of Illinois at Urbana-Champaign
How Soviet foreign policy toward the developing world has changed under Gorbachev, and likely directions in the future. Concludes that, because the Soviet Union will be absorbed in its own problems, it will take a less active role in revolutionary and Leninist movements around the world, but will not end support for existing Leninist regimes. To obtain, call: (217) 333-7086.

From Nyet to Da: Understanding the Russians
Book by Yale Richmond
1992
This book is a guide to dealing with the Russians face to face in social and professional contexts. It offers an analysis of Russian cultural behavior, especially as it differs from that of Americans.

The Future of Soviet-American Relations in a Pluralistic World
Reports
Phase I: May 30, 1991 and Phase II: Feb. 14, 1992
The Atlantic Council of the United States and the Institute of World Economy & International Relations of the Soviet Academy of Sciences
These two reports, labeled joint policy statements and recommendations, are the result of meetings held in

May 1991 in Moscow and February 1992 in Washington DC. They make recommendation for US-Soviet cooperation in a variety of areas, with a substantial section on non-proliferation issues.

Gorbachev: Triumph and Failure
Article by Robert G. Kaiser
Foreign Affairs, Spring 1991, Vol. 70, No, 2
Council on Foreign Relations
Gorbachev, despite his ultimate failures, will have a large place in history for the radical changes he created.

Gorbachev versus Gorbachev
Article by Igor Kliamkin
Global Affairs, Winter 1992, Vol VII, No. 1
International Security Council
Examines how Gorbachev's policies have failed yet he remains in power. To obtain, call: (202) 828-0802.

Gorbachev's Time of Troubles
Article by Dimitri Simes
Foreign Policy, Spring 1991, No. 82
Carnegie Endowment for International Peace
Gorbachev's reform policies have begun to bring about the end of communism in the Soviet empire. Unfortunately, nothing resembling democracy is taking its place. An acceleration of reform or a crackdown to preserve order could end Gorbachev's political life.

The International Sources of Soviet Change
Article by Daniel Deudney and G. John Ikenberry
International Security, Winter 1991-92, Vol. 16, No.3
Center for Science and International Affairs, Harvard University
Argues that the Soviet reorientation is caused by an internal crisis but shaped by the accomodating and attractive Western policy, and will continue to be strongly influenced by future Western policy.

Milestones in Glasnost and Perestroyka: Politics and People
Book, edited by Ed A. Hewett and Victor H. Winston
Brookings Institution, 1991
Selected articles from *Soviet Economy*, an academic journal, by 21 scholars for a broad examination of Soviet culture, political institutions, and cultural values.

Moscow and the Gulf War
Article by Graham E. Fuller
Foreign Affairs, Summer 1991, Vol. 70, No. 3
Council on Foreign Relations
The Gulf War can be seen as the single most formative crisis in the reformulation of the principles and interests of Soviet foreign policy. The US must ensure its policies lead to a more stable Middle East if it wants

continued support from the troubled Soviet Union.

The Parker School Bulletin on Soviet and East European Law (Columbia University)
Periodical: Ten Issues per year
Contains recent Soviet and East European legislation in translation and analysis of the legislation. To order, call Transnational Juris Publications: (914) 693-0089.

Problems of Communism
Periodical: Bimonthly
United States Information Agency
Contains articles analyzing contemporary affairs of the Soviet Union and other communist countries. To order, call The Superintendent of Documents, US Government Printing Office: (202) 619-4230.

The Real Coup
Article by Melor Sturua
Foreign Policy, Winter 1991-92, No. 85
Carnegie Endowment for International Peace
Argues the decline of the Soviet Union began with death of Stalin and the end of his reign of terror. Gorbachev's attempts to make the system work only opened the system up for overthrow by more democratic forces.

Referendum in the Soviet Union: A Compendium of Reports on the March 17, 1991 Referendum on the Future of the USSR
Report
Commission on Security and Cooperation in Europe. April 1991
This report reflects Commission staffers' on-site observations of a number of elections relating to independence and the role of a central government in the former Soviet Union. Contains reportage about the March 17 referendum plus an analysis of its implications.

Russia and the Commonwealth States: Political and Economic Update
Periodical: Bi-monthly
Bulletin
The Atlantic Council of the United States
This four page report provides a summary of recent changes in the political and economic situation in the former Soviet Union.

Russia's Surprising Reactionary Alliance
Article by John B. Dunlop
Orbis: A Journal of World Affairs, Summer 1991, Vol. 35, No. 3
Foreign Policy Research Institute
The alliance of conservative nationalists and neo-Stalinists persists, making the prospects for democracy, pluralism, and a market economy in Russia slim. The

alliance does not enjoy strong support from the Russian public; it does, however, from such critical institutions as the KGB, the military, and the Communist Party.

Soviet Client-States: From Empire to Commonwealth?
Article by Alvin C. Rubenstein
Orbis: A Journal of World Affairs, Winter 1991, Vol. 35, No. 1
Foreign Policy Research Institute

As the situation in the Soviet Union changes, Soviet foreign policy must change as well. Gorbachev wants to maintain a significant role in Eastern Europe and the Third World. He will focus not on the military but on a more prominent Soviet role in international organizations and in the international economic system.

The Soviet Coup and the Benefits of Breakdown
Article by Stephen Miller
Orbis: A Journal of World Affairs, Winter 1992, Vol. 36, No. 1
Foreign Policy Research Institute

The collapse in military authority prepared the way for the coup's failure, Gorbachev's return, and for a collapse in Moscow's political authority, a process now well advanced. Few Americans realize the benefits likely to result as the central government continues to lose power.

The Soviet (Dis)Union
Article by Martha Brill Olcott
Foreign Policy, Summer 1991, No. 82
Carnegie Endowment for International Peace

Gorbachev has unintentionally brought about the disintegration of the Soviet Union. Although maintaining order is in the interest of the US and other Western nations, support cannot be given to Gorbachev if he intends to preserve the Union by force.

Soviet Policy Toward China: A Complex New Relationship
Report by Roger E. Kanet
Occasional Paper, June 1991
Program in Arms Control, Disarmament, and International Security, Univ. of Illinois at Urbana-Champaign

Examines Sino-Soviet relations in recent times. Concludes that, regardless of whether the Soviet Union and China become more or less conservative, both will pursue normal relations and lessen the military build-up past conflict has incurred, allowing each to focus on economic development. To obtain, call: (217) 333-7-086.

Soviet Republics Rebel
Report
CQ Researcher, July 12, 1991, Vol. 1, No. 10
Congressional Quarterly Inc.

Articles and background information on the republics and the realignment of power in the former Soviet Union.

To order, call (202) 887-8500.

Soviet Third World Policy in a Changing Society: Afghanistan to the Gulf War
Report by Marion Recktenwald
Occasional Paper 4, May 1991
Center for International Strategic Studies at Maryland

Presents an assessment of the success of Gorbachev's "New Political Thinking." Concludes that the new thinking has not worked within society, that many structures are still attached to old thinking on security issues, and dangers lie ahead in US-Soviet relations. To obtain, call: (301) 4033-8110.

The Soviet Union
Book by Daniel C. Diller
Congressional Quarterly, 1990

A comprehensive look at the Soviet Union's history, geography and politics with special features such as a chronology, biographies and excerpts from important statements, treaties and other documents.

The Soviet Union 1991
Articles
Current History: A World Affairs Journal, October 1991, Vol. 90, No. 558

This issue includes articles by Jerry Hough, Raymond Garthoff, and other scholars assessing the coup and its aftermath, US policy options, and other key factors.

Suffering from Self-Determination
Article by Viktor Alksnis
Foreign Policy, Fall 1991, No. 84
Carnegie Endowment for International Peace

The only way out of the Soviet crisis lies in democratic reform and a return to lawfulness. Demolishing myths and returning to reality is a difficult and extremely protracted process. Not to understand this point allows the process of disintegration to continue, with all the dangers disintegration entails for the peoples of the Soviet Union.

The Supreme Soviet Defense and Security Committee: Legislative Oversight Capabilities
Report by Jennifer Scheck Lee
Global Outlook, July 1991

Examines the capabilities of the legislative committee charged with oversight of the Soviet defense community. Concludes that the committee, with little experience, no budget control, and little staff, faces serious difficulties.

US Policy Toward a Post-Socialist USSR
Conference Report
The Stanley Foundation, October 24-26, 1991

Daunting problems with high stakes face the peoples of the former Soviet Union. This report defines a set of principles to guide US policy makers through this turbulent period. To order, call: (319) 264-1500

US-USSR: Possibilities in Partnership
Article by Marshall Brement
Foreign Policy, Fall 1991, No. 84
Carnegie Endowment for International Peace
    Gorbachev has transformed the economic and political system of the USSR, bringing it into the modern world. A US-Soviet partnership could benefit both nations and enhance world security.

USSR and Eastern Europe: The Shattered Heartland
Report by John C. Kimball
Headline Series, Winter/Spring 1991, No. 295
Foreign Policy Association
    Explores the reasons for the August 1991 coup and offers an overview of historical, political, and economic factors that led us into and out of the Gorbachev era.

USSR-Germany: A Link Restored
Article by W. R. Smyser
Foreign Policy, Fall 1991, No. 84
Carnegie Endowment for International Peace
    The end of the Cold War presents opportunities for nations to improve relations, as the Soviets and Germans have done. However, it is also essential to avoid straining existing relationships while forming new ones.

Waiting for Democracy
Article by Artyom Borovik
Foreign Policy, Fall 1991, No. 84
Carnegie Endowment for International Peace
    The hardliners in Moscow are trying to maintain order. However, the youth movement is beginning to take control. Eventually, the pressure on the older generation will be too great. A new generation of leaders, with a new philosophy of individual freedom and reform, will help bring true democratic change to the Soviet Union.

Will the Soviet Republics Join the United Nations?
Report by Toby Trister Gati and Ed Piasecki
United Nations Association of the USA, October 1991
    Focuses on the future representation of the former Soviet republics in the UN. It is hoped the republics will be able to agree on how they would like to be represented. Acceptance of the republics could depend largely on their ability to coordinate their foreign policy.

SLAVIC STATES & MOLDOVA

Report on the Moldovan Presidential Election:
December 8, 1991
Report, December 21, 1991
Commission on Security and Cooperation in Europe
    CSCE report discussing the implications of the Moldo-

van presidential election, as witnessed firsthand by Commission staff members.

Report on Ukraine's Referendum on Independence and Presidential Election: December 1, 1991
Report, December 20, 1991
Commission on Security and Cooperation in Europe
    CSCE report discussing the implications of the Ukrainian independence and presidential elections.

Russia: A Chance for Survival
Article by Andrei Kozyrev
Foreign Affairs, Spring 1992, Vol. 71, No. 2
Council on Foreign Relations
    By Russia's Foreign Minister, the article explains the challenges Russia faces.

Russia Reborn
Article by Dimitri Simes
Foreign Policy, Winter 1991-92, No. 85
Carnegie Endowment for International Peace
    The author argues the significance of the Russian Federation, even without its empire, and makes a case for Western support of Russia's reform efforts.

The Ukraine Rising
Article by Vitaly Korotich
Foreign Policy, Winter 1991-92, No. 85
Carnegie Endowment for International Peace
    Discusses the future of Ukraine, the need for development of democratic structures and leaders, and a realization by Ukrainians of their honorable place and role in the world.

Ukraine: The Legacy of Intolerance
Book by David Little
United States Institute of Peace, 1991
    Considers how religion and dissimilar beliefs sometimes contribute to conflict, as well as methods for managing such conflicts and encouraging peaceful pluralism.

TRANSCAUCASUS

Transcaucasus: A Chronology
Periodical: Monthly
Armenian National Committee of America
    A chronological summary of recent significant social, economic and political trends in the Caucasus.

ADDITIONAL RESOURCES

Central Eurasia Daily Report
Periodical: Daily
Foreign Broadcast Information Services

Translations of radio and television broadcasts from the former Soviet Union. To obtain, call: (703) 487-4630.

Meeting Report
Report
Periodical: 24 per year
Kennan Institute for Advanced International Studies
Summarizes lectures, providing a variety of viewpoints from highly respected Russian and American scholars, reporters, academics, and visiting officials.

RFE/RL Research Report
Periodical: Weekly
Radio Free Europe/Radio Liberty
Contains articles based on Radio Liberty broadcasts on political, economic and social issues in the former Soviet Union and Eastern Europe, taken from RFE Daily Reports. To obtain, call (202) 457-6912.

Trip Report: Tallinn, St. Petersburg, Moscow, Alma Ata
Report by Kate M. Hanlon, December 16, 1991
Search for Common Ground Environment Program
A summary of a trip organized by a non-governmental organization to provide assistance to republic government and non-governmental leaders in environmental protection and economic development. Describes conferences, meetings, and initiatives taken by the group.

We/Mbi
Newspaper
Bi-Weekly
"The First Independent Russian-American Newspaper." To obtain, call (800) 289-8747.

DATABASES & ON-LINE SERVICES

ACCESS Database
Computer Database
ACCESS
Includes information on over 2,400 organizations and 6,000 individuals from over 100 countries focusing on international security, peace, and world affairs. Information is available by computer printout or on the telephone.

CDC DataBank
Computer Database
Citizens Democracy Corps
Database of information on organizations working for the peoples of Central and Eastern Europe and the Commonwealth of Independent States. Includes agriculture, arts/culture, business, energy, labor, and others. Information is available by printout or on the telephone.

Coup
Computer Library Files

Nexis - Mead Data Central

Contains documents collected from a wide variety of publications, journals, magazines, and newspapers with information on the August coup and aftermath.
For information, call: (202) 785-3550.

Database of Independent Contacts in the Soviet Union
Computer Database
World Without War Council
Individuals interested in meeting with visitors from the West. Approximately 800 entries, distributed throughout the USSR. Information is regularly updated and databases can be obtained for Moscow or Leningrad only, for a complete republic or the entire former Soviet Union.

EcoNet, PeaceNet, ConflictNet
Computer Network and Communication Services
Institute for Global Communications
Offers a wide variety of computer conferences on the former Soviet Union, including *cdi.sovsis, reg.ussr, en.suur, moscow,news.sam, end.moscow, talk.pol.soviet, glasnost.news, northwest.news,* and *baltic.news.*
For information, call: (415) 442-0220.

Glasnet
Computer Network & Communication Services
Association for Progressive Communications
The Russian computer network for people and organizations working for the environment, peace, conflict resolution, and public interest. To obtain information, call Glasnet at (7 095) 217-6173 or Email: support@glas.apc.org; in the US, call Dave Caulkins at (415) 948-5753.

ISAR Database
Computer Database
ISAR
Includes organizations in Soviet-American Relations, specialists, individuals and organzations with resource information, over 1,000 listings in total. Information is made available by computer printout.

Mead Data Central
Computer Datafiles
Mead Data Central
Contains several datafiles on the former Soviet Union, including *Intlaw USSR* and *World SovLeg.*
For information, call (800) 543-6862.

Registered Joint Ventures
Computer Database
Center for Foreign Policy Development

US, Canadian, and European joint ventures with the former Soviet Union, as registered with the Ministry of Finance of the Soviet Union as of June 1990. Available on computer disk and in pre-printed publications.

Resource Center Database
Computer Database
Institute on Religion and Democracy

When completed (Spring '92), will contain information on over 1,000 Christian organizations of all denominations doing any type of work in the former Soviet Union. Available on computer printouts and over the telephone.

Soviet Elites Database
Computer Database
Columbia University - Harriman Institute

Contains information on nearly 5,000 Russian, Soviet, and CIS scholars and decisionmakers - present and former members of government organizations in the former Soviet Union, the new states and the CIS.

SOVSET'
Computer Database and On-Line Service
Center for Strategic and International Studies

Offers over 30 conferences, including military affairs, domestic and foreign policy, economics and the environment. Many holdings are also available, including Radio Free Europe/Radio Liberty *Daily Reports* and *Research Reports, Ekspress Khronika*, and *PostFactum Analytical Reports*. Electronic mail is also offered.

DIRECTORY & REFERENCE WORKS

The Baltic States: A Reference Book
Reference Book
Moscow Independent Press Publishing

Includes history, political system, economy, religion, business directory, who's who, and government.
To obtain, call: (718) 373-3173.

A Compendium of U.S. Nonprofit Organizaitons Providing Voluntary Assistance to Central and Eastern Europe and the Soviet Union
Directory
Citizens Democracy Corps, July 1991

Information on more than 360 organizations providing some type of assistance to the former Soviet Union and Central and Eastern Europe.

Directory of Contacts for Central and Eastern Europe and the Commonwealth of Independent States
Directory

U.S. Chamber of Commerce, Spring 1992
Contacts in government, chambers of commerce, multilateral agencies, non-government organizations focusing on the CIS and Central and Eastern Europe. To obtain, call: (202) 463-5460.

IREX Bibliography: IREX-Sponsored Research Publications, 1979-1991
Bibliography
International Research & Exchanges Board, Fall 1991

A compilation of contributions by IREX scholars and general surveys of field literature.

Soviet Independent Business Directory
Directory
FYI Information Resources for a Changing World, 1991

Lists over 2,100 cooperatives and independent business ventures. Provides a variety of business-relevant statistics and information.

EDUCATIONAL & CURRICULAR MATERIAL

Breakup of the Soviet Union: US Dilemmas
Citizen education material
Great Decisions, 1992
Foreign Policy Association

This nonpartisan article summarizes the issues and changes in the former Soviet Union through December 1991. It concludes with policy options for the United States, discussion questions, and suggested readings.

Facing a Disintegrated Soviet Union
Curriculum Material
Choices Project, January 1992
Center for Foreign Policy Development

This one-week unit explores US foreign policy after the collapse of communism in the USSR and the establishment of new independent republics. Students come away with a clearer understanding of Soviet history, the Gorbachev era, and emerging issues in US relations toward the former Soviet Union.

Soviet-American Relations: From the Cold War to New Thinking
Curriculum Material
Stanford Program on International and Cross-Cultural Education, 1990

Explores the Cold War (1945-1990) with an emphasis on concepts that clarify the relationship between these two countries. Includes five lessons: Cold War, Arms Buildup, Arms Control, Detente, and Contemporary US-Soviet Relations. To obtain, call (415) 723-1114.

GUIDE TO ORGANIZATIONS

The following is a list of organizations, drawn from the ACCESS database, which focus on the former Soviet Union. Where available, each listing includes specific projects focusing on the many issues confronting the new nations emerging from the Soviet Union, specialists, publications and other resources.

ACCESS: A SECURITY INFORMATION SERVICE

1730 M St., N.W.
Suite 605
Washington, DC 20036
(202) 785-6630: Telephone
(202) 223-2737: Fax
Mary Lord, Executive Director

Purpose: To promote better understanding of war, peace and security issues through the gathering and dissemination of impartial information. Works to improve communication among citizens, research centers, academic programs, advocacy groups and specialists reflecting different perspectives.

Information Strengths:
> Political Issues
> New State Governmental Structures
> CIS Governmental Structures
> Development of Democracy
> Economics
> Military Spending
> Economic Conversion
> Conversion to Market Economy
> Foreign Investment in Businesses
> Foreign Aid/Relief Efforts
> Distributions Problems
> Conversion to Private Property
> Currency/Monetary Issues
> Military Issues
> Command & Control of Military
> Control of Nuclear & Conventional Weapons
> Military Conversion
> Nationalities & Ethnic Disputes
> Human Rights Issues
> Environment
> Entire former USSR

Resources: Reports: *The Future of NATO and US Interests,* (12/91), *Independence for the Baltic States* (9/91), *From Guns to Butter?: USA & USSR,* (9/90). Computer Database, Issue Summaries, Library, Directories, Staff Available to Speak.

Additional information:
❖ ACCESS offers an Information Service to assist in locating resources, speakers, and other materials.
❖ Produced **One Nation Becomes Many: The ACCESS Guide to the Former Soviet Union**.

AMERICAN COMMITTEE ON U.S.-SOVIET RELATIONS

109 11th St., S.E.
Washington, DC 20003
(202) 546-1700: Telephone
(202) 543-3146: Fax
William Miller, President

Purpose: To strengthen official and public understanding of the complex overall relationship between the United States and the former Soviet Union, providing information and analysis, and promoting business-like relations with Russia and the other states of the former Soviet Union.

Project Name: **Cultural relations**
Contact: Moira Ratchford

Project Name: **Trade program**
Contact: Margaret Chapman

Project Name: **Assessment**
Contact: Robert E. Berls, Jr.

Project Name: **Parliamentarian, Legal Reform projects**
Contact: William Miller

Information Strengths:
> Political Issues
> New State Governmental Structures
> CIS Governmental Structures
> Development of Democracy
> Economics
> Economic Conversion
> Conversion to a Market Economy
> Foreign Investment in Business
> Foreign Aid/Relief Efforts
> Conversion to Private Property
> Currency/Monetary Issues
> Military Issues
> Command & Control of Military
> Nationalities
> Environment
> Entire former USSR
> Russia

Specialists: Margaret Chapman, Trade Relations. William Miller, Robert E. Berls, Jr.

Resources: Journal: *New Outlook* (Quarterly). Conferences: Forum on U.S.-Soviet Trade (December 10, 1991). Issue Summaries, Newsletter, Reports or Studies, Staff Available to Speak.

AMERICAN LATVIAN ASSOCIATION

P.O. Box 4578
400 Hurley Ave.
Rockville, MD 20849-4578
(301) 340-8174: Telephone
(301) 762-5438: Fax
Martins Zvaners, Director of Public Affairs

Purpose: To support an independent, democratic, and free-market oriented Republic of Latvia.

Information Strengths:
    Political Issues
    New State Governmental Structures
    Development of Democracy
    Economic Conversion
    Conversion to Market Economy
    Foreign Investment in Businesses
    Foreign Aid/Relief Efforts
    Conversion to Private Property
    Currency/Monetary Issues
    Nationalities & Ethnic Disputes
    Border Disputes
    Human Rights Issues
    Environment
    Relations with International Organizations
    Latvia

Specialists: Martins Zvaners, Latvia.

Resources: Newsletter: *Latvian News Digest* (4/year), Journal, Issue Summaries, Staff Available to Speak.

ARMENIAN NATIONAL COMMITTEE OF AMERICA

1901 Pennsylvania Ave., N.W.
Suite 206
Washington, DC 20006
(202) 775-1918: Telephone
(202) 775-5648: Fax
Vicken Sonentz-Papazian, Executive Director

Purpose: To propose and guide public policy issues of concern to the Armenian American community.

Information Strengths:
    Development of Democracy
    Foreign Aid/Relief Efforts
    Independent Armies/Militias
    Nationalities & Ethnic Disputes
    Border Disputes
    Human Rights Issues
    Armenia
    Azerbaijan
    Georgia
    Iran
    Turkey

Resources: Press Releases, Issue Summaries, Fact Sheets, Newsletter: *TransCaucasus: A Chronology* (12/year).

ARMS CONTROL ASSOCIATION

11 Dupont Circle, NW
Suite 250
Washington, DC 20036
(202) 797-4626: Telephone
(202) 797-4611: Fax
Spurgeon M. Keeny Jr., President & Executive Director

Purpose: To promote public understanding of and support for effective policies and programs in arms control, disarmament, and national security.

Contact: Spurgeon Keeny Jr. or Jack Mendelsohn

Information Strengths:
    Arms Control Issues
    Command & Control
    Nuclear Weapons
    Conventional Weapons
    Arms Transfers
    Compliance with Existing Treaties
    Nonproliferation

Resources: Magazine: *Arms Control Today* (10/year), Issue Summaries, Staff Available to Speak.

Additional Information:
✧ Jan/Feb '92 issue of *Arms Control Today* contains series of articles on nuclear weapons in the former Soviet Union.

ATLANTIC COUNCIL OF THE UNITED STATES

1616 H St., N.W.
Washington, DC 20006
(202) 347-9353: Telephone
(202) 737-5163: Fax
Rozanne L. Ridgeway, President

Purpose: To promote the security of the US and NATO through studies of NATO military, economic, and policy concerns.

Project Name: **The Future of Russian-American Relations in a Pluralistic World**
Contact: Peter Bird Swiers, Vice President
Project Goals: Identifies emerging trends, challenges, opportunities in US relations with the Russian Federation and assesses their effect on the bilateral and multilateral relations of both countries. Formulates specific joint policy recommendations addressed to both governments, to private sector decision-makers and to appropriate international institutions. In collaboration with the Institute of World Economy and International Affairs (IMEMO) of the Russian Academy of Sciences.

Project Name: **Democracy and Federalism**
Contact: Peter Bird Swiers, Vice President
Project Goals: Provides technical assistance to the Supreme Soviet of the Russian Federation in the practi-

cal aspects of governance, environmental policy, defense conversion, economic administration, grass roots action, human needs, and other functional steps to develop an institutional framework and procedures necessary for a modern democratic society and a market economy to function. In collaboration with the Brookings Institution.

Project Name: **Institution Building in Civil-Military Relations**

Contact: Dr. John A. Baker, Director

Project Goals: Familiarizes civilian leaders in the newly sovereign states with the budget and defense policy mechanisms which civilian executive and legislative authorities in democratic governments utilize for oversight of armed services. Aspires to integrate military establishments with the civil societies, and to open them up to greater supervision from and closer working relationships with the democratically elected governments.

Information Strengths:
   Political Issues
   New State Government Structures
   Development of Democracy
   Economics
   Economic Conversion
   Conversion to a Market Economy
   Military Conversion

Specialists: Madeline Albright, CIS, Foreign Policy. Edward B. Atkeson, Military Policy, Jeffrey P. Bialos, CIS. Hans Binnendijk, Military Policy. Lewis W. Bowden, CIS, Foreign Policy, Trade and Economic Policy. William E. Colby, CIS. Jeffrey W. Colyer, Military Policy, Trade and Economic Policy. Russell Dougherty, Military Policy. James A. Duran, Foreign Policy, Trade and Economic Policy. Robert F. Ellsworth, CIS. Richard N. Gardner, CIS. Andrew J. Goodpaster, CIS, Military Policy, Foreign Policy. Lincoln Gordon, Foreign Policy, Trade and Economic Policy. William M. Habeeb, CIS, Georgia, Trade and Economic Policy. Dale R. Herspring, CIS, Military Policy. Robert E. Hunter, CIS. Kempton B. Jenkins, CIS, Foreign Policy, Trade and Economic Policy. Catherine Kelleher, Military Policy, Foreign Policy. Gary L. Matthews, CIS. Paul H. Nitze, CIS, Military Policy. Daniel Nelson, Military Policy, Foreign Policy. Roger F. Pajak, CIS. John Pustay, Military Policy. Stanley R. Restor, Military Policy. Rozanne L. Ridgeway, CIS, Foreign Policy. Dimitri Simes, CIS, Russia. William Y. Smith, Military Policy. Helmut Sonnenfeldt, CIS. Timothy Stanley, CIS. Peter Bird Swiers, CIS, Foreign Policy. Leonard Sullivan, Jr., Military Policy. Randall C. Teague, Sr., Trade and Economic Policy. William C. Turner, CIS, Foreign Policy, Trade and Economic Policy. Harlan K. Ullman, Military Policy. Paul C. Warnke, CIS. John C. Whitehead, CIS. Joseph J. Wolf, Foreign Policy.

Resources: Reports: *Russia and the Commonwealth States: Changes in Security Policies* (Bimonthly), *Russia and the Commonwealth States: Political and Economic Update* (Bimonthly). Conferences, Newsletter.

Additional Information:
✧   Releases Joint Policy Statements and Recommendations with IMEMO, including: *The Future of Soviet-American Relations in a Pluralistic World*, May 30, 1991.

BRITISH AMERICAN SECURITY INFORMATION COUNCIL (BASIC)
1601 Connecticut Ave., N.W.
Suite 302
Washington, DC 20009
(202) 745-2457: Telephone
(202) 387-6298
Daniel Plesch, Director

Purpose: To analyze international security issues afffecting Europe. As part of BASIC's ongoing work, to monitor the security policies of the new independent states, especially in arms control talks and in relation to NATO and the CSCE.

Information Strengths:
   Arms Control Negotiations on Conventional
      Weapons
   Relations with International Organizations
   Entire former USSR.

Specialists: Daniel Plesch, Nuclear & Conventional Forces, Relations with Europe. Natalie Goldring, Arms Transfers, Nuclear & Conventional Arms Control. David Shorr, Conventional Arms Control, Role of Independent States in International Organizations. Sandra Ionno, Nuclear Arms Control.

Resources: Newsletter: *Basic Reports* (6-8/year). Issue Summaries, Staff Available to Speak.

Additional Information:
✧   *Basic Reports* will track the participation of the new independent states in conventional arms talks and other CSCE processes.

BROOKINGS INSTITUTION
1775 Massachusetts Ave., NW
Washington, DC 20036
(202) 797-6000: Telephone
(202) 797-6004: Fax
Bruce MacLaury, President

Purpose: To conduct research, provide education, and produce publications on issues of foreign policy, government, and the social sciences.

Contact: John D. Steinbruner, Director of Foreign Policy Studies

Information Strengths:
- Political Issues
- New State Governmental Structures
- CIS Governmental Structures
- Development of Democracy
- Economics
- Military Spending
- Economic Conversion
- Conversion to Market Economy
- Foreign Investment in Businesses
- Foreign Aid/Relief Efforts
- Distributions Problems
- Conversion to Private Property
- Currency/Monetary Issues
- Military Issues
- Command & Control of Military
- Control of Nuclear Weapons
- Control of Conventional Weapons
- Military Conversion
- Nationalities
- Human Rights Issues
- Entire former USSR

Specialists: Clifford G. Gaddy, Soviet Economy, Soviet Military Conversion. Raymond L. Garthoff, Former Soviet Union, East-West Relations, Eastern Europe. Jerry F. Hough, Former Soviet Union, Soviet-American Relations. Helmut Sonnenfeldt, former Soviet Union, East-West Relations, Eastern Europe, Defense Policy.

Resources: Newsletter: *Brookings* (4/year), Magazine or Journal, Conferences, Curricular Materials, Reports or Studies, Books, Directories, Staff Available to Speak.

Additional Information:
- ❖ Special Soviet Studies: *The Great Transition: American-Soviet Relations (1981-1991)*, *Perestroika and Soviet Military Industry*, *The Relationship of Nationalism and Communism*, and *Soviet-American Relations*.
- ❖ Sponsored a July 1992 visit to the US by high-ranking Russian parliament members for a program designed to impart the basic principles of federalism and democracy.

BUSINESS PARTNERSHIP FOR PEACE
1000 16th St., NW
Suite 810
Washington, DC 20036
(202) 296-9685: Telephone
Neil Schwartzbach, Director

Purpose: To promote aid/assistance to the former Soviet Union with special emphasis on business assistance/training on transition to a free-market economy, and to promote the Management Corps Act of 1991-legislation to send US business people to train/assist Soviet entrepreneurs.

Contact: Sean Meyer

Information Strengths:
- Political Issues
- Conversion to Market Economy
- Foreign Aid/Relief Efforts

Specialists: Sean Meyer, US Congress and legislation regarding Soviet aid/assistance.

Resources: Newsletter: *Capitol Leverage*, Staff Available to Speak.

CAMPAIGN FOR PEACE & DEMOCRACY EAST & WEST
P.O. Box 1640
Cathedral Station
New York, NY 10025
(212) 666-5924: Telephone
Joanne Landy, Director

Purpose: To unite activists in opposition to militarism, interventionism, and the violation of human rights and to build an alternative to the superpower bloc system based on peace, democracy, and social justice throughout the world.

Information Strengths:
- Political Issues
- Development of Democracy
- Economics
- Conversion to Market Economy
- Military Issues
- Control of Nuclear Weapons
- Nationalities
- Human Rights Issues
- Entire former USSR

Specialists: Joanne Landy, Humans Rights/Military & Economic Issues.

Resources: Newsletter, Staff Available to Speak.

CARNEGIE ENDOWMENT FOR INTERNATIONAL PEACE
2400 N St., NW
Washington, DC 20037-1118
(202) 862-7900: Telephone
(202) 862-2610: Fax
Morton I. Abramowitz, President

Purpose: To conduct programs of research, discussion, publication, and education in international relations and US foreign policy.

Information Strengths:
    Political Issues
    New State Governmental Structures
    Command & Control of Military
    Control of Nuclear Weapons
    Control of Conventional Weapons
    Nationalities
    Entire former USSR

Specialists: Paul Goble, Nationalities. Andrew Pierre, Arms Control. Dimitri Simes, Political Issues. Leonard Spector, Nuclear Proliferation.

Resources: Journal: **Foreign Policy**, (4/year), Report: *Nuclear Proliferation Status Report, March, 1992* (includes CIS nuclear states). Books, Staff Available to Speak.

CENTER FOR FOREIGN POLICY DEVELOPMENT
Brown University
PO Box 1948
Providence, RI 02912
(401) 863-3465: Telephone
(401) 274-8440: Fax
Mark Garrison, Director

Purpose: To conduct research and education on US policy concerning the former Soviet Union and related security issues.

Project Name: **Soviet Foreign Economic Policy and International Security**
Contact: Alan Sherr, Associate Director
Project Goals: To assess the impact of domestic and foreign economic policies of the CIS in order to evaluate the meaning of these developments for potential US economic cooperation with the countries of the CIS.

Project name: **US-USSR-Cuba Project**
Contact: James Blight, Senior Research Fellow
Project Goals: A policy-oriented outgrowth of a project on the Cuban Missile Crisis, it focuses on the changing nature of economic and military relations between the former Soviet Union and Cuba and the policy choices they pose for the US.

Project name: **Choices for the 21st Century**
Contact: Susan Graseck, Project Director
Project Goals: To make international issues accessible to high school and college classrooms and to the adult community, in an effort to increase public interest in foreign policy issues, improve participatory citizenship skills, and encourage public judgement on policy priorities.

Project Name: **Naval Strategy Conferences**
Contact: Deana Arsenian, Assistant Director
Project Goals: To bring together US, Soviet, and British active-duty naval officers and civilian specialists on maritime issues to discuss naval strategy and doctrine.

Project Name: **Security for Europe**
Contact: Richard Smoke, Research Director
Project Goals: Working in partnership with institutions in Eastern Europe and the former Soviet Union, to address potential threats (military, political, economic) to European and US security, and to assist institutions in the emerging democracies to attune policies to their publics' choices.

Information Strengths:
    Political Issues
    New State Governmental Structures
    CIS Governmental Structures
    Development of Democracy
    Economics
    Military Spending
    Conversion to Market Economy
    Foreign Investment in Businesses
    Military Issues
    Command & Control of Military
    Control of Nuclear & Conventional Weapons
    Civil-Military Relations
    Military Facilities
    Military Conversion
    Nationalities
    Ethnic Disputes
    Border Disputes
    Entire former USSR

Specialists: Mark Kramer, CIS Strategic/Military Issues. Stephen Shenfield, CIS Political/Interethnic Issues. Michael Spagat, CIS Economy.

Resources: Book: **Soviet Foreign Economic Policy and International Security** (1991); **International Joint Ventures: Soviet and Western Perspectives** (Dec. 1991). Curriculum Material: *Facing a Disintegrated Soviet Union* (Feb 1992). Report: *Future U.S.-Soviet Business Relations: A Manufacturing Strategy Perspective* (Dec. 1991). Computer Database, Issue Summaries, Conferences, Newsletter, Reports or Studies, Books, Staff Available to Speak.

Additional Information:
✧ The US-Russian Academic Teleconferencing Network initiated with the Institute of Space Research at the Russian Academy of Sciences to enhance US-Russian scholarly and academic exchanges by providing affordable and convenient means for organizations and individuals to communicate via compressed-signal video tele-conferencing.
✧ Conferences: *US-Russia-Cuba Conference in Havana, US-CIS-UK Maritime Strategy Conference, The CIS: An Investment Opportunity.*

CENTER FOR POST-SOVIET STUDIES

2 Wisconsin Circle
Suite 410
Chevy Chase, MD 20815
(301) 652-8181: Telephone
(301) 652-8451: Fax
Susan Eisenhower, Director

Purpose: To broaden Western understanding and knowledge of the complex events taking place in the Soviet region. The Center seeks to promote debate on the nature of developments in the region, identify trends, and encourage a long-term, forward-looking Western approach to the former Soviet Union.

Project Name: **The Project on the Future of U.S.-Russian Relations**

Project Name: **Global Security and the Commonwealth Nuclear Establishment**

Information Strengths:
   Political Issues
   CIS Government Structures
   US-Russian Relations
   US-CIS Relations
   Economics
   Commonwealth of Independent States
   Russia

Resources: Conferences, Journal or Magazine, Seminars.

CENTER FOR STRATEGIC & INTERNATIONAL STUDIES

1800 K St., N.W.
Suite 400
Washington, DC 20006
(202) 887-0200: Telephone
(202) 775-3199: Fax
David M. Abshire, President

Purpose: To advance understanding of emerging world issues in the areas of international security, politics, economics, and business by providing a strategic perspective to decision makers that is integrative in nature, international in scope, anticipatory in its timing, and bipartisan in its approach.

Project Name: **Russian and Eurasian Studies**
Contact: Stephen Sestanovich, Director

Project Goals: The Project focuses on the interaction between domestic change in the former Soviet Union and its evolving role in international affairs. It monitors political upheaval, ethnic strife, the economic situation, and societal problems and remedies.

Information Strengths:
   Political Issues
   New State Governmental Structures
   CIS Governmental Structures
   Development of Democracy
   Intra-CIS Treaties/Agreements
   Economics
   Military Spending
   Economic Conversion
   Conversion to Market Economy/Private Property
   Distribution Problems
   Natural Resource Management
   Currency/Monetary Issues
   Military Issues
   Control of Nuclear & Conventional Weapons
   Civil-Military Relations
   Nationalities & Ethnic Disputes
   Human Rights Issues
   Environment
   Entire former USSR
   Armenia
   Azerbaijan
   Byelarus
   Estonia
   Georgia
   Kazakhstan
   Kyrgyzstan
   Latvia
   Lithuania
   Moldova
   Russia
   Tajikistan
   Turkmenistan
   Ukraine
   Uzbekistan

Specialists: Stephen R. Sestanovich, Director, Soviet successor states, East-West relations, post-Soviet/Third World relations. Dauphine M. Sloan, Coordinator, Post-Soviet domestic politics, East-West relations, internal migration in Soviet successor states and emigration. Gabriel Schoenfeld, Senior Fellow, Post-Soviet affairs, East-West relations, environmental pollution, terrorism, disaster management. Sarah Helmstadter, Research Analyst, Post-Soviet socio-economic issues.

Resources: Newsletter: *Post-Soviet Prospects* (8/year). Reports: *Red Armies in Crisis*, 1991; *The Last Leninists: The Uncertain Future of Asia's Communist States*, April 1992. *After Perestroika: Democracy in the Soviet Union*, 1991. Directory: *Dictionary of Political Parties and Organizations in Russia*, April 1992. Books: **From Stagnation to Catastroika: Commentaries on the Soviet Economy, 1983-1991**, 1992. **Soviet Policy toward Israel under Gorbachev**, 1991. Journal: **Washington Quarterly** (4/year). On-Line Service and Computer Database: SOVSET'. Conferences, Staff Available to Speak.

CITIZENS DEMOCRACY CORPS

2021 K St., N.W.
Suite 215
Washington, DC 20006
(202) 872-0933: Telephone
(202) 872-0923: Fax
Sol Polansky, Executive Director

Purpose: To assist the countries of Central and Eastern Europe and the Soviet Republics in their transition to democratic institutions and free market economies by mobilizing and channeling US voluntary assistance.

Project Name: **CDC Clearinghouse**
Contact: Carolyn Stremlau
Project Goals: The CDC Databank provides information on organizations working for the peoples of Central & Eastern Europe (CEE) and the Commonwealth of Independent States (CIS). The CDC Volunteer Registry matches US volunteers with organizations working in CEE and CIS.

Information Strengths:
    Development of Democracy
    Conversion to Market Economy
    Foreign Aid/Relief Efforts
    Distribution Problems
    Environment

Specialists: Carolyn Stremlau and Francis Luzzatto, US private sector assistance.

Resources: Reports: *A Compendium of US Nonprofit Organizations Providing Voluntary Assistance to Central and Eastern Europe and the Soviet Union* (July 1991), *Assistance to the Commonwealth of Independent States: Activities of US Nonprofit Organizations* (1992), Computer Database, Conferences, Newsletter, Directories, Staff Available to Speak.

Additional Information:
- Held "Conference on Private Sector Assistance to the Commonwealth of Independent States" on January 22-23, 1992.
- The *DataBank* publishes a series of country-specific directories on nonprofit organizations and their work in the region, as well as a series of Resource Lists on specialized topics.
- The *Business Entrepreneur Program* enlists the expertise and resources of US entrepreneurs to assist small- and medium-size companies in Central and Eastern Europe.
- The *Volunteer Registry* is a service to match volunteers with organizations working in Central and Eastern Europe and the CIS.

COLUMBIA UNIVERSITY - THE HARRIMAN INSTITUTE

420 W. 118th St.
12th Floor
New York, NY 10027
(212) 854-4623: Telephone
(212) 666-3481: Fax
Robert Legvold, Director

Purpose: To advance knowledge and understanding of the complex and changing society of the former Soviet Union. The Institute is committed to meeting the goals of 1) preparation of graduate students for professional and scholarly careers in Russian, Soviet, and post-Soviet studies; 2) the promotion of advanced research on Russia, the Soviet Union, and the post-Soviet reality; and 3) public dissemination of information, analysis, and opinion derived from Institute-sponsored research and activities.

Information Strengths of Institute Faculty:
    Political Issues
    New State Governmental Structures
    CIS Governmental Structures
    Development of Democracy
    Intra-CIS Treaties/Agreements
    Economics
    Military Spending
    Economic Conversion
    Conversion to a Market Economy
    Distribution Problems
    Conversion to Private Property
    Foreign Investment in Business
    Foreign Aid/Relief Problems
    Natural Resource Management
    Currency/Monetary Issues
    Military Issues
    Control of Nuclear & Conventional Weapons
    Civil-Military Relations
    Military Facilities
    Military Conversion
    Independent Armies/Militias
    Compliance with Existing Treaties
    Nationalities & Ethnic Disputes
    Border Disputes
    Human Rights Issues
    Environment
    Relations with International Organizations
    Entire former USSR

Resources: Reports: *The Harriman Institute Forum*; *Studies of the Harriman Institute.* Newsletter: *News from the Harriman Institute; At the Harriman Institute.* Books: **Thinking Theoretically About Soviet Nationalities: History and Comparison in the Study of the USSR**, edited by Alexander J. Motyl, 1992; **Moscow, Germany, and the West: From Khrushchev to Gorbachev**, by Michael J. Sodaro, 1990. Conferences: *Financing Trade and Investment in the USSR: Soviet, European and American Perspectives* (October 23, 1991),

First Annual Secondary School Curriculum Enrichment Program: Focus on the USSR (December 13, 1991). TV Program, Computer Database, Magazine or Journal, Speakers Bureau, Library, On-Line Services, Curricular Materials, Directories.

Additional Information:
✦ Private sector and media inquiries as well as questions about scholars at the Harriman Institute should be directed to Douglas A. Evans, Program Officer at (212) 854-8487.
✦ Questions on Harriman Institute publications should be directed to the Publications Office.

COMMISSION ON SECURITY AND COOPERATION IN EUROPE
237 Ford House Office Building
Washington, DC 20515
(202) 225-1901: Telephone
(202) 226-4199: Fax
Steny H. Hoyer, Chairman

Purpose: To monitor and encourage compliance of the signatory states with the Helsinki Final Act.

Information Strengths:
  Political Issues
  New State Government Structures
  CIS Government Structures
  Development of Democracy
  Intra-CIS Treaties/Agreements
  Civil-Military Relations
  Compliance with Existing Treaties
  Nationalities & Ethnic Disputes
  Human Rights Issues
  Relations with International Organizations
  Entire former USSR

Resources: Reports: *Report on Turkmenistan'ss Referendum on Independence* (10/26/91); *Report on Moldovan Presidential Election* (12/8/91); *Report on Armenian Referendum on Independence* (9/21/91); *Referendum in the Soviet Union: A Compendium of Reports on the March 17, 1991 Referendum on the Future of the USSR* (4/91); *Report on Ukraine's Referendum on Independence and Presidential Election* (12/1/91).Public Hearings.

Additional Information:
✦ The Commission, also known as the Helsinki Commission, is an independent agency composed of 21 Legislative and Executive Branch officials.
✦ The Commission undertakes human rights casework on behalf of individuals denied visas, separated families, and political prisoners.
✦ The Commission serves on delegations to meetings of the Conference on Security and

Cooperation in Europe (CSCE), particpates in US policy planning and execution toward the CSCE, and holds periodic meetings with officials of the Executive Branch on CSCE policy.

COMMITTEE ON THE PRESENT DANGER
905 16th St., N.W.
Suite 207
Washington, DC 20006
(202) 628-2409: Telephone
Charles Tyroler, II, Director

Purpose: To alert America to the Soviet drive for dominance and the Soviet military buildup.

Project Goals: To provide a non-partisan database and information source for the American public and government.

Information Strengths:
  Military Spending
  Economic Conversion
  Military Issues
  Command & Control of Military
  Control of Nuclear & Conventional Weapons
  Military Facilities
  Military Conversion
  Independent Armies/Militias
  Compliance with Existing Treaties
  Entire former USSR
  Russia
  Ukraine

Specialists: Bob Tarver and David Trachtenberg, Arms Control, US-Russian Military Affairs.

Resources: Report: *Russian Military Expenditures* (April 24, 1991), Library, Staff Available to Speak.

CONGRESSIONAL ROUNDTABLE ON POST-COLD WAR RELATIONS
501 House Annex 2
United States Congress
Washington, DC 20515-6801
(202) 226-3440: Telephone
(202) 225-0081: Fax
Beth C. DeGrasse, Project Director

Purpose: To inform members of Congress about issues relating to US Relations with the former Soviet Union.

Information Strengths:
  Economic Conversion
  Military Issues
  Military Conversion
  Entire former USSR

Resources: Annual Report, Speaker Summaries.

COUNCIL ON ECONOMIC PRIORITIES

30 Irving Pl.
New York, NY 10003
(212) 420-1133: Telephone
(212) 420-0988: Fax
Alice Tepper Marlin, Executive Director

Purpose: To enhance corporate performance as it affects society and perform public policy studies on national security and military spending issues.

Project Name: **Conversion Information Center**
Contact: Dr. John Tepper Marlin

Project Goals: To participate in conferences, legislative initiatives, policy evaluation and information-sharing related to conversion in the former Soviet republics as well as in the USA.

Information Strengths:
    Economics
    Military Spending
    Economic Conversion
    Conversion to Market Economy
    Foreign Investment in Businesses
    Foreign Aid/Relief Efforts
    Distribution Problems
    Conversion to Private Property
    Military Issues
    Command & Control of Military
    Control of Nuclear & Conventional Weapons
    Civil-Military Relations
    Military Facilities
    Military Conversion
    Environment
    Entire former USSR
    Russia
    Ukraine

Specialists: Dr. John Tepper Marlin, Soviet Conversion.

Resources: Conferences, Books, Newsletter, Reports or Studies, Books, Directories, Staff Available to Speak.

Additional Information:
✧ Planning a conference on Soviet conversion to be held in Washington, DC.

COUNCIL ON FOREIGN RELATIONS

58 East 68th St.
New York, NY 10021
(212) 734-0400: Telephone
(212) 861-1789: Fax
Peter Tarnoff, President

Purpose: To improve understanding of American foreign policy and international affairs through the free exchange of ideas.

Project Name: **Project on East-West Relations**
Contact: Michael Mandelbaum

Project Goals: The Project examines: 1) Soviet security policy under Gorbachev, 2) the rise of nationalism in the former Soviet republics, 3) the transition from a planned to a market economy, and 4) the collapse of communism.

Information Strengths:
    Political Issues
    New State Governmental Structures
    CIS Governmental Structures
    Development of Democracy
    Intra-CIS Treaties/Agreements
    Economics
    Military Spending
    Economic Conversion
    Conversion to Market Economy
    Foreign Aid/Relief Efforts
    Distribution Problems
    Conversion to Private Property
    Currency/Monetary Issues
    Military Issues
    Command & Control of Military
    Control of Nuclear & Conventional Weapons
    Civil-Military Relations
    Compliance with Existing Treaties
    Nationalities & Ethnic Disputes
    Border Disputes
    Relations with International Organizations
    Entire former USSR

Specialists: Michael Mandelbaum, Former Soviet Republics. C. Michael Aho, Shafiqul Islam, International Economics. Enid C. B. Schoettle, International Organizations and Law. Peter Tarnoff, Former Soviet Union.

Resources: Journal: **Foreign Affairs** (4/year), Reports: *Critical Issues*, Conferences, Books, Staff Available to Speak.

Additional Information:
✧ Published *The Rise of Nations in the Soviet Union: American Foreign Policy and the Disintegration of the USSR* (1991).
✧ *Foreign Affairs* has published several articles on this topic. Call for a listing of titles.
✧ Published *The Soviet Economy in Crisis* (Critical Issues, 1991, No. 4).
✧ Forthcoming studies on Soviet security policy under Gorbachev and the transition from a planned to a market economy.

DEFENSE BUDGET PROJECT

777 North Capitol St., NE
Suite 710
Washington, DC 20002
(202) 408-1517: Telephone
(202) 408-1526: Fax
Gordon Adams, Director

Purpose: To provide detailed, timely analyses of the defense budget, military spending, and policy issues.

Contact: Carol Lessure

Information Strengths:
Economics
Military Spending
Economic Adjustment
Diversification to Market Economy
Foreign Investment in Businesses
Foreign Aid
Civil-Military Relations
Military Conversion

Specialists: Gordon Adams, US Defense Budget Process, Military Adjustment to Market Economy, Future of Civil-Military Relations in Republics. Conrad Schmidt, Economy, Military Adjustment to Market Economy. Carol Lessure, Civil Military Relations, Foreign Aid Process.

Resources: Conferences, Reports or Studies, Staff Available to Speak.

Additional Information:
✦ Translated Budget Primer on US Defense-Budget Process into Russian.
✦ Held joint meetings with Global Outlook on Defense Budget Process (Moscow, 11/91) and Economic Restructuring and Defense Builddown (Washington, DC, 2/92).

ECONOMISTS AGAINST THE ARMS RACE
70 West 40th St.
New York, NY 10018
(212) 870-3345: Telephone
(212) 870-2207: Fax
Lawrence Klein, Kenneth Arrow, Co-Chairs

Purpose: To provide a base for economists to contribute their skills and professional expertise to demonstrate the destructive nature of military economies.

Contact: Alice Slater, Esq.

Project Goals: To establish an international register of peace economists which will include economists of the CIS.

Information Strengths:
Economics
Military Spending
Economic Conversion
Conversion to Market Economy/Private Property
Foreign Aid/Relief Efforts
Currency/Monetary Issues
Military Conversion
Environment

Specialists: John Tepper Marlin, Soviet Conversion. Betty Lall, Conversion. Jurgen Brauer, Register of Peace Economists.

Resources: Newsletter: *The ECAAR NewsNetwork* (4/year). Book: **Economic Issues of Disarmament** (1991). Conferences, Members Available to Speak.

Additional Information:
✦ Forthcoming publication of **World Register of Peace Economists.**

EDUCATORS FOR SOCIAL RESPONSIBILITY
23 Garden St.
Cambridge, MA 02138
(617) 492-1764: Telephone
(617) 864-5164: Fax
Ruth Bowman, Executive Director

Purpose: To make social responsibility an integral part of education in our nation's schools.

Project Name: **International Education Project**
Contact: Alan Shapiro
Project Goals: Network of former Soviet, Polish, and US teachers working to 1) increase awareness of assumptions and prejudices that block cross-cultural communication and 2) share significant elements in and strategies for teaching for democracy.

Information Strengths:
Development of Democracy
Ethnic Disputes
Entire former USSR
Russia

Specialists: Alan Shapiro, International Education. Art Marquardt, Soviet Educators.

Resources: Newsletter, Staff Available to Speak.

ESTONIAN AMERICAN NATIONAL COUNCIL
Washington Bureau
P.O. Box 11134
Arlington, VA 22210
(703) 522-0345: Telephone
(703) 243-5978: Fax
Mari-Ann Rikken, Director

Purpose: To serve as a clearinghouse for information on Estonia, facilitate US/Estonian relations, liaison with US government agencies, lobby Congress, and liaison with media agencies.

Information Strengths:
Political Issues
New State Governmental Structures
Development of Democracy
Intra-CIS Treaties/Agreements
Economics
Economic Conversion
Conversion to Market Economy
Foreign Investment in Businesses

Foreign Aid/Relief Efforts
Distribution Problems
Conversion to Private Property
Natural Resource Management
Currency/Monetary Issues
Military Issues
Command & Control of Military
Control of Conventional Weapons
Civil-Military Relations
Military Facilities
Independent Armies/Militias
Compliance with Existing Treaties
Nationalities & Ethnic Disputes
Border Disputes
Human Rights Issues
Environment
Relations with International Organizations
Entire former USSR
Estonia

Specialists: Mari-Ann Rikken, Estonian Affairs. Dan Kaszeta, Defense & Political Affairs, Legislative Action.

Resources: Issue Summaries, Reports or Studies, Staff Available to Speak.

ETHICS AND PUBLIC POLICY CENTER

1015 15th St., N.W.
Suite 900
Washington, DC 20005
(202) 682-1200: Telephone
(202) 408-0632: Fax
George Weigel, President

Purpose: To clarify and reinforce the bond between the Judeo-Christian moral tradition and domestic and foreign policy issues.

Project Goals: To produce a newsletter published ten times a year by the Center, being a report and commentary on the peace, freedom, and security debate.

Information Strengths:
   Political Issues
   Conversion to Market Economy

Specialists: Fr. Alexander F.C. Webster, Religion in the Soviet Union and Eastern Europe.

Resources: Newsletter: *American Purpose* (10/year), *American Orthodoxy* (4/year),Conferences, Books, Staff Available to Speak.

Additional Information:
✧   Fr. Webster has a forthcoming book entitled *Price of Prophecy: Eastern Orthodox Churches on Peace, Freedom and Security* (available 9/92).

FEDERATION OF AMERICAN SCIENTISTS

307 Massachusetts Avenue, N.E.
Washington, DC 20002
(202) 546-3300: Telephone
(202) 675-1010: Fax
Jeremy J. Stone, President

Purpose: To provide a scientific perspective to Congress on behalf of peace, arms control, and prevention of the use of nuclear weapons or the misuse of science.

Project Name: **US-CIS Joint Cooperative Program on Arms Control**

Contact: Frank von Hippel. Director

Project Goals: To promote cooperation between American and Soviet scientists on such issues as the technical basis for disarmament; safeguarding and disposing of fissile material; verification of disarmament; and ending the production of fissile material.

Information Strengths:
   Control of Nuclear Weapons
   Control of Conventional Weapons
   Civil-Military Relations
   Military Facilities
   Compliance with Existing Treaties
   Relations with International Organizations

Resources: Reports or Studies, Books, Issue Summaries, Conferences.

Additional Information:
✧   In 1990, FAS began joint sponsorship with the Natural Resources Defense Council of workshops held in the US and the former USSR. The workshops focus on verified storage, dismantlement, and final disposal of nuclear weapons and fissile material.

FELLOWSHIP OF RECONCILIATION

P.O. Box 271
523 North Broadway
Nyack, NY 10960
(914) 358-4601: Telephone
(914) 358-4924: Fax
C. Douglas Hostetter, Executive Secretary

Purpose: To explore the power of love and truth for resolving human conflict, oppose war, support justice and human dignity, and strive for a world at peace.

Contact: Dr. Richard L. Deats

Project Goal: To develop a network of individuals and groups working for nonviolent social change, with special focus on Russia and Lithuania.

Information Strengths:
  Development of Democracy
  Independent Armies/Militias
  Nationalities
  Entire former USSR
  Lithuania
  Russia

Specialists: Richard Deats, Lithuania, Nationalities, Nonviolence/People Power. Joe Peacock, Orthodox Church, Latvia. Jo Becker, Youth in Russia, Lithuania.

Resources: Magazine: *Fellowship*, Staff Available to Speak.

Additional Information:
✧ Provides training in nonviolent action.

FOREIGN POLICY ASSOCIATION
729 7th Ave.
New York, NY 10019
(212) 764-4050: Telephone
(212) 302-6123: Fax
R.T. Curran, President

Purpose: Organizes and develops materials for discussion groups on international issues to foster greater understanding of issues and greater participation in the foreign policy process.

Information Strengths:
  Political Issues
  Military Spending
  Economic Conversion
  Foreign Aid/Relief Efforts
  Military Issues
  Control of Nuclear Weapons
  Nationalities
  Ethnic Disputes
  Human Rights Issues
  Environment
  Relations with International Organizations
  Entire former USSR

Resources: Reports: **Headline Series**: *U.S.S.R and Eastern Europe: The Shattered Heartland* (#295, Winter/Spring 1991), **Great Decisions.** TV Program/Video Tapes, Conferences, Curricular Materials, Newsletters, Books.

FOREIGN POLICY RESEARCH INSTITUTE
3615 Chestnut St.
Philadelphia, PA 19104
(215) 382-0685: Telephone
(215) 382-0131: Fax
Daniel Pipes, Director

Purpose: To study contemporary international developments, publish studies, conduct seminars for business, government and academic leaders, and provide foreign policy analysis training to young scholars.

Project Name: **Inner Asia Turmoil and Its Implications**
Contact: Martha Brill Olcott and Daniel Pipes
Project Goals: To assess turmoil in Soviet Central Asia and its implications for regional stability and US foreign policy.

Project Name: **Transitions to Freedom**
Contact: Patrick L. Clawson or Vladimir Tismaneanu
Project Goals: To assess and analyze the transitions to democratic pluralism and free markets in the ex-Soviet bloc, and to make appropriate recommendations for US foreign policy.

Information Strengths:
  Political Issues
  Nationalities
  Ethnic Disputes
  Border Disputes
  Entire former USSR
  Russia
  Tajikistan

Specialists: Daniel Pipes, Islam and Turkic peoples, David Satter, Alvin Z. Rubinstein, Former USSR. Martha Brill Olcott, Former USSR, (esp. Central Asia). Rens Lee, Drug Trafficking in Central Asia. Herb Levine, Soviet Economy.

Resources: Journal: **Orbis: A Journal of World Affairs** (4/year), Books: **In Search of Civil Society** (1990), **The Soviet War in Afghanistan** (1991). Speakers Bureau, Conferences, Reports or Studies, Staff Available to Speak.

FORUM FOR U.S.-SOVIET DIALOGUE
815 Connecticut Ave., N.W.
Suite 800
Washington, DC 20006
(703) 534-8917: Telephone
(202) 833-8082: Fax
Mark Habeeb, Chair

Purpose: To sponsor, organize, and administer a reciprocal program of educational and cultural exchange with groups in the countries of the former Soviet Union to discuss issues and problems of mutual concern.

Project Goals: To sponsor an annual conference of mid-career professionals from the United States and the states of the former Soviet Union.

Information Strengths:
- Political Issues
- Economics
- Military Issues
- Entire former USSR
- Georgia
- Russia

Specialists: Dr. Mark Habeeb, Negotiations. Dr. Dan Caldwell, Arms Control issues. Prof. Paul Stephan, Legal Issues. Dr. James O'Rourke, Law and Government. Mr. Michael Krepon, Arms Control.

Resources: Newsletter: *Forum Newsletter* (1/year), Magazine or Journal, Issue Summaries, Conferences, Staff Available to Speak.

FREEDOM HOUSE
48 East 21st St.
New York, NY 10010
(212) 473-9691: Telephone
(212) 477-4126: Fax
R. Bruce McColm, Executive Director

Purpose: To promote human rights and democratic institutions throughout the world.

Project Name: **Democracy Corps**
Contact: Penn Kemble
Project Goals: To bring human rights monitors to former USSR.

Information Strengths:
- Political Issues
- New State Governmental Structures
- CIS Governmental Structures
- Development of Democracy
- Economics
- Economic Conversion
- Conversion to Market Economy
- Foreign Aid/Relief Efforts
- Nationalities & Ethnic Disputes
- Border Disputes
- Human Rights Issues
- Entire former USSR

Specialists: George Zarycky, Eastern Europe, Ukraine, Russia and other republics. Ludmilla Thorne, Russia.

Resources: Yearbook: *Freedom in the World*, Magazine or Journal, Conferences, Reports or Studies, Staff Available to Speak.

Additional Information:
- ✧ Sponsors top governmental officials to visit the US Government and media. Contact Ludmilla Thorne for more information.

FYI INFORMATION RESOURCES FOR A CHANGING WORLD
735 8th St., S.E.
Washington, DC 20003
(202) 544-2394: Telephone
(202) 543-9385: Fax
Jonathan J. Halperin, President

Purpose: To provide businesspeople, journalists, institutions, and agencies with timely, accurate information about the former Soviet Union.

Project Goals: To provide information, research, and consulting services related to Soviet business, political, and environmental affairs.

Information Strengths:
- Political Issues
- New State Governmental Structures
- Development of Democracy
- Economics
- Economic Conversion
- Conversion to Market Economy
- Foreign Investment in Businesses
- Foreign Aid/Relief Efforts
- Distribution Problems
- Conversion to Private Property
- Natural Resource Management
- Currency/Monetary Issues
- Civil-Military Relations
- Environment
- Entire former USSR

Specialists: Jonathan J. Halperin, Karen Anderson, Sergei Dascalu.

Resources: Directories: *Soviet Independent Business Directory 1992* (1992); *Oil & Gas USSR; Ukraine Top 100 Exporters.* Library, Conferences, Reports or Studies, Books, Staff Available to Speak.

Additional Information:
- ✧ Also produces resources on Business in the Soviet Region, Environmental and Pollution Control Issues, Agriculture and Food Industry, and other areas.

GEONOMICS INSTITUTE
14 Hillcrest Ave.
Middlebury, VT 05753
(802) 388-9619: Telephone
(802) 388-9627: Fax
Michael P. Claudon, President

Purpose: To accelerate economic reform in the Soviet Union and Eastern Europe.

Project Name: **Gateway Seminar Series**
Project Goals: To transform thoughts/opinions into action/results at the local level. Works to help top policymakers, business people, and regional specialists develop concrete, incentive-based strategies for dealing with reform-related legal, economic, and business policy issues.

Information Strengths:
  Economics
  Conversion to Market Economy
  Foreign Investment in Businesses
  Conversion to Private Property
  Entire former USSR
  Estonia
  Latvia
  Lithuania
  Russia

Specialists: Michael P. Claudon, Privatization, Food Sector Reform, Macroeconomic Problems, Stabilization, Interrepublic Relations. Vera Matusevich, Land Reform, Cooperatives, Agribusiness, Land Privatization, Government-Enterprise Relations, Interrepublic Relations.

Resources: Newsletter: *Geonomics* (6/year), Reports: *Competing for Soviet Business: Reshaping US Foreign Economic Policy and American Business Attitudes* (1992, report on policy workshop, December 1991), *From Field to Table: Reforming Soviet Agriculture* (10/91), *Doing Business in the Baltics and the Union of Sovereign Republics* (10/91), *Competing for Soviet Business: Reshaping US Foreign Economic Policy and American Business Attitudes* (2/92), *Soviet Energy Policy and Consumption in the 1990's: The Need for New Thinking and Price Reform* (2/92), Conferences, Book: *Putting Food on What Was the Soviet Table* (1992), Staff Available to Speak.

Additional Information:
✧ Most recent seminar was *From Field to Table: Reforming Soviet Agriculture* (October 1991).
✧ Conducts intensive training, people-to-people exchanges, and technical cooperation efforts with specific partners through Demonstration Projects and Local Initiatives.

GEORGE WASHINGTON UNIVERSITY - INSTITUTE FOR SINO-SOVIET STUDIES
601 Gelman Library
2130 H St., NW
Washington, DC 20052
(202) 994-6340: Telephone
(202) 994-5436: Fax
James R. Millar, Director

Purpose: To promote and support scholarly research and communication in Soviet, East European, and East Asian affairs encompassing the disciplines of economics, political science, history, and sociology.

Information Strengths:
  Political Issues
  New State Governmental Structures
  CIS Governmental Structures
  Development of Democracy
  Intra-CIS Treaties/Agreements
  Economics
  Military Spending
  Economic Conversion
  Conversion to Market Economy
  Foreign Investment in Businesses
  Foreign Aid/Relief Efforts
  Distribution Problems
  Conversion to Private Property
  Currency/Monetary Issues
  Military Issues
  Command & Control of Military
  Control of Conventional Weapons
  Civil-Military Relations
  Military Facilities
  Military Conversion
  Independent Armies/Militias
  Compliance with Existing Treaties
  Nationalities & Ethnic Disputes
  Border Disputes
  Human Rights Issues
  Relations with International Organizations
  Entire former USSR

Specialists: James R. Millar, Conversion of Centrally Planned Economies to Market Economies. Muriel Atkin, Muslims in USSR. Charles F. Elliott, Soviet Government, Politics, and Military. Carl A. Linden, Soviet Political Leadership and Factional Politics and Ideology. Vladimir Petrov, Soviet Politics and Government. Richard C. Thornton, American, Soviet and Chinese Foreign Policy and History.

Resources: Library, Conferences, Staff Available to Speak.

Additional Information:
✧ Co-sponsored a conference on *The Social Legacy of Communism* (February 1992).

GLOBAL OUTLOOK
405 Lytton Ave.
Palo Alto, CA 94301
(415) 321-3828: Telephone
(415) 321-0805: Fax
Gloria C. Duffy, President

Purpose: To help the public and its institutions play a more informed role in policymaking on issues affecting international peace and security.

Project Name: **Checks and Balances: The Legislative Role In Creating New Approaches to International Peace and Security in the US and the USSR**

Project Goal: To assist republic legislators in furthering the process of democratization, especially in defense areas, through a series of legislative and academic meetings.

Information Strengths:

> CIS Governmental Structures
> Development of Democracy
> Intra-CIS Treaties/Agreements
> Military Spending
> Economic Conversion
> Distribution Problems
> Conversion to Private Property
> Currency/Monetary Issues
> Military Issues
> Command & Control of Military
> Control of Nuclear & Conventional Weapons
> Civil-Military Relations
> Military Facilities
> Military Conversion
> Independent Armies/Militias
> Compliance with Existing Treaties
> Nationalities & Ethnic Disputes
> Human Rights Issues
> Relations with International Organizations
> Entire former USSR
> Byelarus
> Georgia
> Kazakhstan
> Russia
> Ukraine

Specialists: Gloria Duffy, Arms Control/Republic Defense Policy. Jennifer Lee, Political Happenings in Republics/Republic Defense Policy.

Resources: Issue Summaries: *Reactions of the Supreme Soviet During the August 1991 Coup* (10/91), Reports: *The Supreme Soviet Defense and Security Committee: Limited Oversight Capabilities* (7/91), *Legislative War Powers in the US and the Soviet Union* (10/91), Staff Available to Speak.

Additional Information:
✧ Conducts meetings on Legislative Oversight of Defense Industry Transition, and Legislative Oversight of Nuclear Exports and Nonproliferation.

HARVARD UNIVERSITY - RUSSIAN RESEARCH CENTER
1737 Cambridge St.
Cambridge, MA 02138
(617) 495-4037: Telephone
(617) 495-8319: Fax
Adam B. Ulam, Director

Purpose: To promote research on Russia by providing working facilities for graduate students, post-doctoral scholars, lawyers, diplomats, and journalists.

Information Strengths:
> East-West relations
> US-CIS Relations
> Commonwealth of Independent States

Specialists: Timothy J. Colton, Marshall Goldman, Adam B. Ulam.

Resources: Conferences, Workshops or Seminars, Radio or TV Program, Opinion Essays, Library, Staff Available to Speak, Books.

HELSINKI WATCH
Human Rights Watch
485 5th Ave.
3rd Floor
New York, NY 10017
(212) 972-8400: Telephone
(212) 972-0905: Fax
Jeri Laber, Executive Director

Purpose: To monitor domestic and international compliance with the human rights provisions of the 1975 Helsinki Accords and maintain contact with monitoring groups in Eastern and Western Europe.

Information Strengths:
> Human Rights Issues
> Entire former USSR

Specialists: Jeri Laber, Former Soviet Union.

Resources: Newsletter, Reports or Studies, Books.

Additional Information:
✧ Issued book length report titled *Afghanistan: The Forgotten War Human Rights Abuses and Violations of the Laws of War Since the Soviet Withdrawal* (Feb, 1991).

HOOVER INSTITUTION ON WAR, REVOLUTION, AND PEACE AT STANFORD UNIVERSITY
Stanford, CA 94305-6010
(415) 723-0603: Telephone
(415) 723-1687: Fax
John Raisian, Director

Purpose: To advance research in domestic and international affairs.

Project Name: **The Russian Project**
Project Goals: To assist with privatization and economic reform in Russia. Staff are working with the government of the Russian Federation and with coalminers to help them privatize.

Information Strengths:
>   Political Issues
>   Foreign Policy of the CIS
>   East-West Relations
>   Economic Conversion
>   Conversion to Market Economy
>   Conversion to Private Property
>   Commonwealth of Independent States
>   Russia

Specialists: Michael Bernstam, Edward Lazear, Charles McLure, Judy Shelton.

Resources: Reports or Studies, Library, Reference Materials, Staff Available to Speak.

HUDSON INSTITUTE
Herman Kahn Center
5395 Emerson Way
P.O. Box 26-919
Indianapolis, IN 46226
(317) 545-1000: Telephone
(317) 545-9639: Fax
Dr. Leslie Lenkowsky, President

Purpose: To provide policy-relevant analyses and recommendations to senior public and private decision-makers.

Project Name: **International Baltic Economic Commission**
Contact: Richard Judy
Project Goals: To provide policy recommendations and evaluation, advise the Baltic States of Estonia, Latvia and Lithuania in their reform efforts.

Information Strengths:
>   Political Issues
>   New State Governmental Structures
>   Development of Democracy
>   Economics
>   Military Spending
>   Economic Conversion
>   Conversion to Market Economy
>   Foreign Investment in Businesses
>   Conversion to Private Property
>   Currency/Monetary Issues
>   Military Issues
>   Command & Control of Military
>   Control of Nuclear Weapons

>   Civil-Military Relations
>   Military Facilities
>   Military Conversion
>   Independent Armies/Militias
>   Entire former USSR

Specialists: Richard Judy, Russia USSR Economic and Political Transition, Baltic States, Central Europe. William Odom, USSR Military Armed Forces Reform, Naval and Nuclear Strategy. Mary Fitzgerald, Military Doctrine. Christopher Smart, USSR, Russia, Military Conversion. Jamie Wellik, USSR/Russian Politics, Reform of Military. Gary Geidel, Germany, European Security. Charles Jokay, Hungary, Economic Reform.

Resources: Publication: *Triumph After Trial*, Issue Summaries, Speakers Bureau, Library, Conferences, Newsletter, Reports or Studies, Books, Staff Available to Speak.

Additional Information:
✧   The IBEC consists of 9 commissions/working groups.
✧   Conducts conferences on the Baltic economies and post-Communist Russia.

INSTITUTE FOR EAST-WEST STUDIES
360 Lexington Ave.
13th Floor
New York, NY 10017
(212) 557-2570: Telephone
(212) 949-8043: Fax
John Edwin Mroz, President

Purpose: To support the reconstruction of civil societies in Eastern Europe and the former Soviet Union; to strengthen security, cooperation and integration among the nations in the region as well as with the wider international community; to serve as a catalyst for the analysis of social and economic issues in the region; and to consolidate the transformation process.

Information Strengths:
>   Public Policy Analysis
>   Political Culture in Post-Communist Societies
>   Economic Transition
>   Military Spending
>   Western Assistance to East Central Europe
>   Civic Leadership Development
>   Minorities and Nationalism
>   Security Issues in the New Europe

Resources: Task Force Reports, Public Briefings, Occassional Papers, Meeting Reports.

INSTITUTE FOR FOREIGN POLICY ANALYSIS

675 Massachusetts Ave.
10th Floor
Cambridge, MA 02139
(617) 492-2116: Telephone
(617) 492-8242: Fax
Robert L. Pfaltzgraff, President

Purpose: To provide a forum for the examination of the major national security and foreign policy problems facing the United States in the late twentieth century.

Information Strengths:
>   Political Issues
>   Military Issues
>   Command & Control of Military
>   Control of Conventional Weapons
>   Military Facilities
>   Nationalities
>   Ethnic Disputes
>   Entire former USSR

Specialists: Robert L. Pfaltzgraff, US-Soviet Strategic Relations, Arms Control. Charles M. Perry, East-West Relations. David R. Tanks, Arms Control. Jacquelyn K. Davis.

Resources: Report: *The Soviet Union After Perestroika: Change and Continuity* (Spring 1991). Conferences, Books, Library, Staff Available to Speak.

INSTITUTE FOR INTERNATIONAL ECONOMICS

11 Dupont Circle N.W.
Suite 620
Washington, DC 20036
(202) 328-9000: Telephone
(202) 328-5432: Fax
C. Fred Bergsten, Director

Purpose: A private, nonprofit, nonpartisan research institution for the study and discussion of international economic policy.

Contact: Linda Griffin Kean or Fay Gold

Information Strength:
>   Economics
>   Economic Conversion
>   Conversion to Market Economy
>   Distribution Problems
>   Currency/Monetary Issues

Specialists: John Williamson, Currency (esp. Convertibility), Trade, Current Economic Reform Efforts, Relations of the CIS with the IMF/World Bank. Susan Collins, General Economy, Economic Relations with the West.

Resources: Reports: *From Soviet disUnion Toward Eastern Economic Community* (October 1991), *Eastern Europe and the Soviet Union in the World Economy* (May 1991), *The Economic Opening of Eastern Europe* (May 1991), Books, Staff Available to Speak.

Additional Information:
✧   *The Economics of Soviet Disintegration* is due out in June 1992.

INSTITUTE ON RELIGION AND DEMOCRACY

1331 H St., N.W., Suite 900
Washington, DC 20005-4706
(202) 393-3200: Telephone
(202) 638-4948: Fax
Kent R. Hill, President

Purpose: To promote and educate for responsible religious participation in foreign policy issues.

Project Name: **The Christian Resource Center**
Project Goals: To collect and disseminate information on organizations involved in ministries in the former Soviet Union, as well as various works and ministries related to this region.

Information Strengths:
>   Political Issues
>   Development of Democracy
>   Foreign Aid/Relief Efforts
>   Nationalities & Ethnic Disputes
>   Human Rights Issues
>   Entire former USSR

Specialists: Dr. Kent Hill, Human Rights, Religious Liberty, History, Democratic Development. Rev. Stan DeBoe, Human Rights, Religious Liberty, Relief Aid, Democratic Development.

Resources: Computer Database, Speakers Bureau, Library, Reports or Studies, Staff Available to Speak.

Additional Information:
✧   Dr. Hill will be teaching a twenty-week course on Christian apologetics at Moscow State University, and working with sociologists at the International Center on Human Values and the Academy of Sciences in Moscow through August, 1992.

INTERFLO: A SOVIET TRADE NEWS MONITOR

P.O. Box 42
Maplewood, NJ 07040
(212) 763-9493: Telephone
Paul R. Surovell, Editor and Publisher

Purpose: To publish information on Soviet trade, investment, and joint ventures.

Information Strengths:
>   Commonwealth of Independent States
>   East-West Relations
>   US-CIS Relations
>   East-West Trade

Resources: Newsletter, Staff Available to Speak, Reports or Studies, Clipping Service, Bibliographies.

INTERNATIONAL FREEDOM FOUNDATION

200 G St., N.E.
Suite 300
Washington, DC 20002
(202) 546-5788: Telephone
(202) 546-5488: Fax
Carl Runde, Executive Director

Purpose: To promote freedom throughout the world by demonstrating the benefits of freedom for individuals and societies.

Contact: J. Michael Waller

Project Goals: To promote economic reform and business opportunities in the former USSR, and to provide technical assistance to those in Russia charged with demilitarization, including counseling on establishing a body of patent & copyright laws in keeping with international standards.

Information Strengths:
Political Issues
New State Governmental Structures
CIS Governmental Structures
Development of Democracy
Intra-CIS Treaties/Agreements
Economics
Military Spending
Economic Conversion
Conversion to Market Economy
Foreign Investment in Businesses
Foreign Aid/Relief Efforts
Distribution Problems
Conversion to Private Property
Natural Resource Management
Currency/Monetary Issues
Military Issues
Command & Control of Military
Control of Nuclear & Conventional Weapons
Civil-Military Relations
Military Facilities
Military Conversion
Compliance with Existing Treaties
Nationalities & Ethnic Disputes
Border Disputes
Human Rights Issues
Environment
Relations with International Organizations
Entire former USSR

Specialists: J. Michael Waller, Economics, Military, Nationalities, Law, Business.

Resources: Report: *Soviet Perspectives*, Issue Summaries, On-Line Services, Newsletter, Reports or Studies, Staff Available to Speak.

INTERNATIONAL PHYSICIANS FOR THE PREVENTION OF NUCLEAR WAR

126 Rogers St.
Cambridge, MA 02142
(617) 868-5050: Telephone
(617) 868-2560: Fax
Ralph Fine, Executive Director

Purpose: To mobilize the influence of the medical profession against the threat of nuclear weapons and to inform the medical profession, public, and government leaders about the medical consequences of nuclear war and the nuclear arms race.

Project Name: **Parliamentarians Educational Campaign**

Contact: Peter Zheutlin

Project Goal: To encourage nuclear disarmament in the republics by educating political leaders on the various dangers associated with nuclear weapons possession, development and use.

Informations Strengths:
Economic Conversion
Military Issues
Control of Nuclear Weapons
Environment

Specialists: Katherine Yih, Environmental Impact of Nuclear Weapons Program. Peter Zheutlin, Nuclear Disarmament, Nuclear Testing, Kazakhstan.

Resources: Curricular Materials, Staff Available to Speak.

INTERNATIONAL RESEARCH AND EXCHANGES BOARD

126 Alexander St.
Princeton, NJ 08540-7102
(609) 683-9500: Telephone
(609) 683-1511: Fax
Wesley A. Fisher, Director of Soviet Programs
Vivian T. Abbott, Director of East European Programs

Purpose: To guarantee access by US scholars to research resources in Central and Eastern Europe, the Baltic States, Mongolia, and the Soviet successor states and to encourage scholarly cooperation in the humanities and social sciences with those countries. The core activity is the administration of reciprocal scholarly research exchanges and bilateral cooperative projects.

Information Strengths:
Entire former Soviet Union

Resources: Computer Database, Conferences, Newsletter, Directories, Staff Available to Speak, Bibliographies.

Additional Information:
✧ Established in 1989, IREX/Moscow facilitates appropriate research conditions for US scholars in Moscow.

ISAR

(formerly the Institute for Soviet-American Relations)
1601 Connecticut Ave., NW
Suite 301
Washington, DC 20009
(202) 387-3034: Telephone
(202) 667-3291: Fax
Eliza Klose, Executive Director

Purpose: To support efforts which improve conditions for people in the former USSR by collecting and distributing information about joint activities addressing areas of critical need and encouraging personal initiative and democratic approaches. ISAR focuses on practical projects in areas like sustainable economics and agriculture, technical assistance and aid, the environment and indigenous cultural pride.

Project Name: **International Clearinghouse on the Environment**

Contact: Lynn Richards

Project Goal: To develop rapid exchange of information on environmental legislation required by Soviet environmental groups and newly appointed environmental policy makers, identify American and Soviet experts able to consult on issues of specific concern, facilitate joint projects in a wide variety of areas, and develop an environmental resource library.

Information Strengths:
   Development of Democracy
   Sustainable Economics and agricluture
   Foreign Aid/Relief Efforts
   Natural Resource Management
   Nationalities
   Human Rights Issues
   Environment
   Entire former USSR

Specialists: Eliza Klose, Environment, NGO movement, General Soviet issues. Lynn Richards, Environment. Leanne Grossman, Soviet Economy, General Soviet Issues.

Resources: Directory: *1990 Handbook of Organizations Involved in Soviet-American Relations*, Journal: *Surviving Together* (4/year), Computer Database, Library, Seminars, Staff Available to Speak. Conference report: *Proceedings of the Joint US-USSR NGO Conference on the Environment* (March 1991).

JOHNS HOPKINS UNIVERSITY - THE PAUL H. NITZE SCHOOL OF ADVANCED INTERNATIONAL STUDIES

1740 Massachusetts Ave., NW
Washington, DC 20036
(202) 663-5600: Telephone
(202) 663-5656: Fax
George Packard, Dean

Purpose: To relate academic learning to private and public activities involved in relations among governments and national societies, through research and graduate and mid-career education.

Information Strengths:
   Political Issues
   New State Governmental Structures
   CIS Governmental Structures
   Development of Democracy
   Intra-CIS Treaties/Agreements
   Military Spending
   Military Issues
   Command & Control of Military
   Control of Nuclear & Conventional Weapons
   Nationalities & Ethnic Disputes
   Border Disputes
   Entire former USSR

Specialists: Bruce Parrott, Ilya Prizel, Russian Area & East European Studies. Charles Fairbanks, International Politics. Michael Mandelbaum, American Foreign Policy. Hedrick Smith, former Soviet Union.

Resources: Magazine or Journal, Issue Summaries, Curricular Materials, Newsletter, Books, Staff Available to Speak.

JOINT BALTIC AMERICAN NATIONAL COMMITTEE

P.O. Box 4578
Rockville, MD 20850
(301) 340-1954: Telephone
(301) 309-1406: Fax
Sandra M. Aistars, Director, Public Relations

Purpose: To provide information and assistance to the U.S. on events and concerns of the Baltic Republics.

Project Goals: To provide information on Baltic aid needs, to assist Congress and private interests in developing programs to meet those needs.

Information Strengths:
   Political Issues
   Development of Democracy
   Foreign Aid/Relief Efforts
   Nationalities
   Human Rights Issues
   Estonia
   Latvia
   Lithuania

Specialists: Sandra Aistars, Baltics (General), Latvia. Olgerts Pavlovskis, Latvia. Vince Boris, Lithuania. Mari Ann Rikken, Estonia.

Resources: Baltic Information Hotline: *(301) 340-1112*, Issue Summaries, Speakers Bureau, Newsletter, Staff Available to Speak.

KENNAN INSTITUTE FOR ADVANCED RUSSIAN STUDIES

The Woodrow Wilson Center
370 L'Enfant Promenade, SW
Washington, DC 20024-2518
(202) 287-3400: Telephone
(202) 287-3772: Fax
Blair A. Ruble, Director

Purpose: To improve American expertise and knowledge about Rusian and the Soviet Union and to promote dialogue between academic specialists and policy-makers.

Information Strengths:
> Agriculture
> Archival Research
> The Arts
> Demography
> Economy
> Environmental Issues
> Foreign Policy
> Geography
> Industry and Labor
> Law
> Literature
> Military and Defense Issues
> Nationalities and Ethnic Republics
> Political Analysis/Sovietology
> Popular Culture
> Religion
> Russian History
> Science and Technology
> Social Issues
> Sociology
> Soviet History
> Urban Planning
> Women's Studies
> Entire former USSR

Specialists: Through its residential fellowship program, the Institute fosters advanced research on Russian and the former Soviet Union in the humanities and social sciences by academic scholars and specialists from the government, media, and private sector.

Resources: Reports: *Occasional Papers* (6/year), *Meeting Reports* (22/year), Conference and Special Reports, Special Studies, Reference Volumes, Directories and Guides.

Additional Information:
✧ The Kennan Institute sponsors an extensive program of meetings including weekly Noon Discussions, Seminars and Colloquia, Special Lectures and Evening Dialogues, Informal Lunch Discussions, and Conferences led by Russian and American scholars.

LEGACY INTERNATIONAL

346 Commerce St.
3rd Floor
Alexandria, VA 22314
(703) 549-3630: Telephone
(703) 549-0262: Fax
Ira Kaufman, Executive Director

Purpose: To create opportunities to address controversial issues through cooperation by advancing problem solving through cross-cultural understanding.

Project Name: **Working Group on Environmentally Sound Development of Oil in Russia**

Project Goals: To address the social, economic, and environmental impacts, problems and solutions relating to the development of Russian oil reserves.

Information Strengths:
> Foreign Investment in Businesses
> Natural Resource Management
> Energy
> Environment
> Russia

Specialists: Ira Kaufman, Environment/Development issues related to oil.

Resources: TV Program/Video Tapes, Conferences, Reports or Studies, Staff Available to Speak.

Additional Information:
✧ Working Group brings together international experts, Russian ministry officials, the transnational and Russian oil industries, international and Russian environmental organizations, and indigenous groups.

LITHUANIAN CATHOLIC RELIGIOUS AID

351 Highland Blvd.
Brooklyn, NY 11207
(718) 647-2434: Telephone
(718) 827-6696: Fax

Purpose: To provide material and spiritual aid to Lithuania.

Project Name: **Life For Lithuania/ Books For Lithuania**

Contact: Ruta Virkutis, Director of Special Projects

Project Goals: To supply medical aid to local charitable organizations for mass distribution as well as books and periodicals, and other education materials to schools, universities, and libraries.

Information Strengths:
> Foreign Aid/Relief Efforts
> Lithuania
> Catholic Church in Lithuania

Specialists: Ruta Virkutis, Medical Conditions in Lithuania, Needs In Lithuania Today, Humanitarian Aid. Rev. Casimir Pugevicius, Catholic Church in Lithuania.

Resources: Issue Summaries, Audio-Visuals, Staff Available to Speak.

MONTEREY INSTITUTE OF INTERNATIONAL STUDIES
425 Van Buren St.
Monterey, CA 93940
(408) 647-4193: Telephone
(408) 647-4199: Fax
Dr. William Potter, Director, CIS Nonproliferation Project

Project Name: **CIS Nonproliferation Project**
Contact: Gary T. Gardner, Project Manager
Project Goals: To build a community of nuclear and missile proliferation specialists in the former Soviet Union.

Program Name: **Monitoring CIS Environmental Developments Project**
Contact: Scott Monroe
Program Goals: To be a clearinghouse of journalistic and scientific information relating to environmental concerns in the former Soviet Union.

Information Strengths:
  Political Issues
  Natural Resource Management
  Control of Nuclear Weapons
  Nationalities
  Environment
  Relations with International Organizations

Specialists: Dr. William Potter, Nuclear Trade and Proliferation Issues. Amb. Roland Timerbaev, Nuclear Proliferation, CIS and International Organizations. Anna Scherbakova, CIS Environmental Issues and Nationalities Questions.

Resources: Report: *Russian Nuclear Brain Drain: A Chronology of News Reports,* (2/92), Periodical: *CIS Environmental Watch.* Computer Database, Issue Summaries, Library, Conferences, On-Line Services, Curricular Materials,

Additional Information:
✧ The Enviromental Developments project, aided by Russian and US organizations and government agencies, maintains a database of Russian and English language articles and documents on environmental problems in the CIS.
✧ Organizing a conference "The Nonproliferation Predicament in the Former Soviet Union," April 6-9, 1992, in Monterey, CA.

NATIONAL ENDOWMENT FOR DEMOCRACY
1101 15th St., NW
Washington, DC 20005
(202) 293-9072: Telephone
(202) 223-6042: Fax
Carl Gershman, President

Purpose: To award grants to private organizations involved in democratic development abroad, including the areas of democratic governance and political processes, pluralism, international cooperation, education, culture, and communications.

Information Strengths:
  Development of Democracy
  Nationalities
  Entire former USSR

Specialists: Dr. Nadia Diuk, Nationalities. Carl Gershman, Democratic Institution-Building.

Resources: Reports or Studies, Staff Available to Speak.

NATURAL RESOURCES DEFENSE COUNCIL
1350 New York Ave., N.W.
Washington, DC 20005
(202) 783-7800: Telephone
(202) 783-5917: Fax
John H. Adams, Executive Director

Purpose: To design and advocate solutions to critical environmental problems, to promote nuclear arms reduction, and to conduct research on nuclear arms stockpiles and production facilities around the world.

Project Name: **Nuclear Program in the CIS**
Contact: Thomas Cochran, Nuclear Project Director
Project Goals: To promote 1) verified storage and dismantlement of former Soviet nuclear weapons; 2) storage of surplus military and civil stocks of plutonium and highly-enriched uranium under international safeguards; 3) a ban on underground nuclear explosions and alternative employment opportunities for weapons laboratory scientists; 4) direct disposal of nuclear spent fuel without reprocessing; 5) improved legislative and regulatory controls on nuclear energy, technology exports, and radioactive waste management.

Information Strengths:
  Natural Resource Management
  Control of Nuclear Weapons
  Military Facilities
  Intra-CIS Treaties-Agreements
  Compliance with Existing Treaties
  Relations with International Organizations
  Commonwealth of Independent States
  Byelarus
  Kazakhstan
  Russia
  Ukraine

Specialists: Thomas Cochran, Verification Methods, Weapons Systems. Robert S. Norris, Nuclear Weapons, Christopher Paine, Verification.

Resources: Reports or Studies, Books, Audio-Visuals, Workshops or Seminars, Issue Summaries, Opinion Essays, Staff Available to Speak.

Additional Information:
✧ Jointly with the Federation of American Scientists, NRDC has co-sponsored a series of international workshops, involving senior CIS nuclear complex, defense, and foreign ministry officials, on verified storage, dismantlement and final disposal of nuclear weapons and fissile material. The fourth such workshop was held in Washington, DC in late February 1992.
✧ In cooperation with the Soviet Academy of Sciences (SAS), NRDC installed in 1986 a regional seismic monitoring network around the main Soviet nuclear test site in eastern Kazakhstan.
✧ In September 1987, NRDC and the SAS arranged for a Congressional delegation to visit the controversial Kransnoyarsk radar.

New York Univeristy - Center for War, Peace, and the News Media
10 Washington Place
New York, NY 10003
(212) 998-7960: Telephone
(212) 995-4143: Fax
Robert Karl Manoff, Director

Purpose: To study and improve reporting of international security issues by assessing the accuracy, thouroughness, and reliability of the media coverage and, in turn, employing its research to assist journalists improve the coverage.

Project Name: **Moscow Journalism Center**
Contact: Robert Karl Manoff, Co-Chair, Julie Raskin, CIS Programs Coordinator
Project Goals: To assist and promote the process of democratization and professionalization in the CIS media by providing information resources, training, subject-specific seminars, and publications throughout the former Soviet Union.

Resources: On-line computer reference service to allow reporters to access electronic databases in the US and Western Europe. Library of key reference works and journals for reporters. Briefing programs, seminars and conferences on economic, political, environmental, and security issues. Weekly bulletin of information on resources, newly released statistics and policy statements. Information clearinghouse for all media-assis-

tance programs in the CIS for the use of press in identifying fellowship and sources of aid. Forthcoming Directory: *Who's Who in the CIS Media: A Detailed Guide to news Organizations and Journalists, Beat-by-Beat.*

Additional Information:
✧ The Moscow Center encourages proposals for briefings, seminar programs, and press conferences by American organizations interested in reaching the CIS press, and through it the public and policy communities.
✧ The Center for War, Peace, and the News Media has been active in the Soivet Union since 1985, and has held annual meetings in Moscow for the American press corps.
✧ The Center is organizing a program of briefings and information for the CIS press corps on nuclear proliferation and related issues, to be offered in Byelarus, Kazakhstan, Russia, and Ukraine in fall 1992.
✧ "Democratic Russia: A First Anniversary Assessment," conference to be held in fall 1992 with the Foreign Correspondent's Association (Moscow).

Peace Links
747 8th St., S.E.
Washington, DC 20003
(202) 544-0805: Telephone
(202) 544-0809: Fax
Carol Williams, Executive Director

Purpose: To work through traditional community groups, civic clubs, and schools to foster women's awareness and participation in organizing to prevent nuclear war and seek alternative and peaceful ways to resolve conflicts and to sponsor exchanges with American and women of the CIS.

Project Name: **Pen Pals: US/USSR Letter Exchange**
Project Goals: To encourage grassroots citizens of both countries to find common interests and acknowledge the richness in their differences.

Information Strengths:
Entire former USSR

Resources: Newsletter: *The Connection* (2/year), Staff Available to Speak.

PERHAPS . . . KIDS MEETING KIDS CAN MAKE A DIFFERENCE

380 Riverside Dr.
Box 8H
New York, NY 10025
(212) 662-2327: Telephone
Mary Sochet and Marvin Sochet, Co-Chairpersons

Purpose: To help kids around the world find ways to meet and interact with one another creating a safer world for all.

Contact: Mary Sochet or Marvin Sochet

Project Goals: Bringing children together from all nations for the sake of creating a better (more peaceful, socially just) world.

Information Strengths:
   Childrens Rights Issues
   What Kids can do to make the World Better

Resources: Conferences: *International Children's Congress* (annual), Kids' Newsletter, Kids' Computer Network, Kids Available to Speak.

Additional Information:
✧   Sponsors ongoing Kids PenPal Exchanges and Kids Peace Exchanges.

RAND/UCLA CENTER FOR SOVIET STUDIES

1700 Main St.
Santa Monica, CA 90406-2138
(213) 393-0411: Telephone
(213) 393-4818: Fax
Abraham Becker, Director

Purpose: To conduct training and research in Soviet Studies.

Information Strengths:
   Arms Control Negotiations
   US-CIS Relations
   US-USSR Summits
   Foreign Policy of the CIS
   Commonwealth of Independent States
   Crisis Management

Specialists: Abraham Becker, Director. Hans Rogger, Co-Director. Arnold Horelick.

Resources: Staff Available to Speak, Reports or Studies, Books, Conferences.

ROCKFORD INSTITUTE

934 North Main St.
Rockford, IL 61103
(815) 964-5053: Telephone
(815) 965-1826: Fax
Allan C. Carlson, President

Purpose: To influence the moral and intellectual forces that shape social and cultural trends and public issues.

Contact: Michael Warder

Project Goals: To better understand the political, economic, religious and cultural changes that are occurring in the former Soviet Union.

Information Strengths:
   Political Issues
   Development of Democracy
   Economics
   Foreign Aid/Relief Efforts
   Military Issues
   Nationalities & Ethnic Disputes
   Entire former USSR

Specialists: Michael Warder, Political Change, Economics and Cultural Change, Nationalities, US perception of former Soviet Union.

Resources: Issue Summaries, Speakers Bureau, Reports or Studies, Staff Available to Speak.

SEARCH FOR COMMON GROUND

2005 Massachusetts Ave., N.W.
Washington, DC 20036
(202) 265-4300: Telephone
(202) 232-6718: Fax
John Marks, President

Purpose: To find workable solutions to divisive national and international programs by channeling conflict toward constructive outcomes and, hence, to build a more secure and peaceful world.

Project Name: **The Initiative for Conflict Management in Russia**
Contact: Gary Dibianco, Coordinator
Project Goals: To promote peaceful means for managing conflict in Russian labor disputes, among ethnic groups, within the armed forces, between police and demonstrators, and in the nuclear power industry.

Specialists: John Marks, Gary Dibianco.

Resources: Conferences, Newsletter, Staff Available to Speak.

Additional Information:
✧   The project has, to date, provided advice and training for the setting up of a labor mediation service for the Russian government and conducted seminars and trainings in ethnic conflict resolution. During the next year, the project will greatly expand the number of such seminars and training programs.

UNITED NATIONS ASSOCIATION OF THE USA

485 Fifth Avenue
New York, NY 10017-6104
(212) 697-3232: Telephone
(212) 682-9185: Fax
Edward C. Luck, President

Purpose: To strengthen public knowledge about the United Nations, increase effectiveness of international organizations, and promote constructive U.S. policies on matters of global concern.

Project Name: **Parallel Studies Program of the Commonwealth of Independent States (CIS)**

Contact: Toby Trister Gati, Senior Vice President

Project goals: To determine what role the new independent states of the CIS will play in international organizations and to create special mechanisms for incorporating their needs and concerns into the existing international system. This will be done through research and analysis, seminars, policy discussions, scholarly exchanges between existing ties with Russian, Byelorussian, Ukrainian, and Kazakhstan UN Associations, and by establishing ties with UNA's and other NGO's in the other republics.

Information Strengths:
>   Political Issues
>   Development of Democracy
>   Economics
>   Foreign Aid/Relief Efforts
>   Military Issues
>   Nationalities & Ethnic Disputes
>   Border Disputes
>   Human Rights Issues
>   Environment
>   Relations with International Organizations
>   Entire former USSR
>   Byelarus
>   Kazakhstan
>   Kyrgyzstan
>   Russia
>   Ukraine

Specialists: Toby Trister Gati, International Organizations, the Russian Federation. Edward C. Luck, International Organization. Felice Gaer, Human Rights.

Resources: Reports: *Will the Soviet Republics Join the United Nations, The Future of Collective Security: Reflections on the Aftermath of the Gulf War and the Breakup of the Soviet Union.* Summary of Discussion: *U.S..-Soviet Joint Working Group on the Future of the U.N.* Conference: "International Organizations, Collective Security, and the Future of the CIS," Spring 1992. Issue Summaries, Staff Available to Speak.

UNITED STATES INSTITUTE OF PEACE

1550 M St., NW
Suite 700
Washington, DC 20005
(202) 457-1700: Telephone
(202) 429-6063: Fax
Samuel Lewis, President

Purpose: To enhance knowledge and skills in the management of international conflict and in the search for peace among nations.

Project Name: **Study Group on the Southern Tier of the Former Soviet Republics**

Contact: Robert B. Oakley, Kenneth M. Jensen

Project Goals: To provide policy-relevant analysis on the post-Soviet Transcaucasia (including especially Nagorno-Karabakh) and Central Asia.

Information Strengths:
>   Political Issues
>   New State Government Structures
>   Development of Democracy
>   Intra-CIS Treaties/Agreements
>   Economics
>   Conversion to Market Economy
>   Foreign Investment in Business
>   Foreign Aid/Relief Efforts
>   Conversion to Private Property
>   Military Issues
>   Control of Nuclear Weapons
>   Independent Armies
>   Nationalities & Ethnic Disputes
>   Border Disputes
>   Human Rights Issues .
>   Environment
>   Relations with International Organizations
>   Entire former USSR
>   Armenia
>   Azerbaijan
>   Kazakhstan
>   Kyrgyzstan
>   Russia
>   Tajikistan
>   Turkmenistan
>   Uzbekistan

Specialists: Robert B. Oakley, Afghanistan and post-Soviet Central Asia, Islamic States and post-Soviet Central Asia. Kenneth M. Jensen, Trancaucasia and post-Soviet Central Asia.

Resources: Issue Summaries, Conferences, Reports or Studies.

Additional Information:
>   ✧   USIP is holding a public study group conference April 13 on Nagorno-Karabakh and lessons from Afghanistan for post-Soviet Central Asia.

UNIVERSITY OF CALIFORNIA - INSTITUTE ON GLOBAL CONFLICT AND COOPERATION

9500 Gilman Dr.
La Jolla, CA 92093-0518
(619) 534-3352: Telephone
(619) 534-7655: Fax
Susan L. Shirk, Acting Director

Purpose: To encourage research and teaching on international conflict and cooperation, and coordinate research in this field for the University of California system.

Information Strengths:
    Arms Control & Disarmament
    Conflict Resolution
    International Security
    Asia & Pacific
    Nuclear Proliferation
    International Environmental Policy
    Foreign Policy

Resources: Curricular Materials, Workshops or Seminars, Newsletter, Reports or Studies, Books, Conferences, Staff Available to Speak.

UNIVERSITY OF GEORGIA - CENTER FOR EAST-WEST TRADE POLICY

204 Baldwin Hall
Athens, GA 30602
(404) 542-2985: Telephone
(404) 542-4421: Fax
Martin Hillenbrand, Co-Director
Gary Bertsch, Co-Director

Purpose: To contribute to enlightened East-West economic policies and business practices through its research and teaching programs.

Project Name: **Export Controls in the 1990's**
Contact: Dr. Gary K. Bertsch
Project Goals: To promote research and dialogue on export controls in the changing security environment of the 1990's.

Information Strengths:
    Control of Nuclear & Conventional Weapons
    Military Conversion
    Relations with International Organizations
    Entire former USSR

Specialists: Dr. Gary K. Bertsch, CIS Export Controls. Dr. Richard T. Cupitt, Multilateral Export Control Organizations. Dr. Steven Elliott-Gower, Conventional Arms Transfers. Dr. Martin J. Hillenbrand, Germany. Samuel E. Watson, CIS Export Controls, Political Issues.

Resources: Reports: *Export Controls in Transition* (1992), *International Cooperation on Nonproliferation Export Controls.* Library, Conferences, Books, Staff Available to Speak.

UNIVERSITY OF ILLINOIS AT URBANA-CHAMPAIGN - RUSSIAN AND EAST EUROPEAN CENTER

104 International Studies Building
910 South 5th St.
Champaign, IL 61820
(217) 333-1244: Telephone
(217) 244-2429: Fax
Diane P. Koenker, Director

Purpose: To support teaching and research activities in the field of Russian and East European studies.

Information Strengths:
    Political Issues
    New State Governmental Structures
    CIS Governmental Structures
    Development of Democracy
    Intra-CIS Treaties/Agreements
    Military Spending
    Military Issues
    Command & Control of Military
    Control of Nuclear & Conventional Weapons
    Civil-Military Relations
    Military Facilities
    Military Conversion
    Independent Armies/Militias
    Compliance with Existing Treaties
    Nationalities & Ethnic Disputes
    Environment
    Entire former USSR
    Kazakhstan
    Kyrgyzstan
    Russia
    Tajikistan
    Turkmenistan
    Ukraine
    Uzbekistan

Resources: Speakers Bureau, Library, Conferences, Curricular Materials, Staff Available to Speak.

Additional Information:
✧ Offers *Summer Research Laboratory on Russia and Eastern Europe* for scholars who wish to use the resources of the U of I Library for independent research. The Lab organizes numerous Workshops and Discussion Groups on various aspects of the former Soviet Union and Eastern Europe.
✧ Provides *Foreign Language and Area Studies Fellowships* for outstanding graduate studies.

UNIVERSITY OF MICHIGAN, DEARBORN - SOCIETY FOR ARMENIAN STUDIES

4901 Evergreen Rd.
Dearborn, MI 48128-1491
(313) 593-5181: Telephone
(313) 593-5452: Fax
Dennis R. Papazian, Director

Purpose: To promote the study of Armenian culture and society and facilitate the exchange of scholarly information pertaining to Armenian studies around the world.

Project Name: **Armenian Research Center**
Project Goals: To keep abreast of political/economic events in the former USSR, with particular emphasis on Russia, Armenia, Azerbaijan and Georgia.

Information Strengths:
- Political Issues
- New State Governmental Structures
- CIS Governmental Structures
- Intra-CIS Treaties/Agreements
- Economics
- Conversion to Market Economy
- Foreign Aid/Relief Efforts
- Distribution Problems
- Conversion to Private Property
- Independent Armies/Militias
- Nationalities & Ethnic Disputes
- Border Disputes
- Human Rights Issues
- Relations with International Organizations
- Entire former USSR
- Armenia
- Azerbaijan
- Georgia
- Russia

Specialists: Dennis R. Papazian, Former USSR, Armenia, History and Politics.

Resources: Computer Database, Speakers Bureau, Library, Conferences, Reports or Studies, Directories, Staff Available to Speak.

WOMEN FOR MEANINGFUL SUMMITS

1819 H St., NW
Suite 640
Washington, DC 20006
(202) 393-1009: Telephone
Linda Weber, Chair

Purpose: To empower more women to participate in creating a more just and peaceful world.

Information Strengths:
- Political Issues
- Military Issues
- Control of Nuclear Weapons
- Control of Conventional Weapons
- Environment
- Relations with International Organizations
- Armenia
- Russia

Specialists: Sarah Harder, International Organizations. Natalie Goldring (with BASIC), Military/Weapons. Edith Villastrigo, Comprehensive Test Ban. Bella Abzug, Claire Greensfelder, Environment.

Resources: Issue Summaries, Newsletter, Reports or Studies, Staff Available to Speak.

WORLD WITHOUT WAR COUNCIL

1730 Martin Luther King Jr. Way
Berkeley, CA 94709
(510) 845-1992: Telephone
(510) 845-5721: Fax
Robert Pickus, President

Purpose: To make our country a leader in progress toward a world that resolves international conflict without war by building richer, stronger, wiser, and better linked non-governmental organizations in America.

Project Name: **Civil Society: US/CIS**
Contact: Holt Ruffin or Robert Pickus
Project Goal: To introduce those building an independent sector in the CIS to American organizations who might be interested in a supportive linkage.

Information Strengths:
- Political Issues
- New State Governmental Structures
- CIS Governmental Structures
- Development of Democracy
- Intra-CIS Treaties/Agreements
- Conversion to Market Economy
- Control of Nuclear & Conventional Weapons
- Compliance with Existing Treaties
- Nationalities & Ethnic Disputes
- Human Rights Issues
- Relations with International Organizations
- Non-Governmental Organizations
- Conscience & War
- Civic Education
- Georgia
- Lithuania
- Ukraine

Resources: Computer Database, Directories, Staff Available to Speak.

Additional Organizations

The following organizations are contained in the ACCESS database but did not respond to a survey in time to include full information in this directory. Each focuses on the former Soviet Union, US-Soviet relations, or East-West relations. Information listed here is name, address, telephone and fax numbers, and director's name, if available. For additional information, contact ACCESS or the organization.

Academy of Political Science
475 Riverside Dr.
Suite 1274
New York, NY 10115
Telephone: (212) 870-2500
Fax: (212) 870-2202
Frank J. Macchiarola, President

Air University Center for Aerospace
Doctrine, Research, and Education
- Airpower Research Institute
Maxwell Air Force Base
Montgomery, AL 36112-5001
Telephone: (205) 953-6875
Fax: (205) 953-3379
Col. Dennis Drew, USAF, Director

American Defense Foundation
1055 North Fairfax St., 2nd Floor
Alexandria, VA 22314
Telephone: (703) 519-7000
Fax: (703) 519-8627
Michael McDaniel, Exec. Director

American Enterprise Institute for
Public Policy Research
1150 17th St., N.W.
Washington, DC 20036
Telephone: (202) 862-5800
Fax: (202) 862-7178
Christopher C. DeMuth, President

American Friends Service Commit-
tee
1501 Cherry St.
Philadelphia, PA 19102
Telephone: (215) 241-7000
Fax: (215) 864-0104
Asia Bennett, Executive Secretary

American Muslim Council
1212 New York Ave., NW,Suite 525
Washington, DC 20005
Telephone: (202) 789-2262
Fax: (202) 789-2550
Abdurahman Alamoudi, Executive
Director

American Security Council
c/o Washington Communications
Center
Boston, VA 22713
Telephone: (703) 547-1776
John M. Fisher, Director

Armenian National Committee
419A West Colorado, Suite 3
Glendale, CA 91204
Telephone: (818) 500-1918

Bethesda Institute for Soviet Studies
4400 East-West Highway, Suite 806
Bethesda, MD 20814
Telephone: (301) 652-2722

Bridges for Peace
The Norwich Center Inc.
P.O. Box 710
Norwich, VT 05055
Telephone: (802) 649-1000
Fax: (802) 649-2003
Richard Hough-Ross, Executive
Vice President

Capitals Citizen's Exchange
2001 S St., N.W.. Suite 530
Washington, DC 20009
Telephone: (202) 462-5062
Kathleen Donner, Executive Director

Center for Defense Information
1500 Massachusetts Ave., N.W.
Washington, DC 20005
Telephone: (202) 862-0700
Fax: (202) 862-0708
Gene R. La Rocque, USN (Ret.),
Director

Center for Democracy
1101 15th St., N.W., Suite 505
Washington, DC 20005
Telephone: (202) 429-9141
Fax: (202) 293-1768
Allen Weinstein, President

Center for Democracy in the USSR
358 West 30th St., Suite 1-A
New York, NY 10001
Fax: (212) 594-7611
Eduard Gudava, Executive Director

Center for National Policy
317 Massachusetts Ave., NE
Suite 300
Washington, DC 20002
Telephone: (202) 546-9300
Fax: (202) 546-5789
Madeleine Albright, President

Center for Naval Analyses
4401 Ford Ave.
Alexandria, VA 22302
Telephone: (703) 824-2000

Center for Psychosocial Issues in
the Nuclear Age
475 Riverside Dr., Room 634
New York, NY 10115
Telephone: (212) 870-2980
Fax: (914) 235-4403
Harris Peck, M.D., Director

Center for Security Policy
1250 24th St., N.W., Suite 600
Washington, DC 20037
Telephone: (202) 466-0515
Fax: (202) 466-0518
Frank J. Gaffney, Jr., Director

Center for Soviet-American Dialogue
615 2nd Ave., Suite 110
Seattle, WA 98104
Telephone: (215) 965-3036

Chicago Council on Foreign Rela-
tions
116 South Michigan Ave.
Chicago, IL 60603
Telephone: (312) 726-3860
Fax: (312) 726-4491
John E. Reilly, President

Churches' Center for Theology and
Public Policy
4500 Massachusetts Ave., N.W.
Washington, DC 20016-5690
Telephone: (202) 885-9100
James A. Nash, Executive Director

Citizen Exchange Council
12 West 31st St., 4th Floor
New York, NY 10001
Telephone: (212) 643-1985
Fax: (212) 643-1996
Michael Brainerd, President

Committee for National Security
1601 Conn. Ave., NW, Suite 302
Washington, DC 20009
Telephone: (202) 745-2450
Fax: (202) 387-6298
John Parachini, Director

Council for the Defense of Freedom
1275 K St., N.W., Suite 1150
Washington, DC 20005
Telephone: (202) 371-6710
Fax: (202) 371-9054
Donald Irvine, Director

Council on USA-GDR Relations
1267 Newton St., N.E.
Washington, DC 20017
Telephone: (202) 529-0140
Andrew Lang, Director

Duke University - Center for Trade,
Investment, and Communications
2114 Campus Dr.
Durham, NC 27706
Telephone: (919) 684-5551
Fax: (919) 684-8749
Jerry F. Hough, Director

Fairness & Accuracy In Reporting
130 West 25th St.
New York, NY 10001
Telephone: (212) 633-6700
Fax: (212) 727-7668
Jeff Cohen, President

Five College Program in Peace and
World Security Studies
c/o Hampshire College
Social Science Office
Amherst, MA 01002
Telephone: (413) 549-4600
Michael Klare, Director

Forum for U.S.-Soviet Dialogue
815 Connecticut Ave., N.W.
Suite 800
Washington, DC 20006
Telephone: (703) 534-8917
Fax: (202) 833-8082
Mark Habeeb, Chair

Fourth Freedom Forum
803 North Main St.
Goshen, IN 46526
Telephone: (219) 534-3402
Fax: (219) 534-4937
Marc Hardy, Executive Director

Friends Committee on National Leg-
islation
245 2nd St., N.E.
Washington, DC 20002-5795
Telephone: (202) 547-6000
Fax: (202) 547-6019
Joe Volk, Executive Secretary

George Washington University -
Security Policy Studies Program
Elliott School of International Affairs
Washington, DC 20052
Telephone: (202) 994-6425
Fax: (202) 994-0458
Ronald Spector, Director

Georgia Institute of Technology -
International Affairs Department
School of Social Sciences
Atlanta, GA 30332
Telephone: (404) 894-3195
Fax: (404) 853-0535
Daniel Papp, Director

Georgian Association in USA
136 E. 55th St., #3C
New York, NY 10022
Telephone: (212) 308-9433

Global Options
P.O. Box 40601
San Francisco, CA 94140
Telephone: (415) 550-1703
Cecilia O'Leary, President

Harvard University - Center for Inter-
national Affairs
1737 Cambridge St.
Cambridge, MA 02138
Telephone: (617) 495-4420
Fax: (617) 495-8292
Joseph Nye, Director

Harvard University - Nuclear Nego-
tiation Project
Harvard Law School
513 Pound Hall
Cambridge, MA 02138
Telephone: (617) 495-1684
William L. Ury, Director

Harvard University - Program on Ne-
gotiation
Harvard Law School
500 Pound Hall
Cambridge, MA 02138
Telephone: (617) 495-1684
Jeffrey Rubin, Executive Director

Heritage Foundation
214 Massachusetts Ave., N.E.
Washington, DC 20002
Telephone: (202) 546-4400
Fax: (202) 546-8328
Edwin Feulner, Jr., President

Institute for International Coopera-
tion and Development
P.O. Box 103
Williamstown, MA 01267
Telephone: (413) 458-9828
Fax: (413) 458-9466
Michael Norling, Executive Director

Institute for Peace and Justice
4144 Lindell, Suite 122
St Louis, MO 63108
Telephone: (314) 533-4445
James McGinnis, Director

Institute for Policy Studies
1601 Connecticut Ave., N.W.
5th floor
Washington, DC 20009
Telephone: (202) 234-9382
Fax: (202) 387-7915
Richard Healey, Director

International Foreign Policy
Association
1329 Noriega St.. Suite 207
San Francisco, CA 94122
Telephone: (415) 665-1345
Fax: (415) 665-1348

International Peace Walk
4521 Campus Dr., Suite 211
Irvine, CA 92715
Telephone: (714) 856-0200
Allan Affeldt, President

International Security Council
1155 15th St., N.W., Suite 502
Washington, DC 20005
Telephone: (202) 828-0802
Fax: (202) 429-2563
Joseph Churba, President

International Studies Association
The David M. Kennedy Center
216 HRCB
Brigham Young University
Provo, UT 84602
Telephone: (801) 378-5459
Fax: (801) 378-7075
W. Ladd Hollist, Executive Director

Jamestown Foundation
1528 18th St., N.W.
Washington, DC 20036
Telephone: (202) 483-8888
Fax: (202) 483-8337
William W. Geimer, President

Johns Hopkins University - Ameri-
can Institute for Contemporary
German Studies
11 Dupont Circle, N.W., Suite 350
Washington, DC 20036
Telephone: (202) 332-9312
Fax: (202) 265-9531
Robert G. Livingston, Director

Kent State University - Lyman L.
Lemnitzer Center for NATO and
European Community Studies
124 Bowman Hall
Kent, OH 44242-0001
Telephone: (216) 672-7980
Fax: (216) 672-4025
Lawrence W. Kaplan, Director

Kompass Resources International
1635 17th St., N.W., Suite 22
Washington, DC 20009
Telephone: (202) 332-1145
Fax: (202) 234-4953
Melissa L. Stone, Executive Director

Lombard Mennonite Peace Center
528 East Madison
Lombard, IL 60148
Telephone: (708) 627-5310
Fax: (708) 627-9893
Richard G. Blackburn, Director

National Bureau of Asian Research
715 SAFECO Plaza
Seattle, WA 98185
Telephone: (206) 632-7370
Fax: (206) 632-7487
Richard J. Ellings, Exec. Director

National Council of American-Soviet
Friendship
745 Leader Bldg.
Cleveland, OH 44114
Telephone: (216) 861-5542
Alan Thompson, Director

National Institute for Public Policy
3031 Javier Rd., Suite 300
Fairfax, VA 22031-4662
Telephone: (703) 698-0563
Fax: (703) 698-0566
Colin S. Gray, President

National Republican Institute for
International Affairs
1212 New York Ave., NW, Suite 900
Washington, DC 20005
Telephone: (202) 408-9450
Fax: (202) 408-9462
Keith Schuette, President

National Research Council - Com-
mittee on International
Conflict and Cooperation
2101 Constitution Ave., NW
184 Harris Bldg.
Washington, DC 20418
Telephone: (202) 334-3005
Fax: (202) 334-3829
Paul C. Stern, Study Director

Network of Women in Slavic Studies
P.O. Box 20287
Alexandria, VA 22320
Telephone: (703) 548-5877
Jacqueline Hess, President

Ohio State University - Mershon
Center
199 West 10th Ave.
Columbus, OH 43201-2399
Telephone: (614) 292-1681
Fax: (614) 292-2407
Charles Hermann, Director

Peace Child Foundation
9502 B Lee Highway
Fairfax, VA 22031
Telephone: (703) 385-4494
Fax: (703) 273-6568
Mark Sklarow, Executive Director

Public Agenda Foundation
6 East 39th St.
New York, NY 10016
Telephone: (212) 686-6610
Fax: (212) 889-3461

RAND
1700 Main St.
Santa Monica, CA 90406-2138
Telephone: (213) 393-0411
Fax: (213) 393-4818
James Thomson, President

Samantha Smith Foundation
9 Union St.
Hallowell, ME 04347
Telephone: (207) 626-3415
Jane G. Smith, Chair of the Board

Sister Cities International
120 South Payne St.
Alexandria, VA 22314
Telephone: (703) 836-3535
Fax: (703) 836-4815
Thomas W. Gittins, Executive Vice
President

Soviet-American Exchange Center
345 Franklin
San Francisco, CA 94102
Telephone: (415) 563-4731
James A. Garrison, Exec. Director

Stanford University - American As-
sociation for the Advancement of
Slavic Studies
128 Encina Commons
Stanford, CA 94305
Telephone: (415) 723-9668
Fax: (415) 725-7737
Dorothy Atkinson, Exec. Director

Stanford University - Stanford Program on International and Cross-Cultural Education
Littlefield Center, Room 14
300 Lasuen St.
Stanford, CA 94305
Telephone: (415) 723-1114
Fax: (415) 723-6784
Jane Boston, Director

Stanley Foundation
216 Sycamore St., Suite 500
Muscatine, IA 52761
Telephone: (319) 264-1500
Fax: (319) 264-0864

Syracuse University - Program on the Analysis and Resolution of Conflicts
Maxwell School of Citizenship and Public Affairs
712 Ostrom Ave.
Syracuse, NY 13244-4400
Telephone: (315) 443-2367
Fax: (315) 443-3818
Louis Kriesberg, Director

Tufts University - Nuclear Age History and Humanities Center
26 Winthrop St.
Medford, MA 02155
Telephone: (617) 391-0343
Fax: (617) 395-1502
Martin J. Sherwin, Director

US Defense Committee
3238 Wynford Dr.
Fairfax, VA 22031
Telephone: (703) 281-5517
Henry L. Walther, President

US Global Strategy Council
1800 K St., N.W., Suite 1102
Washington, DC 20006
Telephone: (202) 466-6029
Fax: (202) 466-0109
Ray S. Cline, Chairman

US-USSR Trade and Economic Council
805 Third Avenue
New York, NY 10022
Telephone: (212) 644-4550

United Baltic Appeal
115 West 183rd St.
Bronx, NY 10453
Telephone: (212) 367-8802

University of California at Berkeley - Institute of International Studies
215 Moses Hall
Berkeley, CA 94720
Telephone: (510) 642-2472
Fax: (510) 642-9493
Harry Kreisler, Executive Director

University of Illinois at Urbana-Champaign - Program in Arms Control, Disarmament and International Security
330 Davenport Hall
607 South Mathews St.
Urbana, IL 61801
Telephone: (217) 333-7086
Fax: (217) 244-5157
Jeremiah D. Sullivan, Director

University of Kentucky - Patterson School of Diplomacy and International Commerce
Patterson Tower, Suite 455
Lexington, KY 40506-0027
Telephone: (606) 257-4666
Fax: (606) 257-4676
Vincent Davis, Director

University of Maryland - Center for International Development and Conflict Management
Mill Bldg.
College Park, MD 20742
Telephone: (301) 314-7703
Fax: (301) 314-9256

University of Maryland - Center for International Security Studies at Maryland
7100 Baltimore Blvd. Suite 400
College Park, MD 20740
Telephone: (301) 403-8174
Fax: (301) 403-8107
Stephen Crawford, Exec. Director

University of Miami - Institute of Soviet/East European Studies
P.O. Box 248123
Miami, FL 33124
Telephone: (305) 284-5411

University of Michigan - Program for International Peace and Security Research
426 Thompson
Ann Arbor, MI 48109-1220
Telephone: (313) 764-5488
Fax: (313) 764-3341
William Zimmerman, Co-Director

University of Pittsburgh - Ridgway Center for International Security Studies
4G23 Forbes Quadrangle
Pittsburgh, PA 15260
Telephone: (412) 648-7408
Fax: (412) 648-2199
Phil Williams, Director

University of Southern California - Center for International Studies
Social Sciences Building Room B1
Los Angeles, CA 90089-0035
Telephone: (213) 740-4296
Fax: (213) 742-0281
John S. Odell, Director

Veterans for Peace
P.O. Box 3881
Portland, ME 04104
Telephone: (207) 773-1431
Fax: (207) 773-0804
Jerry Genesio, Executive Director

Volunteers For Peace
Tiffany Rd.
Belmont, VT 05730
Telephone: (802) 259-2759
Fax: (802) 259-2922
Peter Coldwell, Executive Director

World Policy Institute
777 UN Plaza
New York, NY 10017
Telephone: (212) 490-0010
Fax: (212) 986-1482

Youth Ambassadors
P.O. Box 5273
Bellingham, WA 98227

TEXTS OF KEY DOCUMENTS AND SPEECHES

LITHUANIA'S DECLARATION OF INDEPENDENCE
DECLARED BY THE LITHUANIAN PARLIAMENT IN VILNIUS ON MARCH 11, 1990

Expressing the will of the people, the Supreme Soviet of the Lithuanian Republic declares and solemnly proclaims the restoration of the exercise of sovereign powers of the Lithuanian state, which were annulled by an alien power in 1940. From now on, Lithuania is once again an independent state.

The February 16, 1918, Act of Independence of the Supreme Council of Lithuania and the May 15, 1920, Constituent Assembly Resolution of the restoration of a democratic Lithuanian state have never lost their legal force and are the constitutional foundation of the Lithuanian state.

The territory of Lithuania is integral and indivisible, and the constitution of any other state has no jurisdiction within it.

The Lithuanian state emphasizes its adherence to universally recognized principles of the inviolability of borders as formulated in Helsinki in 1975 in the Final Act of the Conference on Security and Cooperation in Europe, and guarantees rights of individuals, citizens, and ethnic communities.

The Supreme Council of the Republic of Lithuania, expressing sovereign power, by this act begins to achieve the state's full sovereignty.

DECREE ANNOUNCING THE REMOVAL OF GORBACHEV
SIGNED IN MOSCOW ON AUGUST 19, 1991

In view of Mikhail Sergeyevich Gorbachev's inability, for health reasons, to perform the duties of the U.S.S.R. President and of the transfer of the U.S.S.R. President's powers, in keeping with Paragraph 7, Article 127 of the U.S.S.R. Constitution, to U.S.S.R. Vice President Gennadi Ivanovich Yanayev,

WITH THE AIM OF overcoming the profound and comprehensive crisis, political, ethnic and civil strife, chaos and anarchy that threaten the lives and security of the Soviet Union's citizens and the sovereignty, territory integrity, freedom and independence of our fatherland,

PROCEEDING FROM the results of the nationwide referendum on the preservation of the Union of Soviet Socialist Republics, and

GUIDED BY the vital interests of all ethnic groups living in our fatherland and all Soviet people,
WE RESOLVE:

1. In accordance with Paragraph 3, Article 127, of the U.S.S.R. Constitution and Article 2 of the U.S.S.R. law "on the legal regime of a state of emergency" and with demands by broad popular masses to adopt the most decisive measures to prevent society from sliding into national catastrophe and insure law and order, to declare a state of emergency in some parts of the Soviet Union for six months from 04:00 Moscow time on Aug. 19, 1991.

2. To establish that the Constitution and laws of the U.S.S.R. have unconditional priority throughout the territory of the U.S.S.R.

3. To form a State Committee for the State of Emergency in the U.S.S.R. in order to run the country and effectively exercise the state-of-emergency regime, consisting of:

> O.D. Baklanov, First Deputy Chairman of the U.S.S.R. Defense Council
> V.A. Krhuchkov, chairman of the K.G.B.
> V.S. Pavlov, Prime Minister of the U.S.S.R.
> B.K. Pugo, Interior Minister of the U.S.S.R.
> V.A. Starodutsev, chairman of the Farmer's Union of the U.S.S.R.
> A.I. Tizyakov, president of the Association of State Enterprises and Industrial, Construction, Transport
> and Communications Facilities of the U.S.S.R.
> D.T. Yazov, Defense Minister of the U.S.S.R.
> G.I. Yanayev, Acting President of the U.S.S.R.

4. To establish that the U.S.S.R. State Committee for the State of Emergency's decisions are mandatory for unswerving fulfillment by all agencies of power and administration, officials and citizens throughout the territory of the U.S.S.R.

[Signed by G. Yanayev, V. Pavlov, and O. Baklanov]

Bush's speech the day of the coup against Gorbachev
Speech made in Washington, August 19, 1991

We are deeply disturbed by the events of the last hours in the Soviet Union and condemn the unconstitutional resort to force. While the situation continues to evolve and information remains incomplete, the apparent unconstitutional removal of President Gorbachev, the declaration of a state of emergency, and the deployment of Soviet military forces in Moscow and other cities raise the most serious questions about the future course of the Soviet Union. This misguided and illegitimate effort bypasses both Soviet law and the will of the Soviet peoples.

Accordingly, we support President Yeltsin's call for "restoration of the legally elected organs of power and the reaffirmation of the post of the U.S.S.R. President M.S. Gorbachev."

Greater democracy and openness in Soviet society, including steps toward implementation of Soviet obligations under the Helsinki Final Act and the Charter of Paris, have made a crucial contribution to the welcome improvement in East-West relations during the past few years.

In these circumstances, U.S. policy will be based on the following guidelines:

We believe the policies of reform in the Soviet Union must continue, including democratization, the process of peaceful reconciliation between the center and the republics and economic transformation.

We support all constitutionally elected leaders and oppose the use of force or intimidation to suppress them or restrict their right to free speech.

We oppose the use of force in the Baltic states or against any republics to suppress or replace democratically elected governments.

We call on the U.S.S.R. to abide by its international treaties and commitments, including its commitments to respect basic human rights and democratic practices under the Helsinki Accords, and the Charter of Paris.

We will avoid in every possible way actions that would lend legitimacy or support to this coup effort.

We have no interest in a new cold war or in the exacerbation of East-West tensions.

At the same time, we will not support economic aid programs if adherence to extra-constitutional means continues.

US To Establish Diplomatic Relations with Baltic States
Speech by President Bush in Kennebunkport, Maine, on September 2, 1991

Nearly 2 weeks ago, the world watched with fascination the courage of the Soviet people in foiling a cynical coup - a coup that, thank God, failed. We've marveled since at their efforts to build a new and democratic future.

Major change are now taking place in the Soviet Union, not the least of which is the establishment of new arrangements between the republics and the central government.

While we await the final outcome, I welcome President Gorbachev's support for the concept that the republics will be free to determine their own future. This new Ten-plus-One agreement speaks eloquently to that.

This is a watershed in Soviet political thinking, equal to the dramatic movements toward democracy and market economies that we are witnessing in the republics themselves. The United States strongly supports these efforts.

The Baltic peoples of Estonia, Latvia, and Lithuania and their democratically elected governments have declared their independence and are moving now to control their own national territories and their own destinies. The United States has always supported the independence of the Baltic states and is now prepared immediately to establish diplomatic relations with their governments.

...

Resolution of the Congress of People's Deputies regarding the failed coup.
Passed in Moscow on September 5, 1991,

Resolution of the U.S.S.R. People's Deputies on measures resulting from the joint statement of the U.S.S.R. president and top officials of republics and the decisions of the extraordinary session of the U.S.S.R. Supreme Soviet:

The coup d'etat committed on Aug. 19-21, 1991, endangered the process of the formation of new union relations among sovereign states. The resulting situation may lead to dire consequences inside the country and in relations with foreign states.

The elimination of the coup [and] the victory of democratic forces delivered a serious blow to reactionaries, on all that held back the process of democratic transformations [and] renewal of the country.

In order to prevent the further breakup of power structures, the U.S.S.R. Congress of People's Deputies proclaims a transition period for forming a new system of state relations based on the expression of the will of the republics and the interests of the nations.

The Congress has resolved:

1. To approve, in the main, proposals resulting from the joint statement of the U.S.S.R. president and top officials of the union republics [and] the resolution of the U.S.S.R. Supreme Soviet on the situation created in the country in connection with the coup d'etat.

2. To accelerate the preparation and signing of the treaty on the Union of Sovereign States, in which each of them shall be able to define on its own the form of its participation in the union. The new union must be based on the principles of independence and integrity of states; the observance of the rights of the nations and the individual; social justice; and democracy.

3. To work out and conclude interrepublic agreements on economic, monetary-financial, scientific and technological cooperation; ecological security; defense of the rights and freedoms of citizens; [and] on the principles of collective security and defense, while preserving a single armed forces and single control of nuclear and other arsenals of the means of mass destruction.

The Inter-Republic Economic Committee shall begin immediately to work out and conclude a treaty on the economic union, which would have an open character, and the participation in which would not be tied to the signing of the Union Treaty.

4. [That] the U.S.S.R. president, the U.S.S.R. Supreme Soviet and the State Council shall provide the legal succession of power and government and guarantee a peaceful and orderly transition to a democratic civil society.

5. [That] during the transition period, all international agreements and obligations adopted by the U.S.S.R. shall be strictly observed, including those in the spheres of arms control and reduction, human rights, foreign economic relations.

6. To support the aspiration of republics for their recognition as subjects of international law and for consideration of the question on their membership in the United Nations.

7. [That during the transition period] all state organs, institutions, organizations, and officials shall endure the observance of the rights and freedoms of the people which are proclaimed in the U.S.S.R. Constitution, the Declaration of Human Rights and Freedoms, the laws of the U.S.S.R. and republics, as well as the freedom of the press, the conscience, the right to establish political parties, trade unions and public unions.

While respecting the declarations of sovereignty and acts of independence adopted by republics, the Congress stresses that the gaining of independence by republics which have chosen to refuse to join the new union necessitates negotiations with the U.S.S.R. to resolve the entire complex of problems relating to secession, as well as their immediate joining in the Nuclear Non-Proliferation Treaty, the Final Act of the Conference on Security and Cooperation in Europe and other important international treaties and agreements, including those which guarantee the rights and freedoms of the individual.

FORMATION OF THE COMMONWEALTH OF INDEPENDENT STATES
SIGNED IN MINSK, THE CAPITAL OF BYELORUSSIA, DECEMBER 8, 1991

We, the Republic of Byelorussia, the Russian Federation and Ukraine, as founding members of the Union of Soviet Socialist Republics, having signed the Union Treaty of 1922 and hereafter referred to as the Agreeing Parties, state that the Union of Soviet Socialist Republics as a subject of international law and geopolitical reality has ceased to exist.

Based on historical commonalities of our peoples and on ties that were set up between them, considering bilateral agreements signed between the Agreeing Parties,

Striving to found democratic legal states and intending to develop our relations on the basis of mutual recognition and the respect of state sovereignty, the integral right to self-determination, the principles of equality and noninterference in internal affairs, the refusal to use force or pressure by economic or other means, the settlement of controversial problems through agreement, other common principles and norms of international law,

Taking into account that the further development and strengthening of relations of friendship, good-neighborliness and mutually beneficial cooperation between our states is consistent with the basic national interests of their people and serves in the interests of peace and security,

Confirming our commitment to the goals and principles of the UN Charter, the Helsinki Final Act and other documents from the Conference on Security and Cooperation in Europe,

Obliging to observe common international norms on human and national rights,

We agree on the following:

Article 1

The Agreeing Parties are founding a Commonwealth of Independent States.

Article 2

The Agreeing Parties guarantee their citizens, regardless of nationality or other differences, equal rights and freedoms. Each ... guarantees citizens of other parties and also people on its territory, regardless of nationality or other differences, civil political, social, economic and cultural rights and freedoms in accordance with common international norms on human rights.

...

Article 5

The Agreeing Parties recognize and respect each other's territorial integrity, and the integrity of each other's borders in the framework of the commonwealth. They guarantee openness of borders, and the freedom for citizens to travel and exchange information within the ...commonwealth.

Article 6

Members... will cooperate to ensure international peace and security and to carry out effective measures on limiting weapons and military expenditures. They are striving to liquidate all nuclear arms, to have total and complete disarmament under strict international control.

The Parties will respect each other's striving to achieve the status of a nuclear-free zone and neutral state.

Members of the commonwealth will preserve and support common military and strategic space under a common command, including common control over nuclear armaments, which will be regulated by special agreement.

They also mutually guarantee necessary conditions for the deployment, functioning, material and social maintenance of strategic armed forces. The Parties are obliged to pursue consensual policy on questions of social protection and pensions for military personnel and their families.

Article 7

The Parties recognize that the spheres of their mutual activities conducted on a mutual basis through common coordinating institutions of the commonwealth embrace:

Coordination of foreign policy

Cooperation in forming and developing a common economic space, common European and Eurasian markets, in the sphere of customs policy,

Cooperation to develop transport and communications systems

Cooperation on the sphere of environmental protection, participation in creating of the all-encompassing international system of ecological security

Questions of migration policy

The fight against organized crime

Article 8

The Parties are aware of the universal character of the Chernobyl disaster and are obliged to unite and coordinate their efforts to minimize and overcome its consequences.

...

Article 11

From the moment the current Agreement is signed, the laws of third states, including the U.S.S.R., are not valid on the territories of states which signed the current Agreement.

Article 12

The Parties guarantee the fulfillment of international obligations, treaties and agreements of the former Union of Soviet

Socialist Republics, coming from these obligations.

Article 13

...

The current Agreement is open to all states of the former Union of Soviet Socialist Republics, and also to other states that share the goals and principles of the current Agreement.

Article 14

The official location to station the coordinating organs of the Commonwealth is the city of Minsk.

The activities of the organs of the former Union of Soviet Socialist Republics on the territories of states members of the Commonwealth are stopped.

[Signed on behalf of Byelorussia by Stanislaw Shushkevich and Vyacheslav Kebich, on behalf of Russia by Boris Yeltsin and Gennady Burbulis, and on behalf of Ukraine by Leonid Kravchuk and Vitold Fokin.]

GORBACHEV'S SPEECH FOLLOWING THE CREATION OF THE COMMONWEALTH OF INDEPENDENT STATES

SPEECH MADE IN MOSCOW ON DECEMBER 9, 1991

On December 8, 1991, the leaders of Byelorussia, the Russian Federation and Ukraine signed in Minsk an agreement to found a commonwealth of independent states.

As the country's president, the main yardstick with which to evaluate the document is the measure to which it satisfies the interests of security of its citizens, meets the tasks of overcoming the present crisis and preservation of statehood and furtherance of democratic reforms.

This agreement has its positive moments.

The Ukrainian leadership, which previously showed no activity in the negotiating process, has joined it.

The document stresses the need to create a single economic space, operating on coordinating principles with a single currency and finance and banking system. It expresses readiness for cooperation in the fields of science, education, culture and other spheres. It suggests a definite formula of interaction in the military-strategic field.

But this is a document of special significance. It touches very deeply on the interests of the peoples of our country, of the entire world community, and hence calls for a comprehensive political and legal evaluation.

In any case, it is clear to me that the agreement directly proclaims the end of the U.S.S.R. Undoubtedly, each republic has the right to withdraw from the Soviet Union, but the fate of our multinational country cannot be decided by the will of three republican leaders. This question can only be resolved through constitutional means with the participation of all sovereign states and taking into account the will of their peoples.

Illegal and dangerous is the assertion about the termination of all-union norms, which can only boost chaos and anarchy in the society.

The speed with which the document appeared is baffling. It was not discussed either by the citizens or the Parliamentarians of the republics on behalf of which it was signed.

Even more significantly, it happened at a time when the republics' Parliaments are discussing the draft treaty of the union of sovereign states, drafted by the U.S.S.R. State Council.

I am deeply confident that in the present situation it is necessary for all Supreme Soviets of the republics and the Supreme Soviet of the U.S.S.R. to discuss the draft treaty of the union of sovereign states and the agreement signed in Minsk. As the agreement puts forward a formula of statehood, which is in the competence of the Congress of People's Deputies, it is necessary to convene the Congress. Besides, I do not rule out holding a nationwide referendum on this question.

The Commonwealth Pact
Signed December 21 in Alma-Ata, Kazakhstan.

Protocol to the Commonwealth Pact

The Azerbaijani Republic, the Republic of Armenia, the Republic of Byelorussia, the Republic of Kazakhstan, the Republic of Kirghizia, the Republic of Moldavia, the Russian Federation, the Republic of Tajikistan, Turkmenia, the Republic of Uzbekistan, and Ukraine, on an equal basis, and as high contracting parties, are forming a Commonwealth of Independent States.

...

Alma-Ata Declaration

The independent states - the Azerbaijani Republic, the Republic of Armenia, the Republic of Byelorussia, the Republic of Kazakhstan, the Republic of Kirghizia, the Republic of Moldavia, the Russian Federation, the Republic of Tajikistan, Turkmenia, the Republic of Uzbekistan, and Ukraine,

SEEKING to build democratic law-governed states, the relations between which will develop on the basis of mutual recognition and respect for state sovereignty and sovereign equality, the inalienable right to self-determination, principles of equality and non-interference in internal affairs, the rejection of the use of force, the threat of force and economic and any other methods of pressure, a peaceful settlement of disputes, respect for human rights and freedoms, including the rights of national minorities, a conscientious fulfillment of commitments and other generally recognized principles and standards of international law;

RECOGNIZING AND RESPECTING each other's territorial integrity and the inviolability of existing borders;

BELIEVING that the strengthening of the relations of friendship, good neighborliness and mutually advantageous cooperation, which has deep historic roots, meets the basic interests of nations and promotes the cause of peace and security;

BEING AWARE of their responsibility for the preservation of civil peace and inter-ethnic accord;

BEING LOYAL to the objectives and principles of the agreement on the creation of the Commonwealth of Independent States;

ARE MAKING the following statement:

Cooperation between members of the commonwealth will be carried out in accordance with the principle of equality through coordinating institutions formed on a parity basis and operating in the way established by the agreements between members of the commonwealth, which is neither a state nor a super-state structure.

In order to insure international strategic stability and security, allied command of the military-strategic forces and a single control over nuclear weapons will be preserved, the sides will respect each other's desire to attain the status of a non-nuclear or neutral state.

The Commonwealth of Independent States is open, with the agreement of all its participants, for other states to join - members of the former Soviet Union as well as other states sharing the goals and principles of the commonwealth.

The allegiance to cooperation in the formation and development of the common economic space, and all-Europe and Eurasian markets is being confirmed.

With the formation of the Commonwealth of Independent States, the Union of Soviet Socialist Republics ceases to exist. Member states of the commonwealth guarantee, in accordance with their constitutional procedures, the fulfillment of international obligations stemming from the treaties and agreements of the former U.S.S.R.

Member states of the commonwealth pledge to observe strictly the principles of the declaration.

On the Military

Proceeding from the provision, sealed in the agreement on the establishment of a Commonwealth of Independent States and in the Alma-Ata declaration, for keeping the common military-strategic space under a joint command and for keeping a single control over nuclear weapons, the high contracting parties agreed on the following:

The command of the armed forces shall be entrusted to Marshal Yevgeny I. Shaposhnikov, pending a solution to the question of reforming the armed forces.

Proposals concerning this question shall be submitted by Dec. 30, 1991, for the consideration of the heads of state.

On Institutions

A supreme body of the commonwealth - a "Council of the Heads of State" - as well as a "Council of the Heads of Government" shall be set up with a view to tackling matters connected with coordinating the activities of the states of the new commonwealth in the sphere of common interests.

The plenipotentiary representatives of the states of the new commonwealth shall be instructed to submit proposals concerning the abolition of the structures of the former Soviet Union, as well as the coordinating institutions of the commonwealth for the consideration of the Council of Heads of State.

On U.N. Membership

Member states of the commonwealth, referring to Article 12 of the agreement on the creation of the Commonwealth of Independent States,

PROCEEDING from the intention of each of the states to fulfill its duties stipulated by the U.N. Charter and to take part in the work of that organization as equal members;

TAKING into account that previously the Republic of Byelorussia, the U.S.S.R. and Ukraine were members of the United Nations organization;

EXPRESSING satisfaction that the Republic of Byelorussia and Ukraine continue to U.N. members as sovereign independent states;

BEING full of resolve to promote the consolidation of world peace and security on the basis of the U.N. Charter in the interests of their nations and the whole of the world community;

HAVE DECIDED:

1. Member states of the commonwealth support Russia in taking over the U.S.S.R. membership in the U.N., including permanent membership in the Security Council and other international organizations.

2. The Republic of Byelorussia, the Russian Federation and Ukraine will help other member states of the commonwealth settle problems connected with their full membership in the U.N. and other international organizations.

...

[Signed for the Azerbaijani Republic by A. Mutalibov, for the Republic of Armenia by L. Ter-Petrosyan, for the Republic of Byelorussia by S. Shuchkevich, for the Republic of Kazakhstan by N. Nazarbayev, for the Republic of Kirghizia by A. Akayev, for the Republic of Moldavia by M. Snegur, for the Russian Federation by B. Yeltsin, for the Republic of Tajikistan by R. Nabiyev, for Turkmenia by S. Niyazov, for the Republic of Uzbekistan by I. Karimov, and for Ukraine by L. Kravchuk

On Nuclear Arms

Byelorussia, Kazakhstan, the Russian Federation, and Ukraine, called henceforth the member states,

Confirming their adherence to the non-proliferation of nuclear armaments;

Striving for the elimination of all nuclear armaments, and

Wishing to act to strengthen international stability, have agreed on the following:

Article 1

The nuclear armaments that are part of the unified strategic armed forces insure the collective security of all the members of the Commonwealth of Independent States.

Article 2

The member states...confirm the obligation not to be the first to use nuclear weapons.

...

Article 4

Until nuclear weapons have been completely eliminated on the territory of the Republic of Byelorussia and Ukraine, decisions on the need to use them are taken, by agreement with the heads of member states of the agreement, by the R.S.F.S.R. [Russian Soviet Federated Socialist Republic] President, on the basis of procedures drawn up jointly by the member states.

Article 5

1. The republics of Byelorussia and Ukraine undertake to join the 1968 nuclear non-proliferation treaty as non-nuclear states and to conclude with the International Atomic Energy Agency the appropriate agreements-guarantees.

2. The member states of this agreement undertake not to transfer to anyone nuclear weapons or other triggering devices and technologies, or control over such nuclear triggering devices, either directly or indirectly, as well as not in any way

to help, encourage and prompt any state not possessing nuclear weapons to produce nuclear weapons or other nuclear triggering devices, and also control over such weapons or triggering devices.

3. The provisions of paragraph 2 of this article do not stand in the way of transferring nuclear weapons from Byelorussia, Kazakhstan and Ukraine to R.S.F.S.R. territory with a view to destroying them.

Article 6

The member states of this agreement, in accordance with the international treaty, will assist in the elimination of nuclear weapons. By July 1, 1992 Byelorussia, Kazakhstan and Ukraine will insure the withdrawal of tactical nuclear weapons to central factory premises for dismantling under joint supervision.

Article 7

The Governments of Byelorussia, Kazakhstan, the Russian Federation and Ukraine undertake to submit a treaty on strategic offensive arms for ratification by the Supreme Soviets of their states.

...

US Welcomes New Commonwealth of Independent States
Speech by President Bush to the nation, December 25, 1991

Good evening, and Merry Christmas to all Americans across our great country. During these last few months, you and I have witnessed one of the greatest dramas of the 20th century - the historic and revolutionary transformation of a totalitarian dictatorship, the Soviet Union, and the liberation of its peoples. As we celebrate Christmas - this day of peace and hope - I thought we should take a few minutes to reflect on what these events mean for us as Americans.

For over 40 years, the United States led the West in the struggle against communism and the threat it posed to our most precious values. This struggle shaped the lives of all Americans. It forced all nations to live under the specter of nuclear destruction.

That confrontation is now over. The nuclear threat - while far from gone - is receding. Eastern Europe is free. The Soviet Union itself is no more. This is a victory for democracy and freedom. It's a victory for the moral force of our values. Every American can take pride in this victory, from the millions of men and women who served our country in uniform to millions of Americans who supported their country and a strong defense under nine presidents.

New, independent nations have emerged out the wreckage of the Soviet empire. Last weekend, these former republics formed a Commonwealth of Independent States. This act marks the end of the old Soviet Union, signified today by Mikhail Gorbachev's decision to resign as President.

I'd like to express, on behalf of the American people, my gratitude to Mikhail Gorbachev for years of sustained commitment to world peace, and for his intellect, vision, and courage. I spoke with Mikhail Gorbachev this morning. We reviewed the many accomplishments of the past few years and spoke of hope for the future. Mikhail Gorbachev's revolutionary policies transformed the Soviet Union. His policies permitted the peoples of Russia and the other republics to cast aside decades of oppression and establish the foundation of freedom. His legacy guarantees him an honored place in history and provides a solid basis for the United States to work in equally constructive ways with his successors.

The United States applauds and supports the historic choice for freedom by the new states of the Commonwealth of Independent States. We congratulate them on the peaceful and democratic path they have chosen and for their careful attention to nuclear control and safety during this transition. Despite a potential for instability and chaos, these events clearly serve our national interest.

We stand tonight before a new world of hope and possibilities for our children, a world we could not have contemplated a few years ago. The challenge for us now is to engage these new states in sustaining the peace and building a more prosperous future.

And so today, based on commitments and assurances given to us by some of these states, concerning nuclear safely, democracy, and free markets, I am announcing some important steps designed to begin this process.

First, the United States recognizes and welcomes the emergence of a free, independent, and democratic Russia, led by its courageous President, Boris Yeltsin. Our Embassy in Moscow will remain there as our Embassy to Russia. We will support Russia's assumption of the USSR's seat as a Permanent Member of the UN Security Council. I look forward to working closely with President Yeltsin in support of his efforts to bring democratic and market reform to Russia.

Second, the United States also recognizes the independence of Ukraine, Armenia, Kazakhstan, Byelarus, and

Kyrgyzstan - all states that have made specific commitments to us. We will move quickly to establish diplomatic relations with these states and build new ties with them. We will sponsor membership in the United Nations for those not already members.

Third, the United States also recognizes today as independent states the remaining six former Soviet republics - Moldova, Turkmenistan, Azerbaijan, Tajikistan, Georgia, and Uzbekistan. We will establish diplomatic relations with them when we are satisfied that they have made commitments to responsible security policies and democratic principles, as have the other states we recognized today.

These dramatic events come at a time when Americans are also facing challenges here at home. I know that for many of you, these are difficult times. And I want all Americans to know that I am committed to attacking our economic problems at home with the same determination we brought to winning the Cold War.

I am confident we will meet this challenge as we have so many times before. But we cannot if we retreat into isolationism. We will only succeed in this interconnected world by continuing to lead the fight for free people and free and fair trade. A free and prosperous global economy is essential for America's prosperity; that means jobs and economic growth right here at home.

This is a day of great hope for all Americans. Our enemies have become our partners, committed to building democratic and civil societies. They ask for our support, and we will give it to them. We will do it because as Americans we can do no less.

For our children, we must offer them the guarantee of a peaceful and prosperous future - a future grounded in a world built on strong democratic principles, free from the specter of global conflict.

...

GORBACHEV'S RESIGNATION SPEECH
GIVEN IN MOSCOW ON DECEMBER 25, 1991

Dear compatriots, fellow citizens: As a result of the newly formed situation, creation of the Commonwealth of Independent States, I cease my activities in the post of the USSR President.

I am making this decision out of considerations based on principle. I have firmly stood for independence, self-rule of nations, for the sovereignty of the republics, but at the same time for preservation of the union state, the unity of the country.

Events went a different way. The policy prevailed of dismembering this country and disuniting the state, with which I cannot agree. And after the Alma-Ata meeting and the decisions made there, my position on this matter has not changed. Besides, I am convinced that decisions of such scale should have been made on the basis of a popular expression of will.

Yet I will continue to do everything in my power so that agreements signed there should lead to real accord in society [and] facilitate the escape from the crisis and the reform process.

Addressing you for the last time in the capacity of president of the USSR, I consider it necessary to express my evaluation of the road we have traveled since 1985, especially as there are a lot of contradictory, superficial and subjective judgements on that matter.

Fate had it that when I found myself at the head of the state it was already clear that all was not well in the country. There is plenty of everything: land, oil, and gas, other natural riches, and God gave us lots of intelligence and talent, yet we lived much worse than developed countries and keep falling behind them more and more.

The reason could already be seen. The society was suffocating in the vise of the command-bureaucratic system, doomed to serve ideology and bear the terrible burden of the arms race. It had reached the limit of its possibilities. All attempts at partial reform, and there had been many, had suffered defeat, one after another. The country was losing perspective. We could not go on living like that. Everything had to be changed radically.

...

The process of renovating the country and radical changes in the world community turned out to be far more complicated than could be expected. However, what has been done ought to be given its due. This society acquired freedom, liberated itself politically and spiritually, and this is the foremost achievement - which we have not yet understood completely, because we have not learned to use freedom.

However, work of historic significance has been accomplished. The totalitarian system that deprived the country of an opportunity to become successful and prosperous long ago has been eliminated. A breakthrough has been achieved on the way to democratic changes. Free elections, freedom of the press, religious freedoms, representative organs of power, a multi-party [system] became a reality. Human rights are recognized as the supreme principle.

The movement to a diverse economy has started, equality of all forms of property is becoming established, people who work on the land are coming to life again in the framework of land reform, farmers have appeared, millions of acres of land are being given over to people who live in the countryside and in towns.

Economic freedom of the producer has been legalized, and entrepreneurship, shareholding, privatization are gaining momentum. In turning the economy toward a market, it is important to remember that all this is done for the sake of the individual. ...

We live in a new world. The Cold War has ended; the arms race has stopped, as has the insane militarization that mutilated our economy, public psyche and morals. The threat of a world war has been removed. Once again I want to stress that on my part everything was done during the transition period to preserve reliable control of nuclear weapons.

We opened ourselves to the world, gave up interference into other people's affairs, the use of troops beyond the borders of our country, and trust, solidarity and respect came in response. We have become one of the main foundations for the transformation of modern civilization on peaceful democratic grounds.

...

The August coup brought the general crisis to its ultimate limit. The most damaging thing about this crisis is the breakup of the state. And today I am worried by our people's loss of the citizenship of a great country. The consequences may turn out to be very hard for everyone.

I think it is vitally important to preserve the democratic achievements of the last years. They have been paid for by the suffering of our whole history, our tragic experience. They must not be given up under any circumstances or any pretext, otherwise all our hopes for the better will be buried.

...

I am leaving my post with apprehension, but also with hope, with faith in you, your wisdom and force of spirit. We are the heirs of a great civilization, and its rebirth into a new, modern and dignified life now depends on one and all.

I wish to thank with all my heart all those who have stood together with me all these years for a fair and good cause. Some mistakes could surely have been avoided; many things could have been better done. But I am convinced that sooner or later our common efforts will bear fruit, our nations will live in a prosperous and democratic society

I wish all the best to all of you.

MINSK AGREEMENT ON STRATEGIC FORCES
SIGNED IN MINSK ON DECEMBER 30, 1991

Guided by the necessity for a coordinated and organized solution to issue in the sphere of the control of strategic forces and the single control over nuclear weapons, the Azerbaijan Republic, the Republic of Armenia, the Republic of Byelarus, the Republic of Kazakhstan, the Republic of Kyrgyzstan, the Republic of Moldova, the Russian Federation, the Republic of Tajikistan, Turkmenia, the Republic of Uzbekistan, and Ukraine, henceforth referred to as "the member states of the Commonwealth," have agreed on the following:

...

Article 2
The member states of the Commonwealth undertake to observe the international treaties of the USSR and to pursue a coordinated policy in the area of international security, disarmament and arms control, to participate in the preparation and implementation of programs for reduction in arms and armed forces. ...

Article 3
The member states of the Commonwealth recognize the need for joint command of strategic forces and for maintaining unified control of nuclear weapons and other forms of mass destruction on the armed forces of the former USSR.

Article 4
Until the complete elimination of nuclear weapons, the decision on the need for their use is made by the president of the Russian Federation in agreement with the heads of the Republic of Byelarus, the Republic of Kazakhstan, and Ukraine, and in consultation with the heads of the armed forces of the USSR.

Until their destruction in full, nuclear weapons located on the territory of Ukraine shall be under the control of the Combined Strategic Forces Command, with the aim that they not be used, and dismantled by the end of 1994, including tactical nuclear weapons by 1 July 1992. The process of destruction of nuclear weapons located on the territory of the

Republic of Byelarus and Ukraine shall take place with the participation of the Republic of Byelarus, the Russian Federation and Ukraine under joint control of the Commonwealth states.

....

Joint Declaration announcing the end of the Cold War
Signed in Washington by US President George Bush and Russian President Boris Yeltsin on February 2, 1992

At the conclusion of this meeting between an American President and the President of a new and democratic Russia, we, the leaders of two great peoples and nations, are agreed that a number of principles should guide relations between Russia and America.

1. Russia and the United States do not regard each other as potential adversaries. From now on, the relationship will be characterized by friendship and partnership founded on mutual trust and respect and a common commitment to democracy and economic freedom.

2. We will work to remove any remnants of Cold War hostility, including taking steps to reduce our strategic arsenals.

3. We will do all we can to promote a mutual well-being of our peoples and to expand as widely as possible the ties that now bind our peoples. Openness and tolerance should be the hallmark of relations between our peoples and governments.

4. We will actively promote free trade, investment, and economic cooperation between our two countries.

5. We will make every effort to support the promotion of our shared values of democracy, the rule of law, respect for human rights, including minority rights, respect for borders and peaceful change around the globe.

6. We will work actively together to: Prevent the proliferation of weapons of mass destruction and associated technology, and curb the spread of advanced conventional arms on the basis of principles to be agreed upon; settle regional conflicts peacefully; and counter terrorism, halt drug trafficking and forestall environmental degradation.

In adopting these principles, the United States and Russia have launched a new era in our relationship. In this new era, we seek peace, an enduring peace that rests on lasting common values. This can be an era of peace and friendship that offers hope not only to our peoples but to the peoples of the world.

For a while our conflicts helped divide the world for a generation. Now, working with others, we can help unite the globe through our friendship - a new alliance of partners against the common dangers we face.

Bush's Speech announcing Western Aid to Russia
Speech Given in Washington on April 1, 1992

... I have just met with the Congressional leadership to request their bipartisan backing for a new, comprehensive and integrated program to support the struggle of freedom under way in Russia, Ukraine, and the new states that have replaced the Soviet Union.

The revolution in these states is a defining moment in history, with profound consequences for America's national interest. The stakes are as high for us now as any that we have faced in this century, and our adversary for 45 years, the one nation that posed a worldwide threat to freedom and peace, is now seeking to join the community of democratic nations. A victory for democracy and freedom in the former USSR creates the possibility of a new world of peace for our children and grandchildren.

But if this democratic revolution is defeated, it could plunge us into a world more dangerous in some respects than the dark years of the Cold War. America must meet this challenge, joining with those who stood beside us in the battle against imperialist Communism: Germany, the United Kingdom, Japan, France, Canada, Italy, and other allies. Together, we won the Cold War, and today we must win the peace.

This effort will require new resources from the industrial democracies, but nothing like the price we would pay if democracy and reform failed in Russia and Ukraine and Byelarus and Armenia, and the states of Central Asia. It will require the commitment of a united America strengthened by a consensus that transcends even the heated partisanship of a Presidential election campaign. And today I call upon Congress, Republicans and Democrats alike, and the American people, to stand behind this united effort.

To this end, I would like to announce today a plan to support democracy in the states of the former Soviet Union. This is a complex set of issues which took months to sort out, working with the Administration, working with our major allies and with the leaders of the new independent states of the former Soviet Union. A number of things had to come together to make sure we got it right.

After weeks of intensive consultation in the G-7, Chancellor Kohl, currently serving as chairman of the G-7, has announced today G-7 support for an IMF program for Russia. The program that I'm announcing today builds on this progress and includes three major components.

First, the United States has been working with it Western allies and the international financial institutions on an unprecedented multilateral program to support reform in the newly independent states. The success of this program will depend upon their commitment to reform and their willingness to work with the international community.

Russia is exhibiting that commitment, and I am announcing today that the US is prepared to join in a substantial multilateral financial assistance package in support of Russia's reforms. We are working to develop, with our allies and the IMF, a $6 billion currency stabilization fund, to help maintain confidence in the Russian ruble.

The US will also join in a multilateral effort to marshal roughly $18 billion in financial support in 1992 to assist Russian efforts to stabilize and restructure their economy. We have been working with the Russian Government for three months to help it develop an economic reform plan to permit the major industrialized countries to provide support.

We will work to complete action on this approximately $24 billion package by the end of April, and I pledge the full cooperation of the United States in the effort.

Secondly, the United States will also act to broaden its own capacity to extend assistance to the new states. I am transmitting to Congress a comprehensive bill, the Freedom Support Act, to mobilize the executive branch, the Congress, and indeed, our private sector, around a comprehensive and integrated package of support for the new states.

The US quota increase for the IMF was specifically assumed in the budget agreement and does not require a budget outlay. The package will support my existing authority to work with the G-7 and the IMF to put together this stabilization program for Russia, and support possible subsequent programs for other states of the former Soviet Union, as they embark on landmark reforms, including up to $3 billion for stabilization funds.

It would also repeal restrictive Cold-War legislation so that American business can compete on an even footing in these new markets. ...

Significant new trade relationships can create new jobs right here in this country. The package will broaden the use of $500 million appropriated by Congress last year to encompass not only the safe dismantling and destruction of nuclear weapons, but also, the broader goals of nuclear plant safety, demilitarization, and defense conversion.

It will also establish a major people-to-people program between the United States and the states of the former Soviet Union to create the type of lasting personal bonds among our peoples, and Russian understanding of democratic institutions so critical to long-term peace...
...

Third, in the addition to the $3.75 billion already extended by the US since January 1991, I am announcing today $1.1 billion in new Commodity Credit Corporation credit guarantees for the purchase of American agricultural products. Six hundred million dollars of that will go for US sales to Russia, and an additional $500 million for US sales to Ukraine and other states.

I know there are those who say we should pull back, concentrate our energies, our interest, and our resources on our own pressing domestic problems, and they are - they are very important. But I ask them to think of the consequences here at home of peace in the world. We have got to act right now.

GOVERNMENT AND BUSINESS ASSISTANCE CONTACTS

EMBASSIES

US Embassy Moscow
Chaykovskogo St. 19/21/23
Moscow 121834
Russian Federation
Tel: (7 095) 252-2450-9

Mailing Address:
US Commercial Office
American Embassy - Moscow
APO AE New York 09862

US Embassy Kiev
Vul. Yuriy Kotsubinkoho 10
Kiev, Ukraine
Tel: (70 44) 279-0188
Fax: (70 44) 279-0945

US Embassy Mensk
Hotel Byelarus
Macherov Prospekt
Mensk, Byelarus
Tel: (70 172) 690 802

US Embassy Yerevan
Hotel Hrazdan
Yerevan, Armenia
Tel: (7 885) 215-1144
Fax: (7 885) 215-1122

US Embassy Alma-Ata
Hotel Kazakhstan
Sifulona and Kirova
Alma Ata, Kazakhstan
Tel: (7 3272) 619 056

US Embassy Bishkek
Derzhinskiy Prospekt 66
Bishkek, Kyrgyzstan
Tel: (7 331) 222 2270

CIS REPRESENTATIVES IN THE UNITED STATES

Consulate of the Russian Federation
2790 Green St.
San Francisco, CA 94123
Tel: (415) 202-9800
Fax: (415) 929-0306

Belarus Mission to the UN
136 East 67th St.
New York, NY 10021
Tel: (212) 535-3420
Fax: (212) 743-4810

Russian Mission to the UN
136 East 67th St.
New York, NY 10021
Tel: (212) 861-4900
Fax: (212) 628-0252

Ukrainian Mission to the UN
136 East 67th St.
New York, NY 10021
Tel: (212) 535-3420
Fax: (212) 743-4810

US COMMERCE DEPARMENT

US Commerce Department
14th & Constitution Ave., N.W.
Washington, DC 20230
Tel: (202) 377-2000

Bureau of Export Administration
Room 3898
Tel: (202) 377-1455
Fax: (202) 377--0100
Joan McEntee, Acting Secretary of
Export Administration

Office of East European, Russia
and Independent States
Room 3413, Hoover Building
Tel: (202) 377-3150
Fax: (202) 377-4098
Susan Lotarski, Director
Russian & Independent States Div:
Jack Brougher, Director

Special-American Business
Internship Training Program
(SABIT)
Cynthia Anthony, Manager
Tel: (202) 377-0073
Fax: (202) 377-2443

Places mid- and senior level managers from the CIS in internships with US companies.

Desk Officer, CIS
Susan Lewenz,
International Trade Specialist
Tel: (202) 377-4655
Fax: (202) 377-8042

Export Control Hotline:
Tel: (202) 377-4811

Provides information on export licenses application, commodity classification, and other regulations.

Trade Information Center:
Tel: (800) 872-8723

Provides information on overseas markets and industry trends.

US STATE DEPARTMENT

US State Department
2201 C St., N.W.
Washington, DC 20520
Tel: (202) 647-4000
Fax: (202) 647-0555

Special Advisor
Office of Emerging Eurasian
Democracies
Room 1210 A
Tel: (202) 647-0710
Fax: (202) 647-0414
Ambassador Robert Barry

Assistant Secretary for Bureau of
European/Canadian Affairs
Room 6226
Tel: (202) 647-6402
Fax: (202) 647-0967
Ambassador Thomas Niles

Office of Independent States and
Commonwealth Affairs
Room 4223
Tel: (202) 647-6729
Fax: (202) 647-3506
Larry Napier, Director

Bilateral Political Relations
Tel: (202) 647-8671
Fax: (202) 647-3506
David Hess

OFFICE OF THE US TRADE REPRESENTATIVE

Office of the US Trade
　Representative
600 17th St., N.W.
Washington, DC 20506

Cathy Novelli
Director for East Europe and the
　Soviet Union
Room 319
Tel: (202) 395-3074
Fax: (202) 395-3911

CHAMBERS OF COMMERCE

Armenian Chamber of Commerce
ul. Kutuzov 24
375033 Yeveran, Armenia
Tel: (885) 277 390

Byelarus Chamber of Commerce
65 Ya. Kolasa
220843 Minsk, Byelarus
Tel: (017) 660-460

Georgian Chamber of Commerce
I. Chavchavdze Prospect 1
380079 Tbilisi, Georgia

Kyrgyzstan Chamber of Commerce
ul. Bishkek 24
720345 Bishkek, Kyrgyzstan

Moscow Chamber of Commerce
ul. Chekhova 13-17
Moscow 103050
Russian Federation
Tel: (7 095) 299 7612

Russian Chamber of Commerce
　and Industry
ul. Kuibbysheva 6
103684 Moscow K-5, Russian
　Federation
Tel: (7 095) 921-0811
Tel: (7 095) 923-4323

St. Petersburg Chamber of
　Commerce
Krasny Flot Embankment 10
St. Petersburg 190000
Russian Federation
Tel: (70 812) 314 9953

Tajikistan Chamber of Commerce
ul. Sh. Rustaveli 31
734025 Dunshabe, Tajikistan
Tel: (377) 226 968

Ukrainian Chamber of Commerce
ul. Bolshaya Zhitomirskaya 133
252625 Kiev, Ukraine
Tel: (70 44) 222 911

Uzbekistan Chamber of Commerce
Prospekt Lenina 16-a
700017 Tashkent, Uzbekistan
Tel: (371) 336 282

CIS - American Chamber of
　Commerce
11 E. 36th St.
New York, NY 10016
Tel: 212-689-4440
Fax: 212-689-4465

ADDITIONAL BUSINESS AND CULTURAL CONTACTS

United Nations Industrial
　Development Organization
Investment Promotion Service
Kussinen St. 21B
Moscow 125252
Tel: (7 095) 229 8619

United Nations Industrial
　Development Organization
Investment Promotion Service
Room 215
1660 L St., N.W.
Washington, DC 20036
Tel: 202-659-5165
Fax: 202-659-7674

UNIDO brings promising entrepreneurs in the developing world to the attention of potential partners in industrialized countries. In Russian, information is available on investment opportunities and laws, and possible sources of project finances.

Trade Representation of the
　Russian Federation in the
　United States
2001 Connecticut Ave., NW
Washington, DC 20008
Tel: 202-232-5988

Fax: 202-2332-2917

This organization represents Russia in foreign trade and external economic activities, works on economic cooperation, promotes development of trade and economic activities, assists Russian foreign trade, and provides information on Russian foreign trade policy, organization, and trade contacts.

Russian Trade and Cultural Center
35th Floor, West
One World Trade Center
New York, NY 10048
Tel: 212-432-2989
Fax: 212-432-2814

Amtorg
1755 Broadway Avenue
New York, NY 10019
Tel: 212-956-3010
Fax: 212-956-2995

Represents the Russian Ministry of Foreign Trade - offers assistance to businesses interested in business contacts in Russia.

Intourist
16 Prospekt Marka
Moscow
Tel: (7 095) 292-2260

Intourist
630 Fifth Ave.
Suite 868
New York, NY 1002
Tel: 212-757-3884

Intourist organizes travel itineraries for foreign tourists, and operates hotels and restaurants throughout the CIS.

U.S. Commercial Office Moscow
Chaykovskogo St. 15
Moscow 121834
Tel: (7 095) 255 4848/4660
Fax: (7 095) 230 2101

Source: US Chamber of Commerce

About ACCESS

ACCESS is a non-profit clearinghouse of information on international security and peace issues. ACCESS connects people needing information on these issues with the most appropriate sources. ACCESS is a non-advocacy service, providing reference to sources representing a variety of views.

What kinds of services does ACCESS offer?

◆ **Briefing papers** on current topics in security debates. The 2-page *Resource Brief* (6-8/year) summarizes timely issues like chemical and biological arms control and lists sources of information from various viewpoints. The 4-page *Security Spectrum* (2-3/year) summarizes the major positions taken in debates on controversial subjects, such as US policy toward East Asia, and lists readings and resources from diverse perspectives.

◆ **The Inquiry Service** for individuals with specific questions. We function much like a reference librarian, helping to clarify the question and providing either a referral to the best sources of the information or the answer. In responding to inquiries we draw on our database of over 2,400 organizations in 105 countries, as well as our extensive subject files.

◆ **The Speaker Referral Service.** We work with more than 75 speakers bureaus from a range of perspectives, and can direct callers to organizations that place speakers.

◆ *The ACCESS Guide to the Persian Gulf Crisis.* (ACCESS, 1991) A sixty-page impartial guide to background, resources, information, and organizations on the Persian Gulf war.

◆ *Search for Security: The ACCESS Guide to Foundations in Peace, Security, and International Relations.* (ACCESS, 1989) The new, expanded edition provides valuable information on over 150 foundations, which have spent over $120,000,000 supporting nearly 2,500 grants in the field.

◆ **Lists and Labels** may be produced using the ACCESS database of organizations, which also includes a list of more than 6,400 local groups concerned with international security and peace.

What issues does ACCESS cover?

ACCESS covers many issues relating to international security and peace, including:

◆ *Alternative security*
◆ *Arms control and disarmament*
◆ *Economic dimensions of security*
◆ *Environmental impacts of military activity*
◆ *Military spending & the defense budget*
◆ *Moral and ethical issues*

◆ *Nuclear proliferation*
◆ *Regional security (Central America, Southern Africa, Middle East, etc.)*
◆ *United Nations and international law*
◆ *US foreign and military policy*
◆ *Weapon systems & military balances*

How much does it cost?

ACCESS relies on ACCESS Associates to help support the service. Associates receive ACCESS *Resource Brief, Security Spectrum*, and complimentary or reduced-price copies of other ACCESS materials, as well as regular use ot the Inquiry Service. Individuals are asked to pay only $30 a year ($45 outside of the US); small non-profit organizations may subscribe for $75 a year ($90 international), and large non-profits for $150 a year ($175 international). These are charter rates and cover only part of the costs of the service. A complete list of Associate benefits is on the reverse side. As an introduction to ACCESS, and as a contribution to public education, occasional inquiry calls to ACCESS are free of charge.

ACCESS gratefully acknowledges the generous support of the following foundations: the Carnegie Corporation of New York, the Ford Foundation, the W. Alton Jones Foundation, the John D. and Catherine T. MacArthur Foundation, the Topsfield Foundation, the United States Institute of Peace, and the Winston Foundation for World Peace.

ACCESS •• 1730 M Street, NW •• Suite 605 •• Washington, DC 20036 •• 202-785-6630

ACCESS Associate and Publication Order Form
Order additional copies of One Nation Becomes Many

The ACCESS Associate Program

Regular callers and those wishing to receive our *Brief* and *Spectrum* automatically will want to become ACCESS Associates and take advantage of the benefits listed below. To become an Associate, simply fill out the form below and enclose a check for the proper amount, payable to ACCESS, or charge it on your MasterCard or Visa.

INDIVIDUAL: $30 per year
(international rate: US $45)
✦ Use of a special toll-free number to contact ACCESS Inquiry and Speaker Referral Services with specific questions
✦ *ACCESS Resource Brief* (6-8/year) and *Security Spectrum* (2-3/year)
✦ Associate Discounts on other ACCESS directories, guides, and reports
✦ Associate billing privileges — you may order publications and be billed later

SMALL NON-PROFIT: $75 per year
(Annual budget under $500,000)
(international rate: US $90)
✦ Staff use of ACCESS Inquiry and Speaker Referral Services — includes use of a toll-free number
✦ *ACCESS Resource Brief* and *Security Spectrum*
✦ Complimentary or discounted copies of other ACCESS directories, guides, and reports
✦ Associate billing privileges

LARGE NON-PROFIT: $150 per year
(Annual budget $500,000 or over)
(international rate: US $175)
✦ Staff use of ACCESS Inquiry and Speaker Referral Services — includes use of a toll-free number, limited use by affiliates
✦ *ACCESS Resource Brief* and *Security Spectrum* sent to as many as five addresses
✦ Complimentary or discounted copies of other ACCESS directories, guides, and reports
✦ Associate billing privileges

ACCESS Associate and Publication Order Form

I want ACCESS to the most authoritative information on international security, peace, and world affairs.

My preferred ACCESS Associate Package:
☐ Individual @ $30 per year (int'l rate: US $45)
☐ Small non profit @ $75 (int'l rate: US $90)
☐ Large non-profit @ 150 (int'l rate: US $175)
☐ Send information on commercial rates
☐ Send me a list of other ACCESS publications

I would like to order additional copies of **One Nation Becomes Many**

Number	Normal Rate*	ACCESS Associate Rate
_____	$17.95 each	$14.95 each

*Schools and libraries receive a 20% discount on orders of 10 or more copies. ($14.35 per copy)

Shipping and handling:	Up to $20.00	Add $3
	$20.00 to $50.00	Add $5
	Over $50	Add 10% of total

Associate Package $ _____
Publications Ordered $ _____
Shipping & Handling $ _____
Total Enclosed $ _____

☐ I am making a check payable to ACCESS.
☐ MC/VISA # _____ Exp.Date _____
Name on card _____
Signature _____

Name _____ Organization _____

Address _____

City/Town _____ State _____ Zip _____

Country _____ Phone _____

ACCESS •• 1730 M Street, NW •• Suite 605 •• Washington, DC 20036 •• 202-785-6630